5·11·78

Introductory Readings in Metaphysics

Selected and Edited by

RICHARD TAYLOR

PRENTICE-HALL, INC., Englewood Cliffs, New Jersey 07632

072

78 9421 4

Library of Congress Cataloging in Publication Data

Main entry under title:
    Introductory readings in metaphysics.

    Includes bibliographical references.
    1. Metaphysics—Collected works. I. Taylor, Richard,
1919–
BD111.I5   110'.8   77-15572
ISBN 0-13-502302-5

Printed in the United States of America

10 9 8 7 6 5 4 3 2 1

PRENTICE-HALL INTERNATIONAL, INC., *London*
PRENTICE-HALL OF AUSTRALIA PTY. LIMITED, *Sydney*
PRENTICE-HALL OF CANADA, LTD., *Toronto*
PRENTICE-HALL OF INDIA PRIVATE LIMITED, *New Delhi*
PRENTICE-HALL OF JAPAN, INC., *Tokyo*
PRENTICE-HALL OF SOUTHEAST ASIA PTE. LTD., *Singapore*
WHITEHALL BOOKS LIMITED, *Wellington, New Zealand*

CONTENTS

2011306

v

PREFACE

Collections of readings in philosophy usually present a great array of writers and opinions on every aspect of the subject. One gets little samples of this and that from here and there, but virtually no guidance. As a result, concern for genuine thought tends to give way to interest in mere variety, and a student may get the impression that philosophy is a department store, where you can find almost anything you like.

I have tried instead to reduce the fundamental problems of philosophy, all of them metaphysical, to just four, and instead of presenting samples of thought, I have sought out what seems to me the best thinking that clarifies the central issues in those problems. In doing so I have drawn from both classical and contemporary writers and have not used fame as my criterion. I have eschewed philosophers, even great ones, whose writing on these problems is obscure, turgid, or marred by jargon, believing that thought is not made more profound by being made difficult.

When I was invited to assemble such a collection, I agreed to what appeared to be a generous deadline, only to discover, as I went along, that thrice that amount of time was needed. The difficulty was not in finding literature on the subject, but finding literature that is untechnical, clear, interesting, and of the highest quality. Even so, I found that I had to compose a brief introductory essay for every selection in order to explain the nature and significance of the problem being dealt with, bearing in mind that the subject would be new to most readers. This proved far more difficult than one would suppose.

The problems illustrated here are the same as those discussed in my little book, *Metaphysics*, in the Foundations of Philosophy series, and are presented in the same order. This collection can therefore serve very aptly as a companion volume to that one, providing both text and readings for any course in the basic problems of philosophy.

RICHARD TAYLOR

Introductory
Readings
in Metaphysics

I

Introduction

METAPHYSICS AND DOGMA

1

ARTHUR SCHOPENHAUER

---

introduction

People think of metaphysics as something strange, esoteric, and obscure, something cultivated in universities by a strange and detached minority who are understood only by each other, something, above all, that is remote from the concerns of ordinary human beings.

Schopenhauer maintains that just the opposite is the case, that all people have a deep need for metaphysics, that it is sedulously cultivated everywhere, and almost everywhere utterly corrupted. People have a profound need to answer the most basic questions of existence. Why am I here? Why should I exist at all? What am I? Why should anything exist? Why must I die? What is death? And what is birth? No reflective person can pass his whole life without from time to time dwelling on such questions. They are metaphysical questions. And because they disturb us, we need metaphysics.

Questions such as these do not beset creatures who are less than human. The reason is not merely that they lack the intelligence to grasp them; it is, rather, that they lack a clear conception of their own mortality. Existence for them is something given. But to a human being, who can imagine his own grave, plan for his own inevitable death, and even know of an endless lapse of future time when he will no longer exist, his existence is something enigmatic. It is the most overwhelmingly important thing there is to him, yet it seems quite accidental and most certainly is temporary. So with this awareness deeply implanted in him, he reflects upon his own existence, his approaching nonexistence, the existence of his species, life generally, and the world. In short, he reflects—more or less adequately—upon metaphysics.

The religions of the world, Schopenhauer observed, have arisen in response to this need. They supply the answers, or what their devotees claim are the answers, to the fundamental questions of metaphysics—why there is a world, where it came from, why we are here, what is to become of us, and so on. And most religions, of course, supply answers that are comforting, especially with respect to what is to become of us. Having come into existence at a certain point in time, each of us is going to go right on existing, forever, they say—but for the reassurance of that belief we are expected to pay a certain price, which is devotion to that church and its human representatives, who hold the keys to this everlasting existence, to give or to withhold.

This, Schopenhauer claims, is at the heart of all religion: the assurance that death, which seems so real and inevitable, is not real after all. Belief in a god arises from a need for this reassurance. We believe, because we crave existence, and the gods are the only beings capable of bestowing it.

Religion to Schopenhauer is not metaphysics but merely a substitute for it. It gives believers easy answers, which require no real foundation or proof but are taken on faith alone. And such faith is made easy when one is indoctrinated during childhood, before reason and the critical faculties offer any protection. One who has received his religion during childhood, so that it has become almost part of his thought process, no longer has any need of metaphysics. The questions that give rise to that need have, in him, been answered, however speciously.

Established religion is not the only surrogate metaphysics. Schopenhauer, from his own bitter experience, singled out the established schemes of philosophy professors as being, like religion, counterfeit metaphysics. And the explanation, he thought, was similar: just as priests exploit the need for metaphysics in order to promote the power and well-being of the visible church, so also professors exploit it to promote their own well-being and that of the institutions upon which their salaries and reputations depend. In Schopenhauer's time philosophy professors usually owed their appointments to government ministries, so that metaphysics tended to serve, not the church, but the state. Schopenhauer's observations nevertheless are still apt, for we can substitute for the state the universities themselves and their hierarchies of power, together with the professional guilds that professors create for the advancement of their worldly interests. The result, so far as metaphysics is concerned, is essentially the same as with established religion—the elaboration of artificial metaphysical systems that appear to satisfy, more or less, the universal need for metaphysics but that in fact are skillfully designed to serve other interests altogether, always beginning with the ambitions of the metaphysical practitioners themselves.

How, then, are true and adequate metaphysical theories confirmed? How can we know what is a genuine and true metaphysics, and how can we distinguish it from the pleasant fairy tales of religion and the contrived and artificial games of philosophy professors? Schopenhauer's answer is interesting and novel. Metaphysics, he maintains, is like a puzzle, in which the challenge is to fit all the pieces together into one unified whole. When a piece fits, you have it right. When all the various propositions of a metaphysical system fit together and reinforce each other, each shedding light on the others and rendering the totality intelligible, then you know you have it right. You need not resort to faith in order to believe it, nor to the artificial posturings and pretensions of philosophy professors, nor to any kind of intuition or mysticism. Like a completed jigsaw puzzle, the correct metaphysics is laid out before you, each part fitting the others to yield a completed whole.

Of course Schopenhauer, who was neither a priest nor a professor, believed his own metaphysical system, of which no summary can be given here, to be the true one, the one that truly fulfilled man's need for metaphysics; but he did not think he was its discoverer. He found, instead, that it was embodied in the oldest philosophies known to mankind, particularly that of Buddhism; and this, far more than the applause of his contemporary practitioners of philosophy, was probably his deepest satisfaction.

Schopenhauer, the German philosopher of pessimism who died in 1860, is chiefly known for the central place he assigned to the concept of the *will* in his metaphysics. The essay that follows was written as an elaboration upon his much earlier work, *The World as Will and Representation*, the first edition of which appeared as a single volume. The author's digressions from his main theme, as well as recondite references, have been deleted.

The Need for Metaphysics*

No beings, with the exception of man, feel surprised at their own existence, but to all of them it is so much a matter of course that they do not notice it. Yet the wisdom of nature speaks out of the peaceful glance of the animals, since in them will and intellect are not separated widely enough for them to be capable of being astonished at each other when they meet again.

*Arthur Schopenhauer, "On Man's Need for Metaphysics," from *The World as Will and Representation*, Vol. II, trans. E. F. J. Payne (Indian Hills, Colo.: Falcon's Wing Press, 1958).

Thus in them the whole phenomenon is still firmly attached to the stem of nature from which it has sprung, and partakes of the unconscious omniscience of the great mother. Only after the inner being of nature (the will-to-live in its objectification) has ascended vigorously and cheerfully through the two spheres of unconscious beings, and then through the long and broad series of animals, does it finally attain to reflection for the first time with the appearance of reason (*Vernunft*), that is, in man. It then marvels at its own works, and asks itself what it itself is. And its wonder is the more serious, as here for the first time it stands consciously face to face with *death*, and besides the finiteness of all existence, the vanity and fruitlessness of all effort force themselves on it more or less. Therefore with this reflection and astonishment arises the *need for metaphysics* that is peculiar to man alone; accordingly, he is an *animal metaphysicum*. At the beginning of his consciousness, he naturally takes himself also as something that is a matter of course. This, however, does not last long, but very early, and simultaneously with the first reflection, appears that wonder which is some day to become the mother of metaphysics. In accordance with this, Aristotle says in the introduction to his *Metaphysics* [i, 982]: Διὰ γὰρ τὸ θαυμάζειν οι ἄνθρωποι χαὶ νῦν χαὶ τὸ πρῶτον ἤρξαντο φιλοσοφεῖν. (*Propter admirationem enim et nunc et primo inceperunt homines philosophari*.)[1] Moreover, the philosophical disposition properly speaking consists especially in our being capable of wondering at the commonplace thing of daily occurrence, whereby we are induced to make the *universal* of the phenomenon our problem. Investigators in the physical sciences, on the other hand, marvel only at selected and rare phenomena, and their problem is merely to refer these to phenomena better known. The lower a man is in an intellectual respect, the less puzzling and mysterious existence itself is to him; on the contrary, everything, how it is and that it is, seems to him a matter of course. This is due to the fact that his intellect remains quite true to its original destiny of being serviceable to the will as the medium of motives, and is therefore closely bound up with the world and with nature as an integral part of them. Consequently it is very far from comprehending the world purely objectively, detaching itself, so to speak, from the totality of things, facing this whole, and thus for the time being existing by itself. On the other hand, the philosophical wonder that springs from this is conditioned in the individual by higher development of intelligence, though generally not by this alone; but undoubtedly it is the knowledge of death, and therewith the consideration of the suffering and misery of life, that give the strongest impulse to philosophical reflection and metaphysical explanations of the world. If our life were without end and free from pain, it would possibly not occur to

---

[1]"For on account of wonder and astonishment men now philosophize, as they began to do in the first place." [Tr.]

anyone to ask why the world exists, and why it does so in precisely this way, but everything would be taken purely as a matter of course. In keeping with this, we find that the interest inspired by philosophical and also religious systems has its strongest and essential point absolutely in the dogma of some future existence after death. Although the latter systems seem to make the existence of their gods the main point, and to defend this most strenuously, at bottom this is only because they have tied up their teaching on immortality therewith, and regard the one as inseparable from the other; this alone is really of importance to them. For if we could guarantee their dogma of immortality to them in some other way, the lively ardour for their gods would at once cool; and it would make way for almost complete indifference if, conversely, the absolute impossibility of any immortality were demonstrated to them. For interest in the existence of the gods would vanish with the hope of a closer acquaintance with them, down to what residue might be bound up with their possible influence on the events of the present life. But if continued existence after death could also be proved to be incompatible with the existence of gods, because, let us say, it presupposed originality of mode of existence, they would soon sacrifice these gods to their own immortality, and be eager for atheism. The fact that the really materialistic as well as the absolutely sceptical systems have never been able to obtain a general or lasting influence is attributable to the same reason.

Temples and churches, pagodas and mosques, in all countries and ages, in their splendour and spaciousness, testify to man's need for metaphysics, a need strong and ineradicable, which follows close on the physical. The man of a satirical frame of mind could of course add that this need for metaphysics is a modest fellow content with meagre fare. Sometimes it lets itself be satisfied with clumsy fables and absurd fairy-tales. If only they are imprinted early enough, they are for man adequate explanations of his existence and supports for his morality. Consider the Koran, for example; this wretched book was sufficient to start a world-religion, to satisfy the metaphysical need of countless millions for twelve hundred years, to become the basis of their morality and of a remarkable contempt for death, and also to inspire them to bloody wars and the most extensive conquests. In this book we find the saddest and poorest form of theism. Much may be lost in translation, but I have not been able to discover in it one single idea of value. Such things show that the capacity for metaphysics does not go hand in hand with the need for it. Yet it will appear that, in the early ages of the present surface of the earth, things were different, and those who stood considerably nearer to the beginning of the human race and to the original source of organic nature than do we, also possessed both greater energy of the intuitive faculty of knowledge, and a more genuine disposition of mind. They were thus capable of a purer and more direct comprehension of the inner essence of nature, and were thus in a position to satisfy the need for metaphysics in a more estimable manner. Thus there originated in those primitive ancestors of the Brahmans, the Rishis, the almost superhuman conceptions recorded in the *Upanishads* of the *Vedas*.

On the other hand, there has never been a lack of persons who have endeavoured to create their livelihood out of this need of man's for metaphysics, and to exploit it as much as possible. Therefore in all nations there are monopolists and farmers-general of it, namely the priests. But their vocation had everywhere to be assured to them by their receiving the right to impart their metaphysical dogmas to people at a very early age, before the power of judgement has been roused from its morning slumber, and hence in earliest childhood; for every dogma well implanted then, however sense-less it may be, sticks for all time. If they had to wait till the power of judgement is mature, their privileges could not last.

A second, though not a numerous, class of persons, who derive their livelihood from men's need of metaphysics is constituted by those who live on *philosophy*. Among the Greeks they were called sophists; among the moderns they are called professors of philosophy. Aristotle (*Metaphysics*, ii, 2) without hesitation numbers Aristippus among the sophists. In Diogenes Laërtius (ii, 65) we find the reason for this, namely that he was the first of the Socratics to be paid for his philosophy, on which account Socrates sent him back his present. Among the moderns also those who live *by* philosophy are not only, as a rule and with the rarest exceptions, quite different from those who live *for* philosophy, but very often they are even the opponents of the latter, their secret and implacable enemies. For every genuine and impor-tant philosophical achievement will cast too great a shadow over theirs, and moreover will not adapt itself to the aims and limitations of the guild. For this reason they always endeavour to prevent such an achievement from finding favour. The customary means for this purpose, according to the times and circumstances in each case, are concealing, covering up, suppressing, hushing up, ignoring, keeping secret, or denying, disparaging, censuring, slandering, distorting, or finally denouncing and persecuting. Therefore many a great mind has had to drag itself breathlessly through life unrecog-nized, unhonoured, unrewarded, till finally after his death the world became undeceived as to him and as to them. In the meantime they had attained their end, had been accepted, by not allowing the man with a great mind to be accepted; and, with wife and child, they had lived *by* philosophy, while that man lived *for* it. When he is dead, however, matters are reversed; the new generation, and there always is one, now becomes heir to his achieve-ments, trims them down to its own standard, and now lives *by* him. That Kant could nevertheless live both *by* and *for* philosophy was due to the rare circumstance that, for the first time since Divus Antoninus and Divus Julianus, a philosopher once more sat on the throne. Only under such aus-pices could the *Critique of Pure Reason* have seen the light. Hardly was the king dead when already we see Kant, seized with fear, because he belonged to the guild, modify, castrate, and spoil his masterpiece in the second edition, yet even so, soon run the risk of losing his post, so that Campe invited him to come to Brunswick, to live with him as the instructor of his family (Ring, *Ansichten aus Kants Leben*, p. 68). As for university philosophy, it is as a rule mere juggling and humbug. The real purpose of such philosophy is to give the students in the very depths of their thinking that mental tendency which the ministry that appoints people to professorships regards as in keeping with its views and intentions. From the statesman's point of view, the ministry may even be right, only it follows from this that such philosophy of the chair is a *nervis alienis mobile lignum*,[2] and cannot pass for serious philosophy, but only for philosophy that is a joke. Moreover, it is in any case reasonable that such a supervision or guidance should extend only to chair-philosophy, not to the real philosophy that is in earnest. For if anything in the world is desirable, so desirable that even the dull and uneducated herd in its more reflective moments would value it more than silver and gold, it is that a ray of light should fall on the obscurity of our existence, and that we should obtain some information about this enigmatical life of ours, in which nothing is clear except its misery and vanity. But supposing even that this were in itself attainable, it is made impossible by imposed and enforced solutions of the problem.

We will now, however, subject to a general consideration the different ways of satisfying this need for metaphysics that is so strong.

By *metaphysics* I understand all so-called knowledge that goes beyond the possibility of experience, and so beyond nature or the given phenomenal appearance of things, in order to give information about that by which, in some sense or other, this experience or nature is conditioned, or in popular language, about that which is hidden behind nature, and renders nature possible. But the great original difference in the powers of understanding, and also their cultivation, which requires much leisure, cause so great a variety among men that, as soon as a nation has extricated itself from the uncultured state, no *one* metaphysical system can suffice for all. Therefore in the case of civilized nations we generally come across two different kinds of metaphysics, distinguished by the fact that the one has its verification and credentials *in itself*, the other *outside itself*. As the metaphysical systems of the first kind require reflection, culture, leisure, and judgement for the recognition of their credentials, they can be accessible only to an extremely small number of persons; moreover, they can arise and maintain themselves only in the case of an advanced civilization. The systems of the second kind, on the other hand, are exclusively for the great majority of people who are not capable of thinking but only of believing, and are susceptible not to

---

[2] "A wooden puppet moved by extraneous forces." [Tr.]

arguments, but only to authority. These systems may therefore be described as popular metaphysics, on the analogy of popular poetry and popular wisdom, by which is understood proverbs. These systems are known under the name of religions, and are to be found among all races, with the exception of the most uncivilized of all. As I have said, their evidence is external, and, as such, is called revelation, which is authenticated by signs and miracles. Their arguments are mainly threats of eternal, and indeed also temporal evils, directed against unbelievers, and even against mere doubters. As *ultima ratio theologorum*[3] we find among many nations the stake or things like it. If they seek a different authentication or use different arguments, they make the transition into the systems of the first kind, and may degenerate into a cross between the two, which brings more danger than advantage. For their invaluable prerogative of being imparted to *children* gives them the surest guarantee of permanent possession of the mind, and in this way their dogmas grow into a kind of second inborn intellect, like the twig on the grafted tree. The systems of the first kind, on the other hand, always appeal only to adults, but in them they always find a system of the second kind already in possession of their conviction. Both kinds of metaphysics, the difference between them which can be briefly indicated by the expressions doctrine of conviction and doctrine of faith, have in common the fact that every particular system of them stands in a hostile relation to all others of its kind. Between those of the first kind war is waged only with word and pen; between those of the second kind with fire and sword as well. Many of those of the second kind owe their propagation partly to this latter kind of polemic, and in the course of time all have divided the earth among themselves, and that with such decided authority that the peoples of the world are distinguished and separated rather according to them than according to nationality or government. They alone are *dominant*, each in its own province; those of the first kind, on the contrary, are at most *tolerated*, and even this only because, by reason of the small number of their adherents, they are usually not considered worth the trouble of combating with fire and sword, although, where it has seemed necessary, even these have been employed against them with success; moreover they are found only sporadically. But they have usually been tolerated only in a tamed and subjugated condition, since the system of the second kind that prevailed in the country ordered them to adapt their doctrines more or less closely to its own. Occasionally it has not only subjugated them, but made them serve its purpose, and use them as an additional horse to its coach. This, however, is a dangerous experiment, for, since those systems of the first kind are deprived of power, they believe they can assist themselves by craft and cunning; and they never entirely renounce a secret malice. This malice then occasionally comes on

---

[3]"The ultimate argument of theologians." [Tr.]

the scene unexpectedly, and inflicts injuries that are hard to cure. Moreover, their dangerous nature is increased by the fact that all the physical sciences, not excepting even the most innocent, are their secret allies against the systems of the second kind, and, without being themselves openly at war with these, they suddenly and unexpectedly do great harm in their province. Moreover, the attempt aimed at by the above-mentioned enlistment of the services of the systems of the first kind by those of the second, namely to give a system which originally has its authentication from outside an additional authentication from within, is by its nature perilous; for if it were capable of such an authentication, it would not have required an external one. And in general, it is always a hazardous undertaking to attempt to put a new foundation under a finished structure. Moreover, why should a religion require the suffrage of a philosophy? Indeed, it has everything on its side, revelation, documents, miracles, prophecies, government protection, the highest dignity and eminence, as is due to truth, the consent and reverence of all, a thousand temples in which it is preached and practiced, hosts of sworn priests, and, more than all this, the invaluable prerogative of being allowed to imprint its doctrines on the mind at the tender age of childhood, whereby they become almost innate ideas. With such an abundance of means at its disposal, still to desire the assent of wretched philosophers it would have to be more covetous, or still to attend to their contradiction it would have to be more apprehensive, than appears compatible with a good conscience.

To the above-established distinction between metaphysics of the first kind and of the second, is still to be added the following. A system of the first kind, that is, a philosophy, makes the claim, and therefore has the obligation, to be true *sensu stricto et proprio* in all that it says, for it appeals to thought and conviction. A religion, on the other hand, has only the obligation to be true *sensu allegorico*, since it is destined for the innumerable multitude who, being incapable of investigating and thinking, would never grasp the profoundest and most difficult truths *sensu proprio*. Before the people truth cannot appear naked. A symptom of this *allegorical* nature of religions is the *mysteries*, to be found perhaps in every religion, that is, certain dogmas that cannot even be distinctly conceived, much less be literally true. In fact, it might perhaps be asserted that some absolute inconsistencies and contradictions, some actual absurdities, are an essential ingredient of a complete religion; for these are just the stamp of its *allegorical* nature, and the only suitable way of making the ordinary mind and uncultured understanding *feel* what would be incomprehensible to it, namely that religion deals at bottom with an entirely different order of things, an order of *things-in-themselves*. In the presence of such an order the laws of this phenomenal world, according to which it must speak, disappear. Therefore, not only the contradictory but also the intelligible dogmas are really only allegories and accommodations to the human power of comprehension. It seems to me that Augustine and even Luther adhered to the mysteries of Christianity in this spirit, as opposed to Pelagianism, which seeks to reduce everything to trite and dull comprehensibility. From this point of view it is easy to understand how Tertullian could in all seriousness say: *Prorsus credibile est, quia ineptum est: . . . certum est, quia impossible. (De Carne Christi*, c. 5.)[4] This *allegorical* nature of religions also exempts them from the proofs incumbent on philosophy, and in general from scrutiny and investigation. Instead of this, they demand faith, in other words, a voluntary acceptance that such is the state of affairs. Then, as faith guides conduct, and the allegory is framed so that, as regards the practical, it always leads precisely whither the truth *sensu proprio* would also lead, religion justly promises eternal bliss to those who believe. We therefore see that in the main, and for the great majority unable to devote themselves to thinking, religions fill very well the place of metaphysics in general, the need of which man feels to be imperative. They do this partly for a practical purpose as the guiding star of their action, as the public standard of integrity and virtue, as Kant admirably expresses it; partly as the indispensable consolation in the deep sorrows of life. In this they completely take the place of an objectively true system of metaphysics, since they lift man above himself and above existence in time, as well, perhaps, as such a system ever could. In this their great value, indeed their indispensability is quite clearly to be seen. For Plato rightly says: φιλόσοφον πλῆθοζ ἀδύνατον εἶναι (*vulgus philosophum esse impossibile est*),[5] (*Republic*, VI [494 A], p. 89 *Bip*.). On the other hand, the only stumbling-block is that religions never dare acknowledge their allegorical nature, but have to assert that they are true *sensu proprio*. In this way they encroach on the sphere of metaphysics proper, and provoke its antagonism. Therefore such antagonism is expressed at all times, when metaphysics has not been chained up. The controversy between supernaturalists and rationalists, carried on so incessantly in our own day, is due to the failure to recognize the allegorical nature of all religion. Thus, both want to have Christianity true *sensu proprio*; in this sense, the supernaturalists wish to maintain it without deduction, with skin and hair as it were; and here they have much to contend with in view of the knowledge and general culture of the age. The rationalists, on the other hand, attempt to explain away exegetically all that is characteristically Christian, whereupon they retain something that is not true either *sensu proprio* or *sensu allegorico*, but rather a mere platitude, little better than Judaism, or at most a shallow Pelagianism, and, what is worst of all, an infamous optimism, absolutely foreign to Christianity proper. Moreover, the attempt to found a religion on reason (*Vernunft*) removes it into the other class of metaphysics, namely that which has its

---

[4]"It is thoroughly credible because it is absurd: . . . it is certain because it is impossible." [Tr.]

[5]"It is impossible for the crowd to be philosophically enlightened." [Tr.]

authentication *in itself*, and thus on to a foreign soil, the soil of the philosophical systems, and consequently into the conflict these wage against one another in their own arena; and so this brings it under the rifle-fire of scepticism, and the heavy artillery of the *Critique of Pure Reason*. But for it to venture here would be downright presumption.

It would be most beneficial to both kinds of metaphysics for each to remain clearly separated from the other, and to confine itself to its own province, in order there to develop fully its true nature. Instead of this, the endeavour throughout the Christian era has been to bring about a fusion of the two by carrying over the dogmas and concepts of the one into the other, and in this way both are impaired. In our day this has been done most openly in that strange hybrid or centaur, the so-called philosophy of religion. As a kind of gnosis, this attempts to interpret the given religion, and to explain what is true *sensu allegorico* through something that is true *sensu proprio*. But for this we should have already to know the truth *sensu proprio*, and in that case interpretation would be superfluous. For to attempt first to find metaphysics, i.e., the truth *sensu proprio*, merely from religion by explanation and a fresh interpretation, would be a precarious and perilous undertaking. We could decide to do this only if it were established that truth, like iron and other base metals, could occur only in the ore, and not in the pure unalloyed state, and that it could therefore be obtained only by reduction from that ore.

Religions are necessary for the people, and are an inestimable benefit to them. But if they attempt to oppose the progress of mankind in the knowledge of truth, then with the utmost possible indulgence and forebearance they must be pushed on one side. And to require that even a great mind—a Shakespeare or a Goethe—should make the dogmas of any religion his implicit conviction, *bona fide et sensu proprio*, is like requiring a giant to put on the shoes of a dwarf. . . .

I cannot, as is generally done, put the *fundamental difference* of all religions in the question whether they are monotheistic, polytheistic, pantheistic, or atheistic, but only in the question whether they are optimistic or pessimistic, in other words, whether they present the existence of this world as justified by itself, and consequently praise and commend it, or consider it as something which can be conceived only as the consequence of our guilt, and thus really ought not to be, in that they recognize that pain and death cannot lie in the eternal, original, and immutable order of things, that which in every respect ought to be. The power by virtue of which Christianity was able to overcome first Judaism, and then the paganism of Greece and Rome, is to be found solely in its pessimism, in the confession that our condition is both exceedingly sorrowful and sinful, whereas Judaism and paganism were optimistic. That truth, profoundly and painfully felt by everyone, took effect, and entailed the need for redemption.

I turn to a general consideration of the other kind of metaphysics, that which has its authentication in itself, and is called *philosophy*. I remind the reader of its previously mentioned origin from a *wonder or astonishment* about the world and our own existence, since these obtrude themselves on the intellect as a riddle, whose solution then occupies mankind without intermission. Here I would first of all draw attention to the fact that this could not be the case if, in Spinoza's sense, so often put forth again in our own day under modern forms and descriptions as pantheism, the world were an *"absolute substance,"* and consequently a *positively necessary mode of existence*. For this implies that it exists with a necessity so great, that beside it every other necessity conceivable as such to our understanding must look like an accident or contingency. Thus it would then be something that embraced not only every actual, but also any possible, existence in such a way that, as indeed Spinoza states, its possibility and its actuality would be absolutely one. Therefore its non-being would be impossibility itself, and so it would be something whose non-being or other-being would inevitably be wholly inconceivable, and could in consequence be just as little thought away as can, for instance, time or space. Further, since *we ourselves* would be parts, modes, attributes, or accidents of such an absolute substance, which would be the only thing capable in any sense of existing at any time and in any place, our existence and its, together with its properties, would necessarily be very far from presenting themselves to us as surprising, remarkable, problematical, in fact as the unfathomable and ever-disquieting riddle; on the contrary, they would of necessity be even more self-evident and a matter of course than the fact that two and two make four. For we should necessarily be quite incapable of thinking anything else than that the world is, and is as it is; consequently, we should inevitably be just as little conscious of its existence *as such*, that is to say, as a problem for reflection, as we are of our planet's incredibly rapid motion.

Now all this is by no means the case. Only to the animal lacking thoughts or ideas do the world and existence appear to be a matter of course. To man, on the contrary, they are a problem, of which even the most uncultured and narrow-minded person is at certain more lucid moments vividly aware, but which enters the more distinctly and permanently into everyone's consciousness, the brighter and more reflective that consciousness is, and the more material for thinking he has acquired through culture. Finally, in minds adapted to philosophizing, all this is raised to Plato's θαυμάζειν, μάλα φιλοσοφικὸν πάθος (*mirari, valde philosophicus affectus*),[6] that is, to that *wonder or astonishment* which comprehends in all its magnitude the problem that incessantly occupies the nobler portion of mankind in every age and in every country, and allows it no rest. In fact, the balance wheel

---

[6]"Astonishment as a very philosophical emotion." [*Theaetetus*, 155 D. Tr.]

which maintains in motion the watch of metaphysics that never runs down, is the clear knowledge that this world's non-existence is just as possible as its existence. Therefore, Spinoza's view of the world as an absolutely necessary mode of existence, in other words, as something that positively and in every sense ought to and must be, is a false one. Even simple theism in its cosmological proof tacitly starts from the fact that it infers the world's previous non-existence from its existence; thus, it assumes in advance that the world is something contingent. What is more, in fact, we very soon look upon the world as something whose non-existence is not only conceivable, but even preferable to its existence. Therefore our astonishment at it easily passes into a brooding over that *fatality* which could nevertheless bring about its existence, and by virtue of which such an immense force as is demanded for the production and maintenance of such a world could be directed so much against its own interest and advantage. Accordingly, philosophical astonishment is at bottom one that is dismayed and distressed; philosophy, like the overture to *Don Juan*, starts with a minor chord. It follows from this that philosophy cannot be either Spinozism or optimism. The more specific character, just mentioned, of the astonishment that urges us to philosophize, obviously springs from the sight of the *evil and wickedness* in the world. Even if these were in the most equal ratio to each other, and were also far outweighed by the good, yet they are something that absolutely and in general ought not to be. But as nothing can come out of nothing, they too must have their germ in the origin or the kernel of the world itself. It is hard for us to assume this when we look at the size, the order, and the completeness of the physical world, since we imagine that what had the power to produce such a world must also have been well able to avoid the evil and the wickedness. It is easy to understand that this assumption (the truest expression of which is Ormuzd and Ahriman) is hardest of all for theism. Therefore, the freedom of the will was invented in the first place to dispose of *wickedness*; this, however, is only a disguised way of making something out of nothing, since it assumes an *operari* that resulted from no *esse* (see *Die beiden Grundprobleme der Ethik*, pp. 58 *et seq.*; 2nd ed., pp. 57 *et seq.*). Then the attempt was made to get rid of *evil* by imputing it to matter, or even to an unavoidable necessity, and here the devil, who is really the *expediens ad hoc*,[7] was reluctantly set aside. To evil *death* also belongs; but *wickedness* is merely the shifting of the evil that exists in each case from oneself on to another. Hence, as we have said above, it is wickedness, evil, and death that qualify and intensify philosophical astonishment. Not merely that the world exists, but still more that it is such a miserable and melancholy world, is the *punctum pruriens*[8] of metaphysics, the problem awakening in mankind an unrest that cannot be quieted either by scepticism or criticism.

---

[7]"Means to this end." [Tr.]
[8]"Tormenting problem." [Tr.]

We also find *physics*, in the widest sense of the word, concerned with the explanation of phenomena in the world; but it lies already in the nature of the explanations themselves that they cannot be sufficient. *Physics* is unable to stand on its own feet, but needs a *metaphysics* on which to support itself, whatever fine airs it may assume towards the latter. For it explains phenomena by something still more unknown than are they, namely by laws of nature resting on forces of nature, one of which is also the vital force. Certainly the whole present condition of all things in the world or in nature must necessarily be capable of explanation from purely physical causes. But such an explanation—supposing one actually succeeded so far as to be able to give it—must always just as necessarily be burdened with two essential imperfections (as it were with two sore points, or like Achilles with the vulnerable heel, or the devil with the cloven foot). On account of these imperfections, everything so explained would still really remain un-explained. The first imperfection is that the *beginning* of the chain of causes and effects that explains everything, in other words, of the connected and continuous changes, can positively *never* be reached, but, just like the limits of the world in space and time, recedes incessantly and *in infinitum*. The second imperfection is that all the efficient causes from which everything is explained always rest on something wholly inexplicable, that is, on the origi-nal *qualities* of things and the *natural forces* that make their appearance in them. By virtue of such forces they produce a definite effect, e.g., weight, hardness, impact, elasticity, heat, electricity, chemical forces, and so on, and such forces remain in every given explanation like an unknown quantity, not to be eliminated at all, in an otherwise perfectly solved algebraical equation. Accordingly there is not a fragment of clay, however little its value, that is not entirely composed of inexplicable qualities. Therefore these two inevita-ble defects in every purely physical, i.e., causal, explanation indicate that such an explanation can be only *relatively* true, and that its whole method and nature cannot be the only, the ultimate and hence sufficient one, in other words, cannot be the method that will ever be able to lead to the satisfactory solution of the difficult riddle of things, and to the true under-standing of the world and of existence; but that the *physical* explanation, in general and as such, still requires one that is *metaphysical*, which would furnish the key to all its assumptions, but for that very reason would have to follow quite a different path. The first step to this is that we should bring to distinct consciousness and firmly retain the distinction between the two, that is, the difference between *physics* and *metaphysics*. . . .

Accordingly, naturalism, or the purely physical way of considering things, will never be sufficient; it is like a sum in arithmetic that never comes out. Beginningless and endless causal series, inscrutable fundamental forces, endless space, beginningless time, infinite divisibility of matter, and all this further conditioned by a knowing brain, in which alone it exists just like a dream and without which it vanishes—all these things constitute the labyrinth in which naturalism leads us incessantly round and round. The height to which the natural sciences have risen in our time puts all the previous centuries entirely in the shade in this respect, and is a summit reached by mankind for the first time. But however great the advances which *physics* (understood in the wide sense of the ancients) may make, not the smallest step towards metaphysics will be made in this way, just as a surface never attains cubical contents however far its extension is carried. For such advances will always supplement only knowledge of the *phenomenon*, whereas *metaphysics* strives to pass beyond the phenomenal appearance to that which appears; and even if we had in addition an entire and complete experience, matters would not be advanced in this way as regards the main point. In fact, even if a man wandered through all the planets of all the fixed stars, he would still not have made one step in *metaphysics*. On the contrary, the greatest advances in *physics* will only make the need for a system of *metaphysics* felt more and more, since the corrected, extended, and more thorough knowledge of nature is the very knowledge that always undermines and finally overthrows the metaphysical assumptions that till then have prevailed. . . .

I regard it as a great merit of my philosophy that all its truths have been found independently of one another, through a consideration of the real world; but their unity and agreement, about which I did not concern myself, have always appeared subsequently of themselves. For this reason also it is rich, and has wide-spreading roots in the soil of the reality of perception from which all the nourishment of abstract truths springs. Again, therefore, it is not wearisome and tedious—a quality that might otherwise be regarded as essential to philosophy, to judge from the philosophical writings of the last fifty years. On the other hand, if all the doctrines of a philosophy are derived merely one from another, and ultimately indeed even from one first principle, it must prove to be poor and meagre, and consequently wearisome, for nothing more can follow from a proposition than what in reality it already states itself. Moreover, everything then depends on the correctness of *one* proposition, and by a single mistake in the deduction, the truth of the whole would be endangered. Even less guarantee is given by the systems that start from an intellectual intuition, i.e., a kind of ecstasy or clairvoyance. All knowledge so gained must be rejected as subjective, individual, and consequently problematical. Even if it actually existed, it would not be communicable, for only the normal knowledge of the brain is communicable; if it is abstract knowledge, through concepts and words; if it is knowledge of mere perception, through works of art.

If, as so often happens, metaphysics is reproached with having made so little progress in the course of so many centuries, it should also be borne in mind that no other science has grown up like it under constant oppression, none has been so hampered and hindered from without as it has been at all times by the religion of every country. Everywhere in possession of a monopoly of metaphysical knowledge, religion regards metaphysics as a weed growing by its side, as an unauthorized worker, as a horde of gypsies. As a rule, it tolerates metaphysics only on condition that the latter accommodates itself to serve and emulate it. For where has there ever been true freedom of thought? People have boasted of it often enough, but as soon as it tried to do more than to differ from the religion of the country about some subordinate dogmas, a holy shudder at its audacity seized the proclaimers of tolerance, and they said; "Not a step farther!" What progress in metaphysics was possible under such oppression? Indeed, that pressure or coercion exercised by privileged metaphysics extends not only to the *communication* of thoughts, but to *thinking* itself. This is brought about by its dogmas being so firmly impressed with studied, solemn, and serious airs on the tender, docile, trusting, and thoughtless age of childhood, that henceforth they grow up with the brain, and assume almost the nature of inborn ideas. Therefore some philosophers have considered them to be such, and there are still several who pretend so to regard them. But nothing can so firmly oppose the comprehension of even the *problem* of metaphysics as a previous solution to it forced on the mind, and early implanted in it. For the necessary starting-point of all genuine philosophizing is the deep feeling of the Socratic: "This one thing I know, that I know nothing." In this respect also the ancients had the advantage over us; for it is true that their national religions somewhat restricted the communication of what was thought, but they did not encroach on the freedom of thought itself, because they were not formally and solemnly impressed on children, and in general were not taken so seriously. Therefore the ancients are still our teachers in metaphysics.

Whenever metaphysics is reproached with its slight progress, and with never having yet reached its goal in spite of such constant efforts, we should further reflect that in the meanwhile it has always performed the invaluable service of limiting the infinite claims of the privileged metaphysics, and yet at the same time working against naturalism and materialism proper, which are brought about by this very metaphysics as an inevitable reaction. Consider to what a pitch of arrogance and insolence the priesthood of every religion would go, if belief in its doctrines were as firm and blind as as they really wish. Look back also at all the wars, riots, rebellions, and revolutions in Europe from the eighth to the eighteenth century; how few will be found that have not had as their essence or pretext some controversy about beliefs, that is, metaphysical problems, which became the occasion for making trouble between nations. That whole period of a thousand years is indeed one of constant massacre and murder, now on the battlefield, now on the scaffold, now in the streets—all over metaphysical questions! I wish I had an authentic list of all the crimes that Christianity has actually prevented, and of all the good deeds that it has actually performed, in order to be able to put them in the other pan of the balance.

Finally, as regards the *obligations* of metaphysics, it has but one, for it is one that tolerates no other beside it, namely the obligation to be *true*. If we wished to impose on it other obligations besides this one, such as that it must be spiritualistic, optimistic, monotheistic, or even only moral, we cannot know beforehand whether this would be opposed to the fulfilment of that first obligation, without which all its other achievements would of necessity be obviously worthless. Accordingly, a given philosophy has no other standard of its value than that of truth. For the rest, philosophy is essentially *world-wisdom*; its problem is the world. With this alone it has to do, and it leaves the gods in peace; but in return for this, it expects them to leave it in peace also.

II

What Am I?

MYSELF AND MY BODY

2

PLATO

---

introduction

One of the most important metaphysical questions that occurs to a reflective mind, and one of the first that occurs to persons gifted with the capacity for wonder, is: What am I? One finds a world that is deeply puzzling, and within it, as a minute part, oneself—the most mysterious and overwhelmingly important thing in creation. But what is it? What am I? What, more generally, is a person?

Plato's answer has become so much a part of our intellectual heritage that hardly anyone in the Western world, of whatever education or lack of it, can shake off its influence. Plato declared that a person is not what one sees—not a being with arms and legs and a head, not flesh and bone. That is a person's *body*, not the person himself. A person, or what one truly is, is a mind or soul that governs or directs that body. It is of a divine nature, unlike the body, which is a thing of earthen elements, and it suffers no decay or dissolution; it is immortal. Thus the true person, or soul, is not only distinct in nature from the body in which it is temporarily lodged but in many ways is opposed to it. The soul seeks knowledge, truth, the vision of beauty and goodness, while the body, governed by cravings for earthly things, constantly drags the soul down, hampers it, obscures its vision, and corrupts it.

The death of the body, therefore, cannot be regarded as an evil. Such death leaves the soul, the true person, untouched. Indeed, by the death of the body the soul becomes liberated from its enslavement to the material world, and not only lives on, eternally, but enjoys a divine existence of wisdom and the contemplation of eternal things.

In his writings Plato represented his teacher Socrates as the source of these ideas. Actually, the concept of the human soul as something distinct from the body is much older in Greek thought. The Orphics, whose religious ideas were well known to Socrates, based their practices upon this supposed dual nature of a person, but taught that the soul could obtain liberation from the body through ritual. The Pythagoreans upheld a similar idea of man's dual nature, but sought liberation or a life after the death of the body through the cultivation of knowledge, particularly mathematics. Socrates was thus a part of a tradition, his chief innovation being the contention that the key to salvation lies in philosophical wisdom and the moral goodness that it nourishes.

The Christian Church assimilated this metaphysical conception, the theological claim being that salvation was to be achieved, not merely through ritual, or knowledge, or moral purity, but through religious faith. St. Augustine, who was profoundly influenced by Platonic and Neo-Platonic metaphysics, was one of the most important transmitters of this tradition, which has, with numerous refinements and variations, become an ingredient not only of Christian thought but of our whole culture. Even those who have repudiated religious influences in their thinking are still, often unconsciously, deeply influenced by these ideas.

This dualism of mind and body was taken over from the religious tradition by philosophy. Descartes, usually thought of as the father of modern philosophy, and as the one who had most to do with emancipating philosophy from the Church, never seriously doubted this dualistic conception of a person as a soul and a body. Indeed, he thought it was one of the most elementary deliverances of reason. Despite his insistence upon doubt and skepticism, he could not divest himself of this ancient idea, imbibed from his teachers at a tender age. Nor, it is safe to say, can his contempory descendants. This does not mean that all philosophers still uphold this ancient dualism; many do not. But few do not take it seriously, even while inveighing against it; and even among the most critical, among those who wish to be influenced as little as possible by archaic metaphysics and religion, many find it quite impossible to take seriously the idea that there might be *no* distinction between a person (or what they are apt to refer to as the "mind" or "self") and his body.

Plato's theory, then, is of immense importance, not only because of its inherent profundity and clarity, but also because it has become a basic part of the metaphysics of the whole of Christendom, even for those who have never heard of it, or even profess hostility to the whole historical tradition that was built upon it.

The passages are from the *Phaedo*, and they purport to represent Socrates' reflections upon his own impending death. Simmias and Cebes, who are his partners in conversation, were not philosophers, but they serve well in this dialogue to express the doubts and skepticism that any reader is likely to feel.

The arguments Socrates develops in defense of his metaphysics of the soul are of uneven value, beginning with the rather simple thesis that all opposites arise from each other, such that there is a perpetual alternation between life and death. As one must live in order to die, so also must one die in order to live again. Again, it was a basic principle of Platonic metaphysics, as here enunciated by Socrates, that there are two realms of being: the familiar realm of visible matter, marked by change, impermanence, and decay, and that of eternal and invisible spirit, where things do not suffer any change, this being the realm of perfection. The human soul, it is claimed, resembles the latter more than the former, and in any case tends toward that realm as its true home. This idea, which is really quite foreign to both Jewish and Christian scripture, has nevertheless been assimilated into Christian thought and finds its way, for example, into numerous hymns.

The objection raised to all this by Simmias, to the effect that the soul might be related to the body as the harmony of a musical instrument is related to that instrument itself, is deeply incisive. It is an early expression of the theory of epiphenomenalism, as it eventually came to be called. Changing Simmias' example a bit, consider a violin and the lovely, melodious music that comes from it. The violin is a physical object, but the harmonious and beautiful music is not. The two are quite distinct. Yet this should tempt no one to suppose that, after the violin has been broken and discarded, its music will still be there, eternally. The music must perish with the instrument.

To understand the final and crowning argument of these passages—an argument that has always been much misunderstood—one needs to appreciate another of the ideas of antiquity whose influence is still strongly felt. The idea was that life is something that is possessed by living things. Nonliving things are simply things that lack life. Things that were once living are things that have lost their lives. We speak, for instance, of the gift of life, the spark of life, losing one's life, saving a life, and so on. Conversely, the body of a dead person is referred to as his "remains," or what he has left behind. The Greeks, when they spoke of the life of a living thing, identified that life with the soul of that thing. By virtue of its possession of a soul a man or animal was a living thing. Without that soul it would be something inanimate. To die is thus to lose one's life—that is, one's soul. But in this case, it is incoherent to speak of the *soul* itself as dying. Death is the separation from the body of the life or soul that dwelt there. So the soul itself is not susceptible of death. Hence, it is immortal.

This central thought is expressed with more subtlety in Plato's crowning argument. Thus the soul, though not declared to be identical with life, is said to be living by its very nature—as the number three is odd by its very nature and can never become an even number three, or as snow is cold by its very nature and can never become warm snow. The soul, similarly, can never become dead. The argument, given its metaphysical presupposition, is absolutely conclusive. If, therefore, anyone declares its conclusion—that the soul is immortal—to be doubtful then he must render a different conception of what life is, or what it means for something to be a living thing.

Plato lived in the fifth and fourth centuries B.C. Most of his philosophical thought that has been preserved is expressed in dialogue form, in which Socrates is the central figure, as in the selections that follow. Departures from the main philosophical arguments in this dialogue have been dropped.

The Soul*

Now, O my judges, I desire to prove to you that the real philosopher has reason to be of good cheer when he is about to die, and that after death he may hope to obtain the greatest good in the other world. And how this may be, Simmias and Cebes, I will endeavour to explain. For I deem that the true votary of philosophy is likely to be misunderstood by other men; they do not perceive that of his own accord he is always engaged in the pursuit of dying and death; and if this be so, and he has had the desire of death all his life long, why when his time comes should he repine at that which he has been always pursuing and desiring?

Simmias said laughingly: Though I am not altogether in a laughing humour, you have made me laugh, Socrates; for I cannot help thinking that the many when they hear your words will say how truly you have described philosophers, and our people at home will likewise say that philosophers are in reality moribund, and that they have found them out to be deserving of the death which they desire.

And they are right, Simmias, in thinking so, with the exception of the words 'they have found them out'; for they have not found out either in what sense the true philosopher is moribund and deserves death, or what manner of death he deserves. But enough of them:—let us discuss the matter among ourselves. Do we attach a definite meaning to the word 'death'?

To be sure, replied Simmias.

* From Plato, *Phaedo*, in *The Dialogues of Plato*, trans. Benjamin Jowett, 4th ed. rev. (Oxford: The Clarendon Press, 1953).

Is it not just the separation of soul and body? And to be dead is the completion of this; when the soul exists by herself and is released from the body, and the body is released from the soul. This, I presume, is what is meant by death?

Just so, he replied.

There is another question, which will probably throw light on our present inquiry if you and I can agree about it:—Ought the philosopher to care about such pleasures—if they are to be called pleasures—as those of eating and drinking?

Certainly not, answered Simmias.

And what about the pleasures of love—should he care for them?

By no means.

And will he think much of the other ways of indulging the body, for example, the acquisition of costly raiment or sandals, or other adornments of the body? Instead of caring about them, does he not rather despise anything more than nature needs? What do you say?

I should say that the true philosopher would despise them.

Would you not say that he is entirely concerned with the soul and not with the body? He would like, as far as he can, to get away from the body and to turn to the soul.

Quite true.

First, therefore, in matters of this sort philosophers, above all other men, may be observed in every sort of way to dissever the soul from the communion of the body.

Very true.

Whereas, Simmias, the rest of the world are of opinion that to him who has no taste for bodily pleasures and no part in them, life is not worth having; and that he who is indifferent about them is as good as dead.

Perfectly true.

What again shall we say of the actual acquirement of knowledge?—is the body, if invited to share in the inquiry, a hindrance or a help? I mean to say, have sight and hearing, as found in man, any truth in them? Are they not, as the poets are always repeating, inaccurate witnesses? and yet, if even they are inaccurate and indistinct, what is to be said of the other senses?—for you will allow that they are the best of them?

Certainly, he replied.

Then when does the soul attain truth?—for in attempting to consider anything in company with the body she is obviously deceived by it.

True.

Then must not true reality be revealed to her in thought, if at all?

Yes.

And thought is best when the mind is gathered into herself and none of these things trouble her—neither sounds nor sights nor pain, nor again any pleasure,—when she takes leave of the body, and has as little as possible to do with it, when she has no bodily sense or desire, but is aspiring after true being?

Certainly.

And here again it is characteristic of the philosopher to despise the body; his soul runs away from his body and desires to be alone and by herself?

That is true.

Well, but there is another thing, Simmias: Is there or is there not an absolute justice?

Assuredly there is.

And an absolute beauty[1] and absolute good?

Of course.

But did you ever behold any of them with your eyes?

Certainly not.

Or did you ever reach them with any other bodily sense?—and I speak not of these alone, but of absolute greatness, and health, and strength, and, in short, of the reality or true nature of everything. Is the truth of them ever perceived through the bodily organs? or rather, is not the nearest approach to the knowledge of their several natures made by him who so orders his intellectual vision as to have the most exact conception of the essence of each thing which he considers?

Certainly.

And he attains to the purest knowledge of them who goes to each with the intellect alone, not introducing or intruding in the act of thought sight or any other sense together with reason, but with the intellect in its own purity searches into the truth of each thing in its purity; he who has got rid, as far as he can, of eyes and ears and, so to speak, of the whole body, these being in his opinion distracting elements which when they associate with the soul hinder her from acquiring truth and knowledge—who, if not he, is likely to attain to the knowledge of true being?

What you say has a wonderful truth in it, Socrates, replied Simmias.

And when real philosophers consider all these things, will they not be led to make a reflection which they will express in words something like the following? 'Have we not found,' they will say, 'a path of thought which seems to bring us and our argument to the conclusion, that while we are in the body, and while the soul is mixed with the evils of the body, our desire will not be satisfied? and our desire is of the truth. For the body is a source of countless distractions by reason of the mere requirement of food, and is liable also to diseases which overtake and impede us in the pursuit of truth: it fills us full of loves, and lusts, and fears, and fancies of all kinds, and endless foolery, and in very truth, as men say, takes away from us the power of

---

[1][On 'absolute beauty,' 'absolute justice,' & c., see the note following the introduction to the *Greater Hippias*, p. 563 *infra*.]

thinking at all. Whence come wars, and fightings, and factions? whence but from the body and the lusts of the body? All wars are occasioned by the love of money, and money has to be acquired for the sake of the body and in slavish ministration to it; and by reason of all these impediments we have no time to give to philosophy; and, last and worst of all, even if the body allows us leisure and we betake ourselves to some speculation, it is always breaking in upon us, causing turmoil and confusion in our inquiries, and so amazing us that we are prevented from seeing the truth. It has been proved to us by experience that if we would have pure knowledge of anything we must be quit of the body—the soul by herself must behold things by themselves: and then we shall attain that which we desire, and of which we say that we are lovers—wisdom; not while we live, but, as the argument shows, only after death; for if while in company with the body the soul cannot have pure knowledge, one of two things follows—either knowledge is not to be attained at all, or, if at all, after death. For then, and not till then, the soul will be parted from the body and exist by herself alone. In this present life, we think that we make the nearest approach to knowledge when we have the least possible intercourse or communion with the body, and do not suffer the contagion of the bodily nature, but keep ourselves pure until the hour when God himself is pleased to release us. And thus getting rid of the foolishness of the body we may expect to be pure and hold converse with the pure, and to know of ourselves all that exists in perfection unalloyed, which, I take it, is no other than the truth. For the impure are not permitted to lay hold of the pure.' These are the sort of words, Simmias, which the true lovers of knowledge cannot help saying to one another, and thinking. You would agree; would you not?

Undoubtedly, Socrates.

But, O my friend, if this be true, there is great reason to hope that, going whither I go, when I have come to the end of my journey I shall fully attain that which has been the pursuit of our lives. And therefore I accept with good hope this change of abode which is now enjoined upon me, and not I only. but every other man who believes that his mind has been made ready and that he is in a manner purified.

Certainly, replied Simmias.

And does it not follow that purification is nothing but that separation of the soul from the body, which has for some time been the subject of our argument; the habit of the soul gathering and collecting herself into herself from all sides out of the body; the dwelling in her own place alone, as in another life, so also in this, as far as she can;—the release of the soul from the chains of the body?

Very true, he said.

And this separation and release of the soul from the body is termed death?

To be sure, he said.

And the true philosophers, and they only, are ever seeking to release the soul. Is not the separation and release of the soul from the body their especial study?

That is true.

And, as I was saying at first, there would be a ridiculous contradiction in men studying to live as nearly as they can in a state like that of death, and yet repining when death comes upon them.

Clearly.

In fact, the true philosophers, Simmias, are always occupied in the practice of dying, wherefore also to them least of all men is death terrible. Look at the matter thus:—if they have been in every way estranged from the body, and are wanting to be alone with the soul, when this desire of theirs is being granted, how inconsistent would they be if they trembled and repined, instead of rejoicing at their departure to that place where, when they arrive, they hope to gain that which in life they desired—and their desire was for wisdom—and at the same time to be rid of the company of their enemy. Many a man who has lost by death an earthly love, or wife, or son, has been willing to go in quest of them to the world below, animated by the hope of seeing them there and of being with those for whom he yearned. And will he who is a true lover of wisdom, and is strongly persuaded in like manner that only in the world below he can worthily enjoy her, still repine at death? Will he not depart with joy? Surely he will, O my friend, if he be a true philosopher. For he will have a firm conviction that there, and there only, he can find wisdom in her purity. And if this be true, he would be very absurd, as I was saying, if he were afraid of death.

He would indeed, replied Simmias. . . .

Suppose we consider the question whether the souls of men after death are or are not in the world below. There comes into my mind an ancient doctrine which affirms that they are there after they leave our world, and returning hither, are born again from the dead. Now if it be true that the living come from the dead, then our souls must exist in the other world, for if not, how could they have been born again? And this would be conclusive, if it were established that the living are born from the dead and have no other origin; but if this is not so, then other arguments will have to be adduced.

Very true, replied Cebes.

Then let us consider the whole question, not in relation to man only, but in relation to animals generally, and to plants, and to everything of which there is generation, and the proof will be easier. Are not all things which have opposites generated out of their opposites? I mean such things as the beautiful and the ugly, the just and the unjust—and there are innumerable other cases. Let us consider therefore whether it is necessary that a thing should come to be from its own opposite, if it has one, and from no other source: for example, anything which becomes greater must become greater after being less?

True.

And that which becomes less must have been once greater and then have become less?

Yes.

And the weaker is generated from the stronger, and the swifter from the slower?

Very true.

And the worse is from the better, and the more just is from the more unjust?

Of course.

And is this true of all opposites? and are we convinced that all of them are generated out of opposites?

Yes.

And in this universal opposition of all things, are there not also two intermediate processes which are ever going on, from one to the other opposite, and back again; for example, where there is a greater and a less there is also the intermediate process of increase and diminution, and so a thing is said to increase or to diminish?

Yes, he said.

And there are many other processes, such as analysis and combination, cooling and heating, which equally involve a passage into and out of one another. And this necessarily holds of all opposites, even though not always expressed in words—they are really generated out of one another, and there is a passing or process from one to the other of them?

Very true, he replied.

Well, and is there not an opposite of being alive, as sleep is the opposite of being awake?

True, he said.

And what is it?

Being dead, he answered.

And these, if they are opposites, are generated the one from the other, and have their two intermediate processes also?

Of course.

Now, said Socrates, I will analyse one of the two pairs of opposites which I have mentioned to you, and also its intermediate processes, and you shall analyse the other to me. The two members of the first pair are sleep and waking. The state of sleep is opposed to the state of waking, and out of sleeping waking is generated, and out of waking, sleeping; and the process of generation is in the one case falling asleep, and in the other waking up. Do you agree?

I entirely agree.

Then, suppose that you analyse life and death to me in the same manner. Is not the state of death opposed to that of life?

Yes.

And they are generated one from the other?

Yes.

What is generated from the living?

The dead.

And what from the dead?

I can only say in answer—the living.

Then the living, whether things or persons, Cebes, are generated from the dead?

So it would seem, he replied.

Then the inference is that our souls exist in the world below?

It appears so.

And one of the two processes or generations is visible—for surely the act of dying is visible?

Surely, he said.

What then is to be the result? Shall we exclude the opposite process? and shall we suppose nature to be lame in this respect? Must we not rather assign to the act of dying some corresponding process of generation?

Certainly, he replied.

And what is that?

Return to life.

And return to life, if there be such a thing, is the birth of the dead into the number of the living?

Quite true.

Then here is a new way by which we arrive at the conclusion that the living come from the dead, just as the dead come from the living; and we agreed that this, if true, would be adequate proof that the souls of the dead must exist in some place out of which they come again.

Yes, Socrates, he said; the conclusion seems to flow necessarily out of our previous admissions. . . .

I think, said Simmias, that Cebes is satisfied: although he is the most incredulous of mortals, yet I believe that he is sufficiently convinced of the existence of the soul before birth. But that after death the soul will continue to exist is not yet proven even to my own satisfaction. I cannot get rid of the objection to which Cebes was referring—the common fear that at the moment when the man dies the soul is dispersed, and that this may be the end of her. For admitting that she may have come into being and been framed out of some unknown other elements, and was in existence before entering the human body, why after having entered in and gone out again may she not herself be destroyed and come to an end?

Very true, Simmias, said Cebes; it appears that about half of what was required has been proved; to wit, that our souls existed before we were born;—that the soul will exist after death as well as before birth is the other half of which the proof is still wanting, and has to be supplied; when that is given the demonstration will be complete. . . .

Must we not, said Socrates, ask ourselves what kind of thing that is which is liable to be scattered, and for what kind of thing we ought to fear that fate? and what is that for which we need have no fear? And then we may proceed further to inquire to which of the two classes soul belongs—our hopes and fears as to our own souls will turn upon the answers to these questions.

Very true, he said.

Now that which is compounded and is by nature composite may be supposed to be therefore capable, as of being compounded, so also of being dissolved; but that which is not composite, and that only, must be, if anything is, indissoluble.

Yes; I should imagine so, said Cebes.

And the non-composite may be assumed to be the same and unchanging, whereas the composite is always changing and never the same.

I agree, he said.

Then now let us return to the previous discussion. Is that reality of whose being we give account in the dialectical process—whether equality, beauty, or anything else—are these realities, I say, liable at times to some degree of change? or are they each of them always what they are, having the same uniform self-existent and unchanging natures, not admitting of variation at all, or in any way, or at any time?

They must be always the same, Socrates, replied Cebes.

And what would you say of the many beautiful, for instance, men or horses or garments or any other such things, or of the many equal, or generally of all the things which are named by the same names as the realities—are they the same always? May they not rather be described in exactly opposite terms, as almost always changing and hardly ever the same either with themselves or with one another?

The latter, replied Cebes; they are always in a state of change.

And these you can touch and see and perceive with the senses, but the unchanging things you can only grasp with the mind—they are invisible and are not seen?

That is very true, he said.

Well, then, added Socrates, let us suppose that there are two sorts of existences—one seen, the other unseen.

Let us suppose them.

The seen is the changing, and the unseen is the unchanging?

That may be also supposed.

And, further, of ourselves is not one part body, another part soul?

To be sure.

And to which class is the body more alike and akin?

Clearly to the seen—no one can doubt that.

And is the soul seen or not seen?

Not by man, Socrates.

And what we mean by 'seen' and 'not seen' is that which is or is not visible to the eye of man?

Yes, to the eye of man.

And is the soul seen or not seen?

Not seen.

Unseen then?

Yes.

Then the soul is more like to the unseen, and the body to the seen?

That follows necessarily, Socrates.

And were we not saying some time ago that the soul when using the body as an instrument of perception, that is to say, when using the sense of sight or hearing or some other sense (for the meaning of perceiving through the body is perceiving through the senses)—were we not saying that the soul too is then dragged by the body into the region of the changeable, and wanders and is confused; the world spins round her, and she is like a drunkard, when she touches change?

Very true.

But when returning into herself she reflects, then she passes into the other world, the region of purity, and eternity, and immortality, and unchangeableness, which are her kindred, and with them she ever lives, when she is by herself and is not let or hindered; then she ceases from her wandering, and being in contact with things unchanging is unchanging in relation to them. And this state of the soul is called wisdom?

That is well and truly said, Socrates, he replied.

And to which class is the soul more nearly alike and akin, as far as may be inferred from this argument, as well as from the preceding one?

I think, Socrates, that, in the opinion of everyone who follows the argument, the soul will be infinitely more like the unchangeable—even the most stupid person will not deny that.

And the body is more like the changing?

Yes.

Yet once more consider the matter in another light: When the soul and the body are united, then nature orders the soul to rule and govern, and the body to obey and serve. Now which of these two functions is like to the divine? and which to the mortal? Does not the divine appear to you to be that which is formed to govern and command, and the mortal to be that which is by its nature subject and servant?

True.

And which does the soul resemble?

The soul resembles the divine, and the body the mortal—there can be no doubt of that, Socrates.

Then reflect, Cebes: of all which has been said is not this the conclusion?—that the soul is in the very likeness of the divine, and immortal, and rational, and uniform, and indissoluble, and unchangeable; and that the body is in the very likeness of the human, and mortal, and irrational, and multiform, and dissoluble, and changeable. Can we, my dear Cebes, find any possible ground for rejecting this conclusion?

We cannot.

But if it be true, then is not the body liable to speedy dissolution? and is not the soul almost or altogether indissoluble?

Certainly.

And do you further observe, that after a man is dead, the body, or visible part of him, which is lying in the visible world, and is called a corpse, and would naturally be dissolved and decomposed and dissipated, is not dissolved or decomposed at once, but may remain for some time, nay even for a long time, if the constitution be sound at the time of death, and the season of the year favourable? For the body when shrunk and embalmed, as the manner is in Egypt, may remain almost entire for a prodigious time; and even in decay, there are still some portions, such as the bones and ligaments, which are practically indestructible:—Do you agree?

Yes.

And is it likely that the soul, which is invisible, in passing to the place of the true Hades, which like her is invisible, and pure, and noble, and on her way to the good and wise God, whither, if God will, my soul is also soon to go,—that the soul, I repeat, if this be her nature, is blown away and destroyed immediately on quitting the body, as the many say? That can never be, my dear Simmias and Cebes. The truth rather is that the soul which is pure at departing and draws after her no bodily taint, having never voluntarily during life had connexion with the body, which she is ever avoiding, herself gathered into herself, and making such abstraction her perpetual study—all this means that she has been a true disciple of philosophy; and therefore has in fact been always practising how to die without complaint. For is not such a life the practice of death?

Certainly.

That soul, I say, herself invisible, departs to the invisible world—to the divine and immortal and rational: thither arriving, she is secure of bliss and is released from the error and folly of men, their fears and wild passions and all other human ills, and for ever dwells, as they say of the initiated, in company with the gods. Is not this true, Cebes?

Yes, said Cebes, beyond a doubt.

But the soul which has been polluted, and is impure at the time of her departure, and is the companion and servant of the body always, and is in love with and bewitched by the body and by the desires and pleasures of the body, until she is led to believe that the truth only exists in a bodily form, which a man may touch and see, and drink and eat, and use for the purposes of his lusts,—the soul, I mean, accustomed to hate and fear and avoid that which to the bodily eye is dark and invisible, but is the object of mind and can be attained by philosophy;—do you suppose that such a soul will depart pure and unalloyed?

Impossible, he replied.

She is intermixed with the corporeal, which the continual association and constant care of the body have wrought into her nature. . . .

What do you mean, Socrates?

I will tell you, he said. The lovers of knowledge are conscious that the soul was simply fastened and glued to the body—until philosophy took her in hand, she could only view real existence through the bars of a prison, not in and through herself, and she was wallowing in the mire of every sort of ignorance. This was her original state; and then, as I was saying, and as the lovers of knowledge are well aware, philosophy saw the ingenuity of her prison—a prison built by lust so that a captive might be the principal accomplice in his own captivity—and took her in hand, and gently comforted her and sought to release her, pointing out that the eye and the ear and the other senses are full of deception, and persuading her to retire from them, and abstain from all but the necessary use of them, and be gathered up and collected into herself, bidding her trust only in herself and her own pure apprehension of pure existence, and to mistrust whatever comes to her through other channels and is subject to variation; for such things are sensible and visible, but what she sees in her own nature is of the mind and invisible. And the soul of the true philosopher thinks that she ought not to resist this deliverance, and therefore abstains from pleasures and desires and pains, as far as she is able; reflecting that when a man has great joys or fears or desires, he suffers from them not merely the sort of evil which might be anticipated—as for example, the loss of his health or property which he has sacrificed to his lusts—but an evil greater far, which is the greatest and worst of all evils, and one of which he never thinks.

What is it, Socrates? said Cebes.

The evil is that when the feeling of pleasure or pain is most intense, every soul of man imagines the objects of this intense feeling to be then plainest and truest, though they are not so. And the things of sight are the chief of these objects, are they not?

Yes.

And is not this the state in which the soul becomes most firmly gripped by the body?

How so?

Why, because each pleasure and pain is a sort of nail which nails and rivets the soul to the body, until she becomes like the body, and believes that to be true which the body affirms to be true; and from agreeing with the body and having the same delights she is obliged to have the same habits and haunts, and is not likely ever to be pure at her departure to the world below, but is always infected by the body; and so she sinks into another body and there germinates and grows, and has therefore no part in the communion of the divine and pure and simple.

Most true, Socrates, answered Cebes.

And this, Cebes, is the reason why the true lovers of knowledge are temperate and brave; and not for the reason which the world gives.

Certainly not.

Certainly not! The soul of a philosopher will reason in quite another way; she will not ask philosophy to release her in order that in the very process of release she may deliver herself up again to the thraldom of pleasures and pains, doing a work only to be undone again, weaving and in turn unweaving her Penelope's web. But she will calm passion, and follow reason, and dwell always with her, contemplating the true and the divine and that which is beyond appearance and opinion, and thence, deriving nourishment. Thus she seeks to live while she lives, and after death she hopes to go to her own kindred and to that which is like her, and to be freed from human ills. Thus nurtured, Simmias and Cebes, a soul will never fear that at her departure from the body she will be scattered and blown away by the winds and be nowhere and nothing.

When Socrates had done speaking, for a considerable time there was silence; he himself appeared to be meditating, as most of us were, on what had been said; only Cebes and Simmias spoke a few words to one another. And Socrates observing them asked what they thought of the argument, and whether there was anything wanting? For, said he, there are many points still open to suspicion and attack, if anyone were disposed to sift the matter thoroughly. Should you be considering some other matter I say no more, but if you feel any doubt on the present subject do not hesitate either to give us your own thoughts if you have any improvement to suggest, or, if you think that you will make more progress with my assistance, allow me to help you.

Simmias said: I must confess, Socrates, that doubts do arise in our minds, and each of us has for some time been urging and inciting the other to put the question which we wanted to have answered but which neither of us liked to ask, fearing that our importunity might be troublesome at such a time. . . .

Socrates answered: I dare say, my friend, that you may be right, but I should like to know in what respect the argument is insufficient.

In this respect, replied Simmias:—Suppose a person to use the same argument about harmony[1] and the lyre—might he not say that harmony is a thing invisble, incorporeal, perfect, divine, existing in the lyre which is harmonized, but that the lyre and the strings are matter and material, composite, earthy, and akin to mortality? And when someone breaks the lyre, or cuts and rends the strings, then he who takes this view would argue as you do, and on the same analogy, that the harmony survives, and has not perished—you cannot imagine, he would say, that the lyre without the strings, and the broken strings themselves which are mortal remain, and yet that the harmony, which is of heavenly and immortal nature and kindred, has perished—perished before the mortal. The harmony must still be somewhere, and the wood and strings will decay before anything can happen to that. The thought, Socrates, must have occurred to your own mind that such is our conception of the soul; and that when the body is in a manner strung and held together by the elements of hot and cold, wet and dry, then the soul is the harmony or due proportionate admixture of them. But if so, whenever the strings of the body are unduly loosened or overstrained through disease or other injury, then the soul, though most devine, like other harmonies of music or of works of art, of course perishes at once; although the material remains of the body may last for a considerable time, until they are either decayed or burnt. And if any one maintains that the soul, being an admixture of the elements of the body, is first to perish in that which is called death, how shall we answer him? . . .

Yet once more let me ask you to consider the question from another point of view, and see whether you agree with me:—There is a thing which you term heat, and another thing which you term cold?

Certainly.

But are they the same as fire and snow?

Most assuredly not.

Heat is a thing different from fire, and cold is not the same with snow?

Yes.

And yet I fancy you agree that when snow receives heat (to use our previous phraseology), they will not remain snow and heat; but at the advance of the heat, the snow will either retire or perish?

Very true, he replied.

And the fire too at the advance of the cold will either retire or perish; but it will never receive the cold, and yet insist upon remaining what it was, and so be at once fire and cold.

---

[1]['In Greek the word *harmonia* does not mean "harmony," if "harmony" conveys to us the concord of several sounds. The Greeks called that *symphonia*. *Harmonia* meant originally the orderly adjustment of parts in a complete fabric; then, in particular, the tuning of a musical instrument; and finally the musical scale, composed of several notes yielded by the tuned strings.' (Cornford, *The Unwritten Philosophy and other Essays*. C.U.P., 1950, p. 19.)]

That is true, he said.

And in some cases the name of the form is attached not only to the form in an eternal connexion; but something else which, not being the form, yet never exists without it, is also entitled to be called by that name. I will try to make this clearer by an example:—The odd number is always called by the name of odd?

Very true.

But is this the only thing which is called odd? Here is my point. Are there not other things which have their own name, and yet must be called odd, because, although not the same as oddness, they are essentially never without oddness? I mean such a case as that of the number three, and there are many other examples. Take that case. Would you not say that three may be called by its proper name, and also be called odd, which is not the same with three? and this may be said not only of three but also of five, and of every alternate number—each of them without being oddness is odd; and in the same way two and four, and the other series of alternate numbers, has every number even, without being evenness. Do you agree?

Of course.

Then now mark the point at which I am aiming:—not only do essential opposites seem to exclude one another, but also concrete things, which, although not in themselves opposed, contain opposites; these, I say, likewise reject the form opposed to that which is contained in them, and when it approaches them they either perish or withdraw. For example; Will not the number three endure annihilation or anything sooner than be converted into an even number, while remaining three?

Very true, said Cebes.

And yet, he said, the number two is certainly not opposed to the number three?

It is not.

Then not only do opposite forms repel the advance of one another, but also there are other things which withdraw before the approach of opposites.

Very true, he said.

Suppose, he said, that we endeavour, if possible, to determine what these are.

By all means.

Are they not, Cebes, such as compel anything of which they have possession, not only to take their own form, but also the form of an opposite?

What do you mean?

I mean, as I was just now saying, and as I am sure that you know, that those things which are possessed by the form of the number three must not only be three in number, but must also be odd.

Quite true.

And such things will never suffer the intrusion of the form opposite to that which gives this impress?

No.

And this impress was given by the form of the odd?

Yes.

And to the odd is opposed the even?

True.

Then the form of the even number will never intrude on three?

No.

Then three has no part in the even?

None.

Then the triad or number three is uneven?

Very true.

To return then to my definition of things which are not opposite to one of a pair of opposites, and yet do not admit that opposite—as, in the instance given, three, although not opposed to the even, does not any the more admit of the even, but always brings the opposite into play on the other side; or as two does not receive the odd, or fire the cold—from these examples (and there are many more of them) perhaps you may be able to arrive at the general conclusion, that not only opposites will not receive opposites, but also that nothing which brings an opposite will admit the opposite of that which it brings, in that to which it is brought. And here let me recapitulate—for there is no harm in repetition. The number five will not admit the form of the even, any more than ten, which is the double of five, will admit the form of the odd. The double has itself a different opposite, but nevertheless rejects the odd altogether. Nor similarly will parts in the ratio 3:2 admit the form of the whole, nor will the half or the one-third, or any such fraction: You will agree?

Yes, he said, I entirely agree and go along with you in that.

And now, he said, let us begin again; and do not you answer my question in the words in which I ask it, but follow my example: let me have not the old safe answer of which I spoke at first, but another equally safe, of which the truth will be inferred by you from what has been just said. If you ask me 'what that is, of which the inherence makes the body hot', I shall reply not heat (this is what I call the safe and stupid answer), but fire, a far superior answer, which we are now in a condition to give. Or if you ask me 'why a body is diseased', I shall not say from disease, but from fever; and instead of saying that oddness is the cause of odd numbers, I shall say that the monad is the cause of them: and so of things in general, as I dare say that you will understand sufficiently without my adducing any further examples.

Yes, he said, I quite understand you.

Tell me, then, what is that of which the inherence will render the body alive?

The soul, he replied.

And is this always the case?

Yes, he said, of course.

Then whatever the soul occupies, to that she comes bearing life?

Yes, certainly.

And is there any opposite to life?

There is, he said.

And what is that?

Death.

Then from our previous conclusion it follows that the soul will never admit the opposite of what she always brings.

Impossible, replied Cebes.

And now, he said, what did we just now call that which does not admit the form of the even?

Uneven.

And that which does not admit the musical or the just?

The unmusical, he said, and the unjust.

And what do we call that which does not admit death?

The immortal, he said.

And does the soul admit of death?

No.

Then the soul is immortal?

Yes, he said.

And may we say that this has been proven?

Yes, abundantly proven, Socrates, he replied.

Supposing that the odd were necessarily imperishable, must not three be imperishable?

Of course.

And if that which is cold were necessarily imperishable, when heat came attacking the snow, must not the snow have retired whole and unmelted— for it could never have perished, nor again could it have remained and admitted the heat?

True, he said.

Again, if that which cannot be cooled were imperishable, the fire when assailed by cold would not have perished or have been extinguished, but would have gone away unaffected?

Certainly, he said.

And the same may be said of the immortal: if the immortal is also imperishable, the soul when attacked by death cannot perish; for the preceding argument shows that the soul will not admit death, or exist as dead, any more than three or the odd number will exist as even, or fire, or the heat in the fire, will be cold. Yet a person may say: 'But although the odd will not become even at the approach of the even, why may not the odd perish and the even take the place of the odd?' Now to him who makes this objection, we cannot answer that the odd is imperishable; for this is not the fact. If we had accepted it as a fact, there would have been no difficulty in contending that at the approach of the even the odd and the number three took their departure; and the same argument would have held good of fire and heat and any other thing.

Very true.

And the same may be said of the immortal: if we agree that the immortal is also imperishable, then the soul will be imperishable as well as immortal; but if not, some other proof of her imperishableness will have to be given.

No other proof is needed, he said; for if the immortal, being eternal, is liable to perish, then nothing is imperishable.

Yes, replied Socrates, and all men will agree that God, and the essential form of life, and the immortal in general, will never perish.

Yes, all men, he said—that is true; and what is more, gods, if I am not mistaken, as well as men.

Seeing then that the immortal is indestructible, must not the soul, if she is immortal, be also imperishable?

Most certainly.

Then when death attacks a man, the mortal portion of him may be supposed to die, but the immortal retires at the approach of death and is preserved safe and sound?

True.

Then, Cebes, beyond question, the soul is immortal and imperishable, and our souls will truly exist in another world!

3

JOSEPH BUTLER

---

introduction

Bishop Butler's brief essay, "Of Personal Identity," is one of the clearest specimens of philosophy in any language; yet, partly because of its terseness, it is one of the most difficult for anyone not specially trained in philosophy to understand. Butler wastes no words. He expresses with fastidious care exactly what he means, and he leaves it to the reader to understand what he has said.

His question is, essentially, whether a person remains the very same person throughout his lifetime and, if so, what this implies with respect to the question of what a person is. Briefly, his argument is this: Everyone knows that he is exactly the same person throughout his lifetime; that he is, for example, the same person as the child whom he remembers himself to have been, and the very one who did the various things he remembers having done; and that he is the same person as that person of tomorrow, or a year hence, or of whatever future time, whose affairs he now arranges, in the knowledge that he is arranging his *own* affairs.

For example, a man remembers stealing apples as a child. In that remembrance he is conscious, first, that *someone* stole the apples, and second, that that person is *he*, the very one who now remembers doing it. Or someone, anticipating his own death, composes a will. In so doing, he is conscious that he is making arrangements contingent upon his own eventual death, and not the death of some other person; he is aware that he is one and the same person as him whose death he now anticipates.

Butler considers that such reflections as these, of which everyone is quite certain prior to embracing any philosophical theory, clearly entail (1) that every person remains identically one and the same person throughout his lifetime; (2) that a person is not, therefore, identical with his physical body, which does not remain the same even from one day to the next, and may undergo a complete renewal over a longer period of time; and (3) that a person is not identical with his own acts of remembrance or any of his states of consciousness, which likewise change constantly and are totally different from one day to the next. The implication of all this is that a person is a being or substance, distinct both from its own human body and from its own thought. As such it is capable of surviving the death of the body and of enjoying a conscious future state, as religion teaches.

In the course of these reflections Butler makes an important distinction between two senses of identity. One is illustrated in the kind of identity that a vegetable, such as a tree, can have over the course of time. When one says of some very old tree that it was planted there by his grandfather, he implies that the tiny sapling planted by his grandfather is identical with the aged tree that stands there now. But strictly speaking it is not, for the old tree retains not a single molecule that belonged to the young one. This, then, is what Butler calls identity "in a loose and popular sense." When, on the other hand, a man recalls something that he did as a child, then he knows that he is identical with that child, in a strict and precise sense of identity; for he is recalling the actions, not of some *other* person, but of the very same person who now remembers. Strictly speaking, the trees are two *different* trees, having a continuity with each other through time; the man and the child, however, are *not* two different persons, but one and the same person. The tree, accordingly, can be, and indeed is, one and the same thing as the physical substance of which it is composed; but a man cannot in the same way be the same thing as his body, which does not remain one and the same even though he does.

Butler's little essay was partly inspired by John Locke's reflections on the same subject, which he considered seriously misleading. Locke believed that a person is not one and the same thing as his body; he then tended sometimes to speak as though he must, therefore, be identical with his own consciousness. But Butler points out that, from the fact that one is conscious of himself—that he remembers various things he has done, for example—it certainly does not follow that he is the same as that consciousness. And indeed he cannot be, for he is conscious of his being the same person today as one whose acts he now remembers, even though his consciousness is itself not the same.

Butler's conclusion is therefore rather like Socrates', namely, that he is a being distinct from his own body, and therefore capable of surviving the dissolution of the latter. The beauty of his essay lies in the rigor with which he deduces this from his fundamental premise, that every person is perfectly aware of being, during any considerable part of his lifetime, one and the same person, and not several different people.

Joseph Butler, who died in 1752, was widely known in his day as a clergyman and writer and is still highly esteemed for his contributions to moral philosophy and natural theology. The following essay appeared as an appendix to his book, *The Analogy of Religion*.

*The Identity of a Person through Time**

Whether we are to live in a future state, as it is the most important question which can possibly be asked, so it is the most intelligible one which can be expressed in language. Yet strange perplexities have been raised about the meaning of that identity or sameness of person, which is implied in the notion of our living now and hereafter, or in any two successive moments. And the solution of these difficulties hath been stranger than the difficulties themselves. For, personal identity has been explained so by some, as to render the inquiry concerning a future life of no consequence at all to us the persons who are making it. And though few men can be misled by such subtleties; yet it may be proper a little to consider them.

Now when it is asked, wherein personal identity consists, the answer should be the same, as if it were asked, wherein consists similitude, or equality; that all attempts to define would but perplex it. Yet there is no difficulty at all in ascertaining the idea. For as, upon two triangles being compared or viewed together, there arises to the mind the idea of similitude; or upon twice two and four, the idea of equality: so likewise, upon comparing the consciousnesses of one's self, or one's own existence, in any two moments, there as immediately arises to the mind the idea of personal identity. And as the two former comparisons not only give us the ideas of similitude and equality; but also shew us, that two triangles are alike, and twice two and four are equal: so the latter comparison not only gives us the idea of personal identity, but also shews us the identity of ourselves in those two moments;

*Joseph Butler, "Of Personal Identity," in *The Analogy of Religion* (London: Macmillan & Co., 1900).

the present, suppose, and that immediately past; or the present, and that a month, a year, or twenty years past. Or in other words, by reflecting upon that, which is myself now, and that, which was myself twenty years ago, I discern they are not two, but one and the same self.

But though consciousness of what is past does thus ascertain our personal identity to ourselves, yet to say, that it makes personal identity, or is necessary to our being the same persons, is to say, that a person has not existed a single moment, nor done one action, but what he can remember; indeed none but what he reflects upon. And one should really think it self-evident, that consciousness of personal identity presupposes, and therefore cannot constitute, personal identity; any more than knowledge, in any other case, can constitute truth, which it presupposes.

This wonderful mistake may possibly have arisen from hence; that to be endued with consciousness is inseparable from the idea of a person, or intelligent being. For, this might be expressed inaccurately thus, that consciousness makes personality: and from hence it might be concluded to make personal identity. But though present consciousness of what we at present do and feel is necessary to our being the persons we now are; yet present consciousness of past actions or feelings is not necessary to our being the same persons who performed those actions, or had those feelings.

The inquiry, what makes vegetables the same in the common acceptation of the word, does not appear to have any relation to this of personal identity: because, the word *same*, when applied to them and to person, is not only applied to different subjects, but it is also used in different senses. For when a man swears to the same tree, as having stood fifty years in the same place, he means only the same as to all the purposes of property and uses of common life, and not that the tree has been all that time the same in the strict philosophical sense of the word. For he does not know, whether any one particle of the present tree be the same with any one particle of the tree which stood in the same place fifty years ago. And if they have not one common particle of matter, they cannot be the same tree in the proper philosophical sense of the word *same*: it being evidently a contradiction in terms, to say they are, when no part of their substance, and no one of their properties is the same: no part of their substance, by the supposition; no one of their properties, because it is allowed; that the same property cannot be transferred from one substance to another. And therefore when we say the identity or sameness of a plant consists in a continuation of the same life, communicated under the same organization, to a number of particles of matter, whether the same or not; the word *same*, when applied to life and to organization, cannot possibly be understood to signify, what it signifies in this very sentence, when applied to matter. In a loose and popular sense then, the life and the organization and the plant are justly said to be the same, notwithstanding the perpetual change of the parts. But in a strict and

philosophical manner of speech, no man, no being, no mode of being, no
anything, can be the same with that, with which it hath indeed nothing the
same. Now sameness is used in this latter sense, when applied to persons.
The identity of these, therefore, cannot subsist with diversity of substance.

The thing here considered, and demonstratively, as I think, determined,
is proposed by Mr. Locke in these words, *Whether it*, i.e., the same self or
person, *be the same identical substance?* And he has suggested what is a
much better answer to the question, than that which he gives it in form. For
he defines Person, *a thinking intelligent being*, etc., and personal identity,
the sameness of a rational being.[1] The question then is, whether the same
rational being is the same substance: which needs no answer, because Being
and Substance, in this place, stand for the same idea. The ground of the
doubt, whether the same person be the same substance, is said to be this;
that the consciousness of our own existence, in youth and in old age, or in
any two joint successive moments, is not the *same individual action*,[2] i.e.,
not the same consciousness, but different successive consciousnesses. Now it
is strange that this should have occasioned such perplexities. For it is surely
conceivable, that a person may have a capacity of knowing some object or
other to be the same now, which it was when he contemplated it formerly:
yet in this case, where, by the supposition, the object is perceived to be the
same, the perception of it in any two moments cannot be one and the same
perception. And thus though the successive consciousnesses, which we have
of our own existence, are not the same, yet are they consciousnesses of one
and the same thing or object; of the same person, self, or living agent. The
person, of whose existence the consciousness is felt now, and was felt an hour
or a year ago, is discerned to be, not two persons, but one and the same
person; and therefore is one and the same.

Mr. Locke's observations upon this subject appear hasty: and he seems to
profess himself dissatisfied with suppositions, which he has made relating to
it.[3] But some of those hasty observations have been carried to a strange
length by others; whose notion, when traced and examined to the bottom,
amounts, I think, to this:[4] "That Personality is not a permanent, but a
transient thing: that it lives and dies, begins and ends continually: that no one
can any more remain one and the same person two moments together, than
two successive moments can be one and the same moment: that our substance is indeed continually changing; but whether this be so or not, is, it
seems, nothing to the purpose; since it is not substance, but consciousness

[1]Locke's *Works*, vol. i. p. 146. [*Essay concerning Human Understanding*, II. xxvii. 10.]
[2]Locke, pp. 146, 147.
[3]Locke, p. 152. [*Essay concerning Human Understanding*, II. xxvii. 27.]
[4]See an Answer to Dr. Clarke's *Third Defence of his Letter to Mr. Dodwell*, 2nd edit. pp. 44,
56, etc. [The paradoxical view which Butler here exposes was that of Collins. Just four years
before Berkeley had printed in *Alciphron* (vii. sec. II) some paragraphs in which he argues, as
Butler does, against the doctrine that personal identity consists in consciousness.]

alone, which constitutes personality: which consciousness, being successive, cannot be the same in any two moments, nor consequently the personality constituted by it." And from hence it must follow, that it is a fallacy upon ourselves, to charge our present selves with anything we did, or to imagine our present selves interested in anything which befell us yesterday; or that our present self will be interested in what will befall us to-morrow: since our present self is not, in reality, the same with the self of yesterday, but another like self or person coming in its room, and mistaken for it; to which another self will succeed to-morrow. This, I say, must follow: for if the self or person of to-day, and that of to-morrow, are not the same, but only like persons; the person of to-day is really no more interested in what will befall the person of to-morrow, than in what will befall any other person. It may be thought, perhaps, that this is not a just representation of the opinion we are speaking of: because those who maintain it allow, that a person is the same as far back as his remembrance reaches. And indeed they do use the words, *identity* and *same* person. Nor will language permit these words to be laid aside; since if they were, there must be I know not what ridiculous periphrasis substituted in the room of them. But they cannot, consistently with themselves, mean, that the person is really the same. For it is self-evident, that the personality cannot be really the same, if, as they expressly assert, that in which it consists is not the same. And as, consistently with themselves, they cannot, so, I think it appears, they do not, mean that the person is *really* the same, but only that he is so in a fictitious sense: in such a sense only as they assert, for this they do assert, that any number of persons whatever may be the same person. The bare unfolding this notion, and laying it thus naked and open, seems the best confutation of it. However, since great stress is said to be put upon it, I add the following things.

First, This notion is absolutely contradictory to that certain conviction, which necessarily and every moment rises within us, when we turn our thoughts upon ourselves, when we reflect upon what is past, and look forward upon what is to come. All imagination of a daily change of that living agent which each man calls himself, for another, or of any such change throughout our whole present life, is entirely borne down by our natural sense of things. Nor is it possible for a person in his wits to alter his conduct, with regard to his health or affairs, from a suspicion, that, though he should live to-morrow, he should not, however, be the same person he is to-day. And yet, if it be reasonable to act, with respect to a future life, upon this notion, that personality is transient; it is reasonable to act upon it, with respect to the present. Here then is a notion equally applicable to religion and to our temporal concerns; and every one sees and feels the inexpressible absurdity of it in the latter case; if, therefore, any can take up with it in the former, this cannot proceed from the reason of the thing, but must be owing to an inward unfairness, and secret corruption of heart.

Secondly, It is not an idea, or abstract notion, or quality, but a being only, which is capable of life and action, of happiness and misery. Now all beings confessedly continue the same, during the whole time of their existence. Consider then a living being now existing, and which has existed for any time alive: this living being must have done and suffered and enjoyed, what it has done and suffered and enjoyed formerly, (this living being, I say, and not another,) as really as it does and suffers and enjoys, what it does and suffers and enjoys this instant. All these successive actions, enjoyments, and sufferings, are actions, enjoyments, and sufferings, of the same living being. And they are so, prior to all consideration of its remembering or forgetting: since remembering or forgetting can make no alteration in the truth of past matter of fact. And suppose this being endued with limited powers of knowledge and memory, there is no more difficulty in conceiving it to have a power of knowing itself to be the same living being which it was some time ago, of remembering some of its actions, sufferings, and enjoyments, and forgetting others, than in conceiving it to know or remember or forget anything else.

Thirdly, every person is conscious, that he is now the same person or self he was as far back as his remembrance reaches: since when any one reflects upon a past action of his own, he is just as certain of the person who did that action, namely, himself, the person who now reflects upon it, as he is certain that the action was at all done. Nay, very often a person's assurance of an action having been done, of which he is absolutely assured, arises wholly from the consciousness that he himself did it. And this he, person, or self, must either be a substance, or the property of some substance. If he, if person, be a substance; then consciousness that he is the same person is consciousness that he is the same substance. If the person, or he, be the property of a substance, still consciousness that he is the same property is as certain a proof that his substance remains the same, as consciousness that he remains the same substance would be: since the same property cannot be transferred from one substance to another.

But though we are thus certain, that we are the same agents, living beings, or substances, now, which we were as far back as our remembrance reaches; yet it is asked, whether we may not possibly be deceived in it? And this question may be asked at the end of any demonstration whatever: because it is a question concerning the truth of perception by memory. And he who can doubt, whether perception by memory can in this case be depended upon, may doubt also, whether perception by deduction and reasoning, which also include memory, or indeed whether intuitive perception can. Here then we can go no further. For it is ridiculous to attempt to prove the truth of those perceptions, whose truth we can no otherwise prove, than by other perceptions of exactly the same kind with them, and which there is just the same ground to suspect; or to attempt to prove the truth of our faculties, which can no otherwise be proved, than by the use or means of those very suspected faculties themselves.

4

RENÉ DESCARTES

introduction

The Socratic and Platonic conception of a person as a mind or soul, quite distinct from the human body, became crystallized, almost ossified, in Descartes' metaphysics—which is somewhat astonishing in view of Descartes' deliberate and resolute attempt to divest himself of all received philosophical opinions, particularly those of antiquity, and begin afresh on metaphysical foundations that not even almighty God could overturn. The severance of mind and body that Descartes, following Plato, reaffirmed, persists still, and many contemporary philosophers, as scornful of their predecessors as Descartes was, are no more able than he was to shake it off. In Descartes' reflections we see clearly how an ingrained prejudice can appear to its possessor as the most indubitable discovery, vouchsafed by reason itself.

Descartes refers to these speculations as meditations on "first philosophy," an expression derived from Aristotle and meaning, simply, metaphysics. And his approach to metaphysics was, in his day, unique indeed. For instead of trying at the outset to see what truths he can discover, either through philosophical argument (following the example of Socrates) or through experience (following the example of most people), he tries instead to see how much *error* he can find in his own opinions. And his test for error is very rigorous, for he decides to treat as *false* everything that he is capable of even *doubting*. He will endorse as true, and therefore acceptable into his

metaphysics, only those beliefs that are incapable of being doubted. This
would appear to lead to the most extreme skepticism—for what beliefs, after
all, are we incapable of entertaining the slightest doubt about? But Descartes, it turns out, has a way out of this—namely, trust in his own reasoning or understanding, whose reliability will in the end be guaranteed by
God!

Can I doubt my own senses? Do they not tell me reliably what the world is
like, and what it contains? Of course they do not, for there are many illusions
of sense. A stick half submerged in water looks bent, the moon looks like a
small object not far away, things feel cold to a fevered hand, and so on. How,
then, do we know that all our sense experience is not illusory? Concerning
anything that our senses tell us, we can at least consider that it *might* not be
true—and on Descartes' criterion we must therefore treat it as false.

Then what of my own body? Can I doubt that I have arms and legs, that I
am sitting in a room, doing what I seem to be doing? Of course I can, for
these are exactly like the things that sometimes seem true in my dreams,
from which I awaken to find they were false. Perhaps what now seems to me
most clearly to be true about my body, where it is and what it is doing, will
one day turn out to have been only a dream.

Then what of the truths of geometry and mathematics? Can I really doubt
that squares have four sides and triangles three, that the sum of the angles of
the latter is equal to a straight line, and so on? Yes, even such seeming
certainties as these can be doubted; for it is possible that a God has created
me to think these things erroneously, endowing me with powers of reasoning
so arranged that they will mislead me every time I use them.

Thus Descartes pursues his method of doubting everything, until he en-
counters a truth that remains unshaken: the truth of his own existence. Even
if you make the wildest suppositions imaginable about your senses, your
reason, and the power of God to deceive you, you cannot possibly be deceived in believing in your own existence. This is incapable of being
doubted—for even in trying to doubt it, you affirm the existence of yourself,
the doubter.

This brings us back to the question with which we began: What am I? Not,
Descartes infers, my body, since I can doubt that this even exists while not
doubting my own existence. I am, then, that which doubts. And since it is I
who, besides doubting, also will, sense, feel, and so on, then I am, more
generally, just a thing that thinks—in short, a mind.

Knowing, then, exactly what he is, and what he is not, Descartes asks:
How can one know what *anything* is? I know that I am a thinking thing, a
mind, because this is the clearest idea of my self that my understanding
yields. What, then, of matter? What is it? Descartes reaches for an answer,
not through reliance on his senses, which have already been dismissed as
misleading, but by forming a perfectly clear idea of matter in his understand-

ing. This is his point in his example of the piece of beeswax. Whatever such a substance may appear to be to the senses, what the understanding clearly grasps of it is that it has shape, size, and is capable of motion—in short, it is an *extended* thing. This applies to matter generally. Thus we are confronted with two basic realities: mind, which thinks, and matter, which is extended. A person is a being of the former kind, a mind—but in some sense he "has" something of the second kind, a body. The main problem, after that, for Descartes and all of his successors, has been to show how these two beings, thus metaphysically sundered, are related to each other—for clearly, every person (mind) has *some* rather close relationship to his own body. Descartes, though much preoccupied with this question throughout his life, was never able to answer it satisfactorily. Nor, having once accepted this ultimate metaphysical distinction, has anyone else. The distinction itself goes back to the religious ideas of the Orphics and Pythagoreans, who transmitted it to us through Plato, but every generation of philosophers seems, like Descartes, to think of it as a fresh deliverance of reason.

René Descartes died in 1650 at the age of 54. Often described as the father of modern philosophy, he was most famous during his own lifetime for his contributions to mathematical and physical theory. The following are the first two of his six *Meditations*.

The Distinction between the Mind and the Body*

MEDITATION I

Of the things which may be brought within the sphere of the doubtful.

It is now some years since I detected how many were the false beliefs that I had from my earliest youth admitted as true, and how doubtful was everything I had since constructed on this basis; and from that time I was convinced that I must once for all seriously undertake to rid myself of all the opinions which I had formerly accepted, and commence to build anew from the foundation, if I wanted to establish any firm and permanent structure in the sciences. But as this enterprise appeared to be a very great one, I waited until I had attained an age so mature that I could not hope that at any later date I should be better fitted to execute my design. This reason caused me to delay so long that I should feel that I was doing wrong were I to occupy in deliberation the time that yet remains to me for action. To-day, then, since very opportunely for the plan I have in view I have delivered my mind from every care [and am happily agitated by no passions] and since I have procured for myself an assured leisure in a peaceable retirement, I shall at last seriously and freely address myself to the general upheaval of all my former opinions.

Now for this object it is not necessary that I should show that all of these are false—I shall perhaps never arrive at this end. But inasmuch as reason already persuades me that I ought no less carefully to withhold my assent from matters which are not entirely certain and indubitable than from those which appear to me manifestly to be false, if I am able to find in each one some reason to doubt, this will suffice to justify my rejecting the whole. And for that end it will not be requisite that I should examine each in particular, which would be an endless undertaking; for owing to the fact that the destruction of the foundations of necessity brings with it the downfall of the rest of the edifice, I shall only in the first place attack those principles upon which all my former opinions rested.

All that up to the present time I have accepted as most true and certain I have learned either from the senses or through the senses; but it is sometimes proved to me that these senses are deceptive, and it is wiser not to trust entirely to any thing by which we have once been deceived.

But it may be that although the senses sometimes deceive us concerning things which are hardly perceptible, or very far away, there are yet many others to be met with as to which we cannot reasonably have any doubt, although we recognise them by their means. For example, there is the fact that I am here, seated by the fire, attired in a dressing gown, having this paper in my hands and other similar matters. And how could I deny that these hands and this body are mine, were it not perhaps that I compare myself to certain persons, devoid of sense, whose cerebella are so troubled and clouded by the violent vapours of black bile, that they constantly assure us that they think they are kings when they are really quite poor, or that they are clothed in purple when they are really without covering, or who imagine that they have an earthenware head or are nothing but pumpkins or are made of glass. But they are mad, and I should not be any the less insane were I to follow examples so extravagant.

At the same time I must remember that I am a man, and that consequently I am in the habit of sleeping, and in my dreams representing to myself the same things or sometimes even less probable things, than do those who are insane in their waking moments. How often has it happened to me that in the night I dreamt that I found myself in this particular place, that I was dressed and seated near the fire, whilst in reality I was lying undressed in bed! At this moment it does indeed seem to me that it is with eyes awake that

I am looking at this paper; that this head which I move is not asleep, that it is deliberately and of set purpose that I extend my hand and perceive it; what happens in sleep does not appear so clear nor so distinct as does all this. But in thinking over this I remind myself that on many occasions I have in sleep been deceived by similar illusions, and in dwelling carefully on this reflection I see so manifestly that there are no certain indications by which we may clearly distinguish wakefulness from sleep that I am lost in astonishment. And my astonishment is such that it is almost capable of persuading me that I now dream.

Now let us assume that we are asleep and that all these particulars, e.g., that we open our eyes, shake our head, extend our hands, and so on, are but false delusions; and let us reflect that possibly neither our hands nor our whole body are such as they appear to us to be. At the same time we must at least confess that the things which are represented to us in sleep are like painted representations which can only have been formed as the counterparts of something real and true, and that in this way those general things at least, i.e., eyes, a head, hands, and a whole body, are not imaginary things, but things really existent. For, as a matter of fact, painters, even when they study with the greatest skill to represent sirens and satyrs by forms the most strange and extraordinary, cannot give them natures which are entirely new, but merely make a certain medley of the members of different animals; or if their imagination is extravagant enough to invent something so novel that nothing similar has ever before been seen, and that then their work represents a thing purely fictitious and absolutely false, it is certain all the same that the colours of which this is composed are necessarily real. And for the same reason, although these general things, to wit, [a body], eyes, a head, hands, and such like, may be imaginary, we are bound at the same time to confess that there are at least some other objects yet more simple and more universal, which are real and true; and of these just in the same way as with certain real colours, all these images of things which dwell in our thoughts, whether true and real or false and fantastic, are formed.

To such a class of things pertains corporeal nature in general, and its extension, the figure of extended things, their quantity or magnitude and number, as also the place in which they are, the time which measures their duration, and so on.

That is possibly why our reasoning is not unjust when we conclude from this that Physics, Astronomy, Medicine and all other sciences which have as their end the consideration of composite things, are very dubious and uncertain; but that Arithmetic, Geometry and other sciences of that kind which only treat of things that are very simple and very general, without taking great trouble to ascertain whether they are actually existent or not, contain some measure of certainty and an element of the indubitable. For whether I am awake or asleep, two and three together always form five, and the square can never have more than four sides, and it does not seem possible that truths so clear and apparent can be suspected of any falsity [or uncertainty].

Nevertheless I have long had fixed in my mind the belief that an all-powerful God existed by whom I have been created such as I am. But how do I know that He has not brought it to pass that there is no earth, no heaven, no extended body, no magnitude, no place, and that nevertheless [I possess the perceptions of all these things and that] they seem to me to exist just exactly as I now see them? And, besides, as I sometimes imagine that others deceive themselves in the things which they think they know best, how do I know that I am not deceived every time that I add two and three, or count the sides of a square, or judge of things yet simpler, if anything simpler can be imagined? But possibly God has not desired that I should be thus deceived, for He is said to be supremely good. If, however, it is contrary to His goodness to have made me such that I constantly deceive myself, it would also appear to be contrary to His goodness to permit me to be sometimes deceived, and nevertheless I cannot doubt that He does permit this.

There may indeed be those who would prefer to deny the existence of a God so powerful, rather than believe that all other things are uncertain. But let us not oppose them for the present, and grant that all that is here said of a God is a fable; nevertheless in whatever way they suppose that I have arrived at the state of being that I have reached—whether they attribute it to fate or to accident, or make out that it is by a continual succession of antecedents, or by some other method—since to err and deceive oneself is a defect, it is clear that the greater will be the probability of my being so imperfect as to deceive myself ever, as is the Author to whom they assign my origin the less powerful. To these reasons I have certainly nothing to reply, but at the end I feel constrained to confess that there is nothing in all that I formerly believed to be true, of which I cannot in some measure doubt, and that not merely through want of thought or through levity, but for reasons which are very powerful and maturely considered; so that henceforth I ought not the less carefully to refrain from giving credence to these opinions than to that which is manifestly false, if I desire to arrive at any certainty [in the sciences].

But it is not sufficient to have made these remarks, we must also be careful to keep them in mind. For these ancient and commonly held opinions still revert frequently to my mind, long and familiar custom having given them the right to occupy my mind against my inclination and rendered them almost masters of my belief; nor will I ever lose the habit of deferring to them or of placing my confidence in them, so long as I consider them as they really are, i.e., opinions in some measure doubtful, as I have just shown, and at the same time highly probable, so that there is much more reason to believe in than to deny them. That is why I consider that I shall not be acting amiss, if, taking of set purpose a contrary belief, I allow myself to be deceived, and for a certain time pretend that all these opinions are entirely false and imaginary, until at last, having thus balanced my former prejudices with my latter [so that they cannot divert my opinions more to one side than to the other], my judgment will no longer be dominated by bad usage or turned away from the right knowledge of the truth. For I am assured that there can be neither peril nor error in this course, and that I cannot at present yield too much to distrust, since I am not considering the question of action, but only of kn owledge.

I shall then suppose, not that God who is supremely good and the fountain of truth, but some evil genius not less powerful than deceitful, has employed his whole energies in deceiving me; I shall consider that the heavens, the earth, colours, figures, sound, and all other external things are nought but the illusions and dreams of which this genius has availed himself in order to lay traps for my credulity; I shall consider myself as having no hands, no eyes, no flesh, no blood, nor any senses, yet falsely believing myself to possess all these things; I shall remain obstinately attached to this idea, and if by this means it is not in my power to arrive at the knowledge of any truth, I may at least do what is in my power [i.e., suspend my judgment], and with firm purpose avoid giving credence to any false thing, or being imposed upon by this arch deceiver, however powerful and deceptive he may be. But this task is a laborious one, and insensibly a certain lassitude leads me into the course of my ordinary life. And just as a captive who in sleep enjoys an imaginary liberty, when he begins to suspect that his liberty is but a dream, fears to awaken, and conspires with these agreeable illusions that the deception may be prolonged, so insensibly of my own accord I fall back into my former opinions, and I dread awakening from this slumber, lest the laborious wakefulness which would follow the tranquillity of this repose should have to be spent not in daylight, but in the excessive darkness of the difficulties which have just been discussed.

MEDITATION II

Of the Nature of the Human Mind; and that it is more easily known than the Body.

The Meditation of yesterday filled my mind with so many doubts that it is no longer in my power to forget them. And yet I do not see in what manner I can resolve them; and, just as if I had all of a sudden fallen into very deep water, I am so disconcerted that I can neither make certain of setting my feet on the bottom, nor can I swim and so support myself on the surface. I shall nevertheless make an effort and follow anew the same path as that on which I yesterday entered, i.e. I shall proceed by setting aside all that in which the least doubt could be supposed to exist, just as if I had discovered that it was absolutely false; and I shall ever follow in this road until I have met with something which is certain, or at least, if I can do nothing else, until I have learned for certain that there is nothing in the world that is certain. Archimedes, in order that he might draw the terrestrial globe out of its place, and transport it elsewhere, demanded only that one point should be fixed and immoveable; in the same way I shall have the right to conceive high hopes if I am happy enough to discover one thing only which is certain and indubitable.

I suppose, then, that all the things that I see are false; I persuade myself that nothing has ever existed of all that my fallacious memory represents to me. I consider that I possess no senses; I imagine that body, figure, extension, movement and place are but the fictions of my mind. What, then, can be esteemed as true? Perhaps nothing at all, unless that there is nothing in the world that is certain.

But how can I know there is not something different from those things that I have just considered, of which one cannot have the slightest doubt? Is there not some God, or some other being by whatever name we call it, who puts these reflections into my mind? That is not necessary, for is it not possible that I am capable of producing them myself? I myself, am I not at least something? But I have already denied that I had senses and body. Yet I hesitate, for what follows from that? Am I so dependent on body and senses that I cannot exist without these? But I was persuaded that there was nothing in all the world, that there was no heaven, no earth, and there were no minds, nor any bodies: was I not then likewise persuaded that I did not exist? Not at all; of a surety I myself did exist since I persuaded myself of something [or merely because I thought of something]. But there is some deceiver or other, very powerful and very cunning, who ever employs his ingenuity in deceiving me. Then without doubt I exist also if he deceives me, and let him deceive me as much as he will, he can never cause me to be nothing so long as I think I am something. So that after having reflected well and carefully examined all things, we must come to the definite conclusion that this proposition: I am, I exist, is necessarily true each time that I pronounce it, or that I mentally conceive it.

But I do not yet know clearly enough what I am, I who am certain that I am; and hence I must be careful to see that I do not imprudently take some other object in place of myself, and thus that I do not go astray in respect of this knowledge that I hold to be the most certain and most evident of all that I have formerly learned. That is why I shall now consider anew what I believed myself to be before I embarked upon these last reflections; and of my former opinions I shall withdraw all that might even in a small degree be invalidated by the reasons which I have just brought forward, in order that there may be nothing at all left beyond what is absolutely certain and indubitable.

What then did I formerly believe myself to be? Undoubtedly I believed myself to be a man. But what is a man? Shall I say a reasonable animal? Certainly not; for then I should have to inquire what an animal is, and what is reasonable; and thus from a single question I should insensibly fall into an infinitude of others more difficult; and I should not wish to waste the little time and leisure remaining to me in trying to unravel subtleties like these. But I shall rather stop here to consider the thoughts which of themselves spring up in my mind, and which were not inspired by anything beyond my own nature alone when I applied myself to the consideration of my being. In the first place, then, I considered myself as having a face, hands, arms, and all that system of members composed of bones and flesh as seen in a corpse which I designated by the name of body. In addition to this I considered that I was nourished, that I walked, that I felt, and that I thought, and I referred all these actions to the soul: but I did not stop to consider what the soul was, or if I did stop, I imagined that it was something extremely rare and subtle like a wind, a flame, or an ether, which was spread throughout my grosser parts. As to body I had no manner of doubt about its nature, but thought I had a very clear knowledge of it; and if I had desired to explain it according to the notions that I had then formed of it, I should have described it thus: By the body I understand all that which can be defined by a certain figure: something which can be confined in a certain place, and which can fill a given space in such a way that every other body will be excluded from it; which can be perceived either by touch, or by sight, or by hearing, or by taste, or by smell: which can be moved in many ways not, in truth, by itself, but by something which is foreign to it, by which it is touched [and from which it receives impressions]: for to have the power of self-movement, as also of feeling or of thinking, I did not consider to appertain to the nature of body: on the contrary, I was rather astonished to find that faculties similar to them existed in some bodies.

But what am I, now that I suppose that there is a certain genius which is extremely powerful, and, if I may say so, malicious, who employs all his powers in deceiving me? Can I affirm that I possess the least of all those things which I have just said pertain to the nature of body? I pause to consider, I revolve all these things in my mind, and I find none of which I can say that it pertains to me. It would be tedious to stop to enumerate them. Let us pass to the attributes of soul and see if there is any one which is in me? What of nutrition or walking [the first mentioned]? But if it is so that I have no body it is also true that I can neither walk nor take nourishment. Another attribute is sensation. But one cannot feel without body, and besides I have thought I perceived many things during sleep that I recognised in my waking moments as not having been experienced at all. What of thinking? I find here that thought is an attribute that belongs to me; it alone cannot be separated from me. I am, I exist, that is certain. But how often? Just when I think; for it might possibly be the case if I ceased entirely to think, that I should likewise cease altogether to exist. I do not now admit anything which is not necessarily true: to speak accurately I am not more than a thing which thinks, that is to say a mind or a soul, or an understanding, or a reason, which are terms whose significance was formerly unknown to me. I am, however, a real thing and really exist; but what thing? I have answered: a thing which thinks.

And what more? I shall exercise my imagination [in order to see if I am not something more]. I am not a collection of members which we call the human body: I am not a subtle air distributed through these members, I am not a wind, a fire, a vapour, a breath, nor anything at all which I can imagine or conceive; because I have assumed that all these were nothing. Without changing that supposition I find that I only leave myself certain of the fact that I am somewhat. But perhaps it is true that these same things which I supposed were non-existent because they are unknown to me, are really not different from the self which I know. I am not sure about this, I shall not dispute about it now; I can only give judgment on things that are known to me. I know that I exist, and I inquire what I am, I whom I know to exist. But it is very certain that the knowledge of my existence taken in its precise significance does not depend on things whose existence is not yet known to me; consequently it does not depend on those which I can feign in imagination. And indeed the very term *feign* in imagination proves to me my error, for I really do this if I image myself a something, since to imagine is nothing else than to contemplate the figure or image of a corporeal thing. But I already know for certain that I am, and that it may be that all these images, and, speaking generally, all things that relate to the nature of body are nothing but dreams [and chimeras]. For this reason I see clearly that I have as little reason to say, 'I shall stimulate my imagination in order to know more distinctly what I am,' than if I were to say, 'I am now awake, and I perceive somewhat that is real and true: but because I do not yet perceive it distinctly enough, I shall go to sleep of express purpose, so that my dreams may represent the perception with greatest truth and evidence.' And, thus, I know for certain that nothing of all that I can understand by means of my imagination belongs to this knowledge which I have of myself, and that it is necessary to recall the mind from this mode of thought with the utmost diligence in order that it may be able to know its own nature with perfect distinctness.

But what then am I? A thing which thinks. What is a thing which thinks? It is a thing which doubts, understands, [conceives], affirms, denies, wills, refuses, which also imagines and feels.

Certainly it is no small matter if all these things pertain to my nature. But why should they not so pertain? Am I not that being who now doubts nearly everything, who nevertheless understands certain things, who affirms that one only is true, who denies all the others, who desires to know more, is averse from being deceived, who imagines many things, sometimes indeed despite his will, and who perceives many likewise, as by the intervention of the bodily organs? Is there nothing in all this which is as true as it is certain that I exist, even though I should always sleep and though he who has given me being employed all his ingenuity in deceiving me? Is there likewise any one of these attributes which can be distinguished from my thought, or which might be said to be separated from myself? For it is so evident of itself that it is I who doubts, who understands, and who desires, that there is no reason here to add anything to explain it. And I have certainly the power of imagining likewise; for although it may happen (as I formerly supposed) that none of the things which I imagine are true, nevertheless this power of imagining does not cease to be really in use, and it forms part of my thought. Finally, I am the same who feels, that is to say, who perceives certain things, as by the organs of sense, since in truth I see light, I hear noise, I feel heat. But it will be said that these phenomena are false and that I am dreaming. Let it be so; still it is at least quite certain that it seems to me that I see light, that I hear noise and that I feel heat. That cannot be false; properly speaking it is what is in me called feeling; and used in this precise sense that is no other thing than thinking.

From this time I begin to know what I am with a little more clearness and distinction than before; but nevertheless it still seems to me, and I cannot prevent myself from thinking, that corporeal things, whose images are framed by thought, which are tested by the senses, are much more distinctly known than that obscure part of me which does not come under the imagination. Although really it is very strange to say that I know and understand more distinctly these things whose existence seems to me dubious, which are unknown to me, and which do not belong to me, than others of the truth of which I am convinced, which are known to me and which pertain to my real nature, in a word, than myself. But I see clearly how the case stands: my mind loves to wander, and cannot yet suffer itself to be retained within the just limits of truth. Very good, let us once more give it the freest rein, so that, when afterwards we seize the proper occasion for pulling up, it may the more easily be regulated and controlled.

Let us begin by considering the commonest matters, those which we believe to be the most distinctly comprehended, to wit, the bodies which we touch and see; not indeed bodies in general, for these general ideas are usually a little more confused, but let us consider one body in particular. Let us take, for example, this piece of wax: it has been taken quite freshly from the hive, and it has not yet lost the sweetness of the honey which it contains; it still retains somewhat of the odour of the flowers from which it has been culled; its colour, its figure, its size are apparent; it is hard, cold, easily handled, and if you strike it with the finger, it will emit a sound. Finally all the things which are requisite to cause us distinctly to recognise a body, are met with in it. But notice that while I speak and approach the fire what remained of the taste is exhaled, the smell evaporates, the colour alters, the figure is destroyed, the size increases, it becomes liquid, it heats, scarcely can one handle it, and when one strikes it, no sound is emitted. Does the same wax remain after this change? We must confess that it remains; none would judge otherwise. What then did I know so distinctly in this piece of wax? It could certainly be nothing of all that the senses brought to my notice, since all these things which fall under taste, smell, sight, touch, and hearing, are found to be changed, and yet the same wax remains.

Perhaps it was what I now think, viz. that this wax was not that sweetness of honey, nor that agreeable scent of flowers, nor that particular whiteness, nor that figure, nor that sound, but simply a body which a little while before appeared to me as perceptible under these forms, and which is now perceptible under others. But what, precisely, is it that I imagine when I form such conceptions? Let us attentively consider this, and, abstracting from all that does not belong to the wax, let us see what remains. Certainly nothing remains excepting a certain extended thing which is flexible and movable. But what is the meaning of flexible and movable? Is it not that I imagine that this piece of wax being round is capable of becoming square and of passing from a square to a triangular figure? No, certainly it is not that, since I imagine it admits of an infinitude of similar changes, and I nevertheless do not know how to compass the infinitude by my imagination, and consequently this conception which I have of the wax is not brought about by the faculty of imagination. What now is this extension? Is it not also unknown? For it becomes greater when the wax is melted, greater when it is boiled, and greater still when the heat increases; and I should not conceive [clearly] according to truth what wax is, if I did not think that even this piece that we are considering is capable of receiving more variations in extension than I have ever imagined. We must then grant that I could not even understand through the imagination what this piece of wax is, and that it is my mind alone which perceives it. I say this piece of wax in particular, for as to wax in general it is yet clearer. But what is this piece of wax which cannot be understood excepting by the [understanding or] mind? It is certainly the same that I see, touch, imagine, and finally it is the same which I have always believed it to be from the beginning. But what must particularly be observed is that its perception is neither an act of vision, nor of touch, nor of imagination, and has never been such although it may have appeared formerly to be so, but only an intuition of the mind, which may be imperfect and confused as it was formerly, or clear and distinct as it is at present, according as my attention is more or less directed to the elements which are found in it, and of which it is composed.

Yet in the meantime I am greatly astonished when I consider [the great feebleness of mind] and its proneness to fall [insensibly] into error; for although without giving expression to my thoughts I consider all this in my own mind, words often impede me and I am almost deceived by the terms of ordinary language. For we say that we see the same wax, if it is present, and not that we simply judge that it is the same from its having the same colour and figure. From this I should conclude that I knew the wax by means of vision and not simply by the intuition of the mind; unless by chance I remember that, when looking from a window and saying I see men who pass in the street, I really do not see them, but infer that what I see is men, just as I say that I see wax. And yet what do I see from the window but hats and coats which may cover automatic machines? Yet I judge these to be men. And similarly solely by the faculty of judgment which rests in my mind, I comprehend that which I believed I saw with my eyes.

A man who makes it his aim to raise his knowledge above the common should be ashamed to derive the occasion for doubting from the forms of speech invented by the vulgar; I prefer to pass on and consider whether I had a more evident and perfect conception of what the wax was when I first perceived it, and when I believed I knew it by means of the external senses or at least by the common sense as it is called, that is to say by the imaginative faculty, or whether my present conception is clearer now that I have most carefully examined what it is, and in what way it can be known. I would certainly be absurd to doubt as to this. For what was there in this first perception which was distinct? What was there which might not as well have been perceived by any of the animals? But when I distinguish the wax from its external forms, and when, just as if I had taken from it its vestments, I consider it quite naked, it is certain that although some error may still be found in my judgment, I can nevertheless not perceive it thus without a human mind.

But finally what shall I say of this mind, that is, of myself, for up to this point I do not admit in myself anything but mind? What then, I who seem to perceive this piece of wax so distinctly, do I not know myself, not only with much more truth and certainty, but also with much more distinctness and clearness? For if I judge that the wax is or exists from the fact that I see it, it certainly follows much more clearly that I am or that I exist myself from the fact that I see it. For it may be that what I see is not really wax, it may also be that I do not possess eyes with which to see anything; but it cannot be that when I see, or (for I no longer take account of the distinction) when I think I see, that I myself who think am nought. So if I judge that the wax exists from the fact that I touch it, the same thing will follow, to wit, that I am; and if I judge that my imagination, or some other cause, whatever it is, persuades me that the wax exists, I shall still conclude the same. And what I have here remarked of wax may be applied to all other things which are external to me [and which are met with outside of me]. And further, if the [notion or] perception of wax has seemed to me clearer and more distinct, not only after the sight or the touch, but also after many other causes have rendered it quite manifest to me, with how much more [evidence] and distinctness must it be said that I now know myself, since all the reasons which contribute to the knowledge of wax, or any other body whatever, are yet better proofs of the nature of my mind! And there are so many other things in the mind itself which may contribute to the elucidation of its nature, that those which depend on body such as these just mentioned, hardly merit being taken into account.

But finally here I am, having insensibly reverted to the point I desired, for, since it is now manifest to me that even bodies are not properly speaking known by the senses or by the faculty of imagination, but by the understanding only, and since they are not known from the fact that they are seen or touched, but only because they are understood, I see clearly that there is nothing which is easier for me to know than my mind. But because it is difficult to rid oneself so promptly of an opinion to which one was accustomed for so long, it will be well that I should halt a little at this point, so that by the length of my meditation I may more deeply imprint on my memory this new knowledge.

5

PIERRE GASSENDI

---

introduction

Pierre Gassendi, when he was given Descartes' *Meditations* to read, had
long since decided, unlike Descartes, that knowledge was to be gained only
through observation and experience, not through the kind of isolated,
abstract reflection on ideas of which Descartes' philosophy is a perfect example.

Gassendi was a follower of the philosophy of Epicurus, the most scientifi-
cally advanced philosophical outlook of antiquity. According to this
philosophy, nothing exists except tiny material particles called "atoms." This
term was used by the ancients to mean, literally, that which is indivisible.
According to the Epicureans, all changes that take place in the world, and
thus in the human body as well, are changes in the velocity, direction, and
position of atoms. All knowledge of such changes and of the laws governing
them arises from experience. The mind itself, according to this philosophy,
must also consist of atoms, since it exists and is subject to change. It is
therefore not really distinct from the body, and the actual process of thinking, to which Descartes attached such importance, must be a process that
occurs in matter.

Gassendi and Descartes were, then, poles apart in their ideas. Gassendi, a
younger contemporary and admirer of Galileo, was one of the forerunners of
modern science. Descartes, on the other hand, while strongly influenced by
the scientific revolution that began in his day, nevertheless reverted to the

abstract and rationalistic philosophy of Platonism in his metaphysical speculation.

Gassendi's deference and excessive modesty, in his communication with
Descartes, is essentially ironic and sarcastic, as becomes evident when we
find him addressing his opponent "O Soul," "O Mind," and eventually "O
Ghost"! His preliminary acknowledgment of the existence of Almighty God
and of the immortality of the soul was a fairly standard practice among
writers of that age whose thinking was in discord with that of the Church; it
was meant mainly to protect themselves from censorship and persecution.
Galileo's forced recantation was very fresh in Gassendi's memory. These
characteristics of his writing can mislead a contemporary reader, concealing
the truly devastating character of Gassendi's remarks.

Essentially what Gassendi does in these criticisms is to show, as Gilbert
Ryle would do again three centuries later, that nothing in Descartes'
philosophy refutes the supposition that a man is a material being only, and
that his mind or "soul" is therefore likewise material in nature. It is certainly
true that we think, and that nothing can be more certain. And if we simply
mean by the "the mind" that which thinks, then it does follow that we are
minds, or that each of us is, as Descartes put it, "a thinking thing." But,
Gassendi points out, it has not been shown that this mind that thinks is not
material in nature. Air, which we do not ordinarily think of as matter,
nevertheless *is* matter. Why cannot the mind be composed of matter as well?
It is fair to say that Descartes never really answered this question. Indeed,
he never really understood it, so obsessed was he with the *concept* of the
mind as something immaterial in nature, a concept which he had simply
inherited from a very long tradition. Even today this trenchant criticism of
Gassendi's is sometimes unappreciated by philosophers, whose thought has
been so thoroughly conditioned by Descartes and the metaphysical tradition
to which he belonged.

Pierre Gassendi, a contemporary of Descartes, was a priest whose main
interests were in astronomy and empirical philosophy. Much of his writing
was aimed at diminishing the authority of Aristotle. His lengthy set of objections to Descartes' first two *Meditations* has been abridged in what follows.

Against the Immateriality
of the Mind*

Sir,

Our friend Mersenne did me a great kindness in communicating to me
your magnificent work—your Meditations on First Philosophy. The excel-

*Pierre Gassendi, "The Fifth Set of Objections," from *Philosophical Writings* by René Descartes, trans. Haldane and Ross. Copyright 1911, Cambridge University Press, by permission
of Cambridge Univeristy Press.

lence of your arguments, the perspicuity of your intellect, and the brilliance of your expression have caused me extraordinary delight. It gives me great pleasure to compliment you on the sublimity and felicity with which your mind assails the task of extending the boundaries of the sciences and bringing to light those matters that preceding ages have found most difficult to drag from their obscurity. To me it has proved hard to comply, as friendship obliged me to do, with the request M. Mersenne also made, and let you know if I took any exception to your doctrine and had any scruple unsatisfied. Especially I foresaw that, if I did not agree with your arguments, I should merely display my own lack of acuteness, or rather should merely manifest rashness, if I dared to utter my dissent in the smallest matter, and appear to oppose you. Nevertheless I have yielded to my friend, thinking besides that you would approve of his plan rather than of mine; since indeed your candour will easily let you see that my intention is solely to display to you without disguise the reasons I have for doubting. I testify that this will be amply confirmed if you have patience to scrutinize them thoroughly; for as to any influence they may have in causing you the slightest sense of insecurity in your reasonings, or in causing you to consume, in replying, any time destined for more valuable studies, I declare myself not responsible for this. Nay, I cannot without shame-facedness expose my difficulties to your gaze, sure as I am that there is none of them that has not often suggested itself to you in your reflections, and which you have not with full consciousness dismissed as of no account, or determined to keep out of sight. Consequently, though I bring forward certain hypotheses, I bring them forward merely as hypotheses, and they are hypotheses that affect not the truths themselves of which you have undertaken the proof, but the method and the cogency of your proof. I unaffectedly acknowledge the existence of Almighty God and the immortality of our souls; my doubts concern merely the validity of the reasoning by which you prove those matters, as well as other things involved in the scheme of Metaphysical science.

RELATIVE TO MEDITATION I.

Of the things which may be brought within the sphere of the doubtful.

In the matter of the first Meditation, there is really little for me to linger over; I agree with your plan of freeing your mind from every prejudice. On one point only I am not clear; that is, why you should not have preferred to indicate simply and with few words that what you previously knew was uncertain, in order subsequently to choose what might be found to be true, rather than by regarding everything as false, not so much to dismiss an old prejudice, as to take up with a new one. Thus, for example, it became necessary to feign that God was a deceiver, or some evil spirit that mocks us, in order to convince yourself; whereas it would have seemed to be sufficient to ascribe that to the obscurity of the human mind and the weakness of its nature alone. Further, you feign that you are dreaming in order to cast doubt on everything, and consider that everything that happens is done to make sport of us. But will that compel you to believe that you are not awake and to deem uncertain and false the events that occur before your eyes? Say what you will, no one will be convinced that you have convinced yourself that none of the things you have learned are true, and that your senses, or a dream, or God, or an evil spirit have imposed on you. Would it not have been better and more consonant with philosophic candour and the love of the truth to state the actual facts in a straightforward and simple manner, rather than to incur the possible objection of having recourse to an artifice, of eagerness for verbal trickery and seeking evasions? Yet, since you have been pleased to take this way, I shall make no further criticism on it.

RELATIVE TO MEDITATION II.

Of the Nature of the Human Mind; and that it is more easily known than the Body.

When it comes to the second Meditation, I see that you still persist in keeping up the game of pretence, and yet that you recognize at least that *you exist*; which thus establishes the *conclusion that this proposition: —I am, I exist, is true each time that you pronounce it, or that you mentally conceive it.* But I don't see that you needed all this mechanism, when you had other grounds for being sure, and it was true, that you existed. You might have inferred that from any other activity, since our natural light informs us that whatever acts also exists.

You add *that this does not yet let you know clearly enough what you are.* But this is admitted, and in quite a serious spirit; we grant it quite willingly: to know this requires toil and exertion. But surely this knowledge might have been sought for without all that circumlocution and all those suppositions.

You next wish to contemplate yourself *as what you have believed yourself to be, in such a way that, when every doubtful element is withdrawn, nothing may be left beyond what is absolutely certain and indubitable.* But you will do this with the approval of everyone. You tackle the matter; and believing that you are a man, you ask, *what is man?* Purposely dismissing the common definition you select those characteristics *which at the first glance presented themselves to you, e.g. that you had a face, hands, and other members which you designated by the name body; and likewise that you were nourished, that you walked, that you felt, that you thought, features which you referred to the soul.* So far, so good, only what becomes of the distinction you draw between the soul and the body? You say *that you did not then perceive what the soul was, but imagined merely that it was like a wind, a flame, or an ether, which was spread throughout your grosser parts.* That is worth noting. *But body you did not doubt to have a nature identical with*

*whatever can be defined by figure, or can be confined in a certain place, can
fill a space from which it can exclude every other body, can be perceived by
touch, sight, hearing, smell or taste, and can be moved in many ways.* But
these things you can even at present attribute to bodies, provided you do not
attribute all of them to every corporeal thing; inasmuch as wind is a body,
and yet is not perceived by sight. And you cannot exclude the other attributes which you mention next in order, for wind, fire, also move many
things. Moreover, what you subjoin, viz. that you denied to body the power
of moving itself, cannot, so far as it appears, be successfully maintained; for
this implies that every body must by its own nature be without motion, and
that all its motions must proceed from an incorporeal principle; and it must
be thought that neither can water flow nor an animal move, unless through
the agency of some incorporeal mover.

Next you investigate whether, *the existence of a deceiving agent being up
to this point supposed, you can affirm that any of the things which you
judged to belong to the nature of body exist in you. You say that after the
most careful scrutiny nothing of such a sort can be found in you.* Already at
this point you consider yourself not as a complete human being, but as that
inner and more hidden part, such as you deemed the soul to be. Wherefore I
ask thee, O soul, or whatever the name be by which you choose to be
addressed, have you by this time corrected that notion in virtue of which you
previously imagined that you were something similar to wind, or a like
substance, diffused throughout the members of the body? You certainly have
not. Why then, cannot you be a wind, or rather a very subtle spirit, which,
by means of the heat of the heart, is distilled from the purest of the blood or
from some other source; or may there not be some other cause by which you
are evoked and preserved; and may you not, being diffused throughout the
members, attribute life to them, and see with the eye, hear with the ear,
think by means of the brain and discharge the other functions which by
common consent are ascribed to you? If that be so, why may you not have
the same figure as the whole of this body has, just as the air takes the shape of
the vessel which contains it? Why may you not believe that you are bounded
too by the same circumambient medium as surrounds the body, or by the
bodily epidermis? May you not occupy space, or those parts of space which
the solid body or its parts do not completely fill? In truth, the solid body
possesses pores through which you yourself may be diffused, in such a way
that, where the parts of which you consist are found none of its parts exist;
just as in a mixture of wine and water, where the particles of the former are,
the parts of the second are not found, howsoever much sight be unable to
distinguish between the two. Why will it be impossible for you to exclude
another body from the same space as you occupy, when the parts composing
the solid body are incapable of existing in the same tiny portions of space in
which you are found? Why cannot you participate in many motions? For
when you assign many motions to the members themselves, how can you

move them unless you yourself are moved? Certainly you must not be un-
moved if you are to cause movement, where exertion is called for; nor can
you rest immoveable when the body itself is moved. If this be so, why do you
say that *none of those things exist in you which are relative to the nature of
the body?*

You proceed to say *that, of the things ascribed to soul, neither nourishment nor walking belong to you.* But, in the first place, a thing may be a body
and yet not be nourished. Secondly, if you are such a body as we have
described breath to be, why, if your more solid members are nourished by
more solid substance, may you—a more rarefied one—not be also nourished
by a rarer substance? Further, are you not young and vigorous when that
body, of which these are the parts, is in the vigour of youth? And when it is
weak, are you not yourself weak? In the matter of moving, when it is owing
to you that your members move and never pass into any position except you
move and transport them thither, how can that be possible without movement on your part? But, you say, *if now I do not possess a body, these are
nothing but figments.* But whether you are making game of us or playing
with yourself, there is no reason for our delaying here. If, however, you are
speaking seriously, you must prove that you neither have any body which
you inform, nor are of such a nature as to be nourished and to move along
with it.

You proceed, saying *that you are without sensation.* But yourself assuredly
are such as to see colour, hear sounds, etc. *This,* you say, *cannot occur apart
from the body.* I grant you that; but, in the first place, a body is present to
you and you yourself reside within the eye, which certainly does not see
without you; and secondly you may be a rarefied body operating by means of
the sense-organs. You say *I have thought I perceived many things during
sleep that subsequently I recognised as not having been experienced at all.*
But though you go wrong if, without using the eye, you seemed to have
experiences which do not occur without the eye coming into play, nevertheless so to err is not your universal experience, nor have you not employed
your eye, by which you perceive and by which you take in the images, which
now you can use without employing the eye.

At length you come to the conclusion *that thought belongs to you.* True,
that is not to be denied; but you still have to prove that the power of thinking
is so much superior to the nature of body, that neither breath nor any other
mobile, pure, and rarefied body, can by any means be so adapted as to be
capable of exercising thought. You will have to prove at the same time that
the souls of the brutes are incorporeal inasmuch as they think, or, over and
above the functioning of the external senses, are aware of something internal, not only while awake, but when dreaming. Again, you must prove that
this solid body contributes absolutely nothing to your thinking (though you
have never existed without it nor have ever hitherto had any thought in

isolation from it), and that your thinking is hence independent of it; so that you can neither be impeded nor disturbed by the foul and dense vapours or fumes, which sometimes so afflict the brain.

Your conclusion is: *I am, to speak accurately, a Thing which thinks, that is to say, a mind or a soul, or an understanding, or a reason.* Here I confess that I have been suffering from a deception. For I believed that I was addressing the human soul, or that internal principle, by which a man lives, feels, moves from place to place and understands, and after all I was only speaking to a mind, which has divested itself not only of the body but of the soul itself. Have you, my worthy sir, in attaining to this result, followed the example of those ancients, who, though they thought that the soul was diffused throughout the whole body, believed that its principal part—the dominating part—was located in a determinate region of the body, e.g. in the brain, or in the heart? Not that they judged that the soul was not also to be found there, but that they believed that the mind was, as it were, added to the soul existing there, was linked to it, and along with it informed that region. I ought really to have remembered that from the discussion in your Discourse on Method. There you appeared to decide that all those offices, ascribed both to the vegetative and to the sensitive soul, do not depend on the rational soul and can be exercised without it before it is introduced into the body, as does happen in the case of the brutes, in whom your contention is that no reason is found. I do not know how I managed to forget this, except for the reason that I remained in doubt as to whether that principle by means of which we and the brutes alike exercise the vegetative function and feel, was not according to your nomenclature to be styled soul, soul being exclusively reserved for the human mind. Yet since it is that principle that is properly said to animate us, mind is capable of no other function than to make us think, as you indeed assert. And, since this is so, call it now *Mind*, and let it be, taken precisely, *a Thing which thinks*.

You add that it is *thought alone which cannot be separated from you*. Truly it is impossible to deny this of you, if you are primarily Mind alone and refuse to allow that your substance can be distinguished from the substance of the soul except in thought; though here I pause and ask whether, when you say *that thought cannot be separated from you*, you mean that you, as long as you exist, think to an indefinite extent. This is indeed in conformity with the pronouncement of those celebrated philosophers who, in order to prove your immortality, assumed that you were in perpetual motion, or, as I interpret it, thought continuously. But this will not gain the adhesion of those who cannot comprehend how you can think during a lethargic sleep, or while in the womb. Besides, I have a difficulty here as to whether you think that you have been infused into the body or one of its parts during the uterine stage of existence or at birth. But I should be loth to be troublesome with my enquiries, or to reflect whether you remember what your thoughts were when in the womb, or in the days, months, and years succeeding your birth; or, if you replied that you had forgotten, to ask why this was so. Yet I suggest that you should remember how obscure, how meagre, how nearly nonexistent your thought must have been during those periods of life.

Proceeding, you maintain *that you are not the complex of members which we call the human body.* But that must be admitted because you are considering yourself solely as a thing which thinks, as a part of the concrete human whole, distinct from this exterior and more solid part. *'I am not,'* you say, *'a subtle air distributed through these members, I am not a wind, a fire, a vapour, nor a breath, nor anything which I can construct in imagination. For I have assumed that all these were nothing; and let that supposition be unchanged.'* But halt here, O Mind, and let those suppositions or rather those fictions take themselves off. You say, *'I am not air or anything of such a nature.'* But, if the total soul be something of the kind, wherefore may not you who are thought to be the noblest part of the soul, be deemed to be, as it were, the flower, or the subtlest, purest, and most active part of it. You say *'perhaps those same things which I supposed were non-existent, are real things and are not different from the self which I know? I do not know about this, I shall not dispute about it now.'* But if you do not know, if you do not dispute the matter, why do you assume that you are none of these things? *'I know,'* you say, *'that I exist; but the knowledge of my existence taken in its precise significance cannot depend on that which I do not know.'* Granted, but remember that you have not proved that you are not air, or a vapour, or many other things. . . .

You next add: *But what should I say of this mind, that is of myself, for up to this point I do not admit in myself anything but mind? What then am I who seem to perceive this wax so distinctly, do I not know myself not only with much more truth, and certainty, but also with much more distinctness and clearness? For, if I judged that the wax is or exists from the fact that I see it, how much more clearly does it follow that I exist? For it may be that what I see is not really wax. It may also happen that I do not even possess eyes with which to see anything. But it cannot be that when I see, or (for I do not now take account of the distinction), when I think I see, that I myself who think am nought. So if I judge that wax exists from the fact that I touch it, the same thing will follow, to wit, that I am; and so if I judge from the fact that I imagine it, or from any other cause, the same result will follow. But what I have here remarked of wax may be applied to all other things which are external to me.* These are your own words; and I here repeat them in order to let you see that while they indeed prove that you distinctly perceive that you exist, from the fact that you distinctly see and are aware of the existence of wax and those accidents of it, they yet do not prove that you for this reason know what or of what nature you are, either distinctly or indistinctly. Yet to do so had been worth your while, for of your existence there is no doubt.

Notice meanwhile, though I do not mean to dwell on the point, that neither have I previously raised the objection that, since you do not admit the existence in you of anything beyond mind alone, and therefore rule out eyes, hands and the rest of the organs, it is vain to talk of wax and its accidents, which you see, touch, etc.; you certainly cannot see them without using your eyes, touch them without employing the hands (or, to adopt your mode of expression, think that you see and touch them).

You proceed: *If the perception of wax has seemed to me clearer and more distinct not only after the sight and touch, but also after many other causes have rendered it quite manifest to me, with how much more distinctness must it be said that I now know myself, since all the reasons which contribute to the knowledge of wax, or to any other body whatever, are yet better proof of the nature of my mind?* But, just as your conclusions about wax prove only the perception of the existence of mind, and fail to reveal its nature, so will all other examples fail to prove anything more. But, if you wish to deduce something more from the perception of the substance of wax and other things, the only conclusion you can arrive at will be that just as we conceive that substance confusedly only and as an unknown somewhat, so we must also conceive of the mind. Hence you may well repeat that phrase of yours—that *obscure and unknown part of me.*

Your conclusion is: *And finally, behold I have without premeditation re-verted to the point I desired. For, since it is now manifest that the mind itself and bodies are not, properly speaking, known by the senses or by the faculty of imagination, but by the understanding only; and since they are not known owing to the fact that they are seen and touched, I see clearly that there is nothing which is easier for me to know than my mind.* So you have it; but I do not see how you deduce or are clearly aware, that anything else can be known of your Mind than that it exists. Whence that also which was prom-ised by the very title of the Meditation, viz. that the human mind considered by itself would be shown to be better known than the body, cannot in my estimation be complied with. For it was not your project to prove that the human mind existed and that its existence was better known than that of the body, when really no one disputed its existence; rather you doubtless wished to make its nature better known than that of the body and this is what you, however, have not achieved. Truly, O Mind, you have recounted of cor-poreal nature the very things, the list of which we know, viz. extension, figure, occupation of space, etc. But what about yourself? You are not a material complex, not air, not wind, not a fire, or one of many other things. To grant you these results (though some of them you yourself refuted), they are not however what we expected. They are forsooth negatives and we want to know, not what you are not, but what you really are. Hence, you refer us to your main conclusion, viz. that you are a *Thing which thinks, i.e. doubts, affirms,* etc. But first, to say that you are a Thing is to say nothing which is known. For "*thing*" is a general term, undifferentiated and vague and not applying to you more than to anything else in the entire world, to anything which is not wholly non-existent. You are a Thing? That is to say, you are not nothing; or, what is precisely the same, you are something. But a stone is not nothing, i.e. is something; and so is a fly, and so on with everything else. Next, in saying that you are a Thinking being, though you do assign a predicate known to us, yet it was not previously unknown and was not the object of your enquiry. Who doubts your thinking? That which baffles us, that which we seek to discover is that inner substance belonging to you, the property of which is to think. Wherefore, your conclusion should correspond with your quest, and that is to discover, not that you are a Thinking thing, but of what nature you, the thing which thinks, are. Is it not the case that it will not be sufficient for you to say, when a knowledge of wine superior to the vulgar is sought for: wine is a thing which is liquid, extracted from grapes, is white or red, is sweet, intoxicating and so on? Rather you will try to discover and to declare how that internal substance, in accordance with what you have observed of its fabrication, has been compounded out of a mixture of spirits, humour, tartar and other elements, in some or other particular quantity and proportion. Hence, similarly, since a knowledge of yourself superior to the vulgar, i.e. to what you previously possessed, is called for, you see quite clearly that it is not enough to inform us that you are a thing which thinks, doubts, understands, etc., but that you ought to scrutinise yourself, as it were, by a chemical method of procedure in order to be able to reveal and demonstrate to us your internal substance. If you accomplish this, we shall certainly ourselves discover by investigation whether you are better known than the body itself, of which anatomy, chemistry and many other sciences, many senses and numbers of experiments of all kinds tell us so much.

6

GILBERT RYLE

---

introduction

Gilbert Ryle's book,*The Concept of Mind*, from which this selection is taken, appeared in 1949 and soon became one of the most widely discussed philosophical works of the present age. What its author attempted to do was completely reorient our thinking with respect to the question, What is a person? For almost the whole of our intellectual history, beginning with the dualism of Socrates and Plato, people have spoken, and thought, of human nature as having two parts, the mental and the physical. This conception became fixed and settled in Cartesian philosophy, and while not all philosophers were Cartesians, virtually all accepted in one way or another the fundamental distinction between mind and matter upon which that philosophy rested. Philosophers who did not, such as Gassendi, were rare exceptions. Ryle, accordingly, picks Descartes as the ostensible target of his attack. His real target, however, is one of the presuppositions of the prevailing philosophical outlook of our entire culture.

Ryle's writing is so clear and forceful that little interpretative comment is needed. It is, however, necessary to appreciate the nature of his argument. It is broadly empirical, rather than rational and dialectical. That is to say, Ryle does not, in the manner of Plato, Descartes, and most other philosophers, develop deductive arguments from antecedent premises. Instead, he examines with great care and describes in detail some philosophical conception, much as a skilled portrait artist might render, in fastidious and faithful detail, a human likeness. Then, having gotten the picture clearly before us, Ryle invites us to step back and *look* at it, to see whether it in fact resembles anything in the world.

The selection that follows, which is the entire first chapter of his book, constitutes a preliminary sketch. The remainder of the book fills in the details. What is here set forth is a picture of a human being as composed of two radically different things, a body that has shape and mass and is therefore subject to the laws of mechanics, and, somehow inside that body, a mind that has neither size nor weight, is not subject to the laws of mechanics, and constitutes the true self or person. This picture Ryle calls, in a now famous expression, "The Ghost in the Machine," and his argument for its lack of correspondence with anything in the world consists simply in inviting us to look at it and see for ourselves what an absurd caricature it is.

How, then, did an entire culture become captivated by this picture? Part of the answer lies in the clash between the scientific conception of the world that began to emerge at about the time of Descartes and the then prevailing philosophical and religious conception of the soul. But much of the rest of the answer lies in the human propensity to treat certain forms of linguistic expression as literally descriptive when in fact they serve only as abbreviated references to things and relationships of a sometimes very complex kind. This is what Ryle refers to as a "category mistake." If, for instance, upon hearing that the average father has 2.3 children, anyone were to set out to find that father and his strange household, containing a fractional child, he would have fallen victim to a category mistake. The statement about the average father—which might well be a *true* statement—really describes something fairly complex, namely, the result of certain computations as applied to families within a given context. Similarly, if, upon hearing someone described as tall, muscular, and possessed of a brilliant mind, one were to set out to find, along with the tall and muscled frame, the additional thing here referred to as a mind and described as brilliant, he would have fallen victim to a category mistake. The expression "brilliant mind" no more denotes a part of a person than the expression "average father" denotes a member of the human race. Like the latter, its use is to describe, often truly, human capacities and modes of behavior of a rather complex nature.

People are not, of course, really misled by certain common expressions such as "the average father," "the University," and so on, but they have been most seriously misled by the expression "the mind" in its many contexts. And philosophers, building upon the reflections of the ancients, of Christian theologians, and particularly upon the thought of Descartes, have tended to reinforce that very error. Ryle conceives it as his philosophical mission to shatter that myth.

Gilbert Ryle, who was born in 1900, was Waynflete professor of metaphysics at Oxford University.

The Concept of the Human Mind*

(I) THE OFFICIAL DOCTRINE

There is a doctrine about the nature and place of minds which is so prevalent among theorists and even among laymen that it deserves to be described as the official theory. Most philosophers, psychologists and religious teachers subscribe, with minor reservations, to its main articles and, although they admit certain theoretical difficulties in it, they tend to assume that these can be overcome without serious modifications being made to the architecture of the theory. It will be argued here that the central principles of the doctrine are unsound and conflict with the whole body of what we know about minds when we are not speculating about them.

The official doctrine, which hails chiefly from Descartes, is something like this. With the doubtful exceptions of idiots and infants in arms every human being has both a body and a mind. Some would prefer to say that every human being is both a body and a mind. His body and his mind are ordinarily harnessed together, but after the death of the body his mind may continue to exist and function.

Human bodies are in space and are subject to the mechanical laws which govern all other bodies in space. Bodily processes and states can be inspected by external observers. So a man's bodily life is as much a public affair as are the lives of animals and reptiles and even as the careers of trees, crystals and planets.

But minds are not in space, nor are their operations subject to mechanical laws. The workings of one mind are not witnessable by other observers; its career is private. Only I can take direct cognisance of the states and processes of my own mind. A person therefore lives through two collateral histories, one consisting of what happens in and to his body, the other consisting of what happens in and to his mind. The first is public, the second private. The events in the first history are events in the physical world, those in the second are events in the mental world.

It has been disputed whether a person does or can directly monitor all or only some of the episodes of his own private history; but, according to the

*From Gilbert Ryle, *The Concept of Mind*, Chap. 1 (London: Hutchinson's University Library, 1949). Reprinted by permission of Hutchinson Publishing Group Ltd.

official doctrine, of at least some of these episodes he has direct and unchallengeable cognisance. In consciousness, self-consciousness and introspection he is directly and authentically apprised of the present states and operations of his mind. He may have great or small uncertainties about concurrent and adjacent episodes in the physical world, but he can have none about at least part of what is momentarily occupying his mind.

It is customary to express this bifurcation of his two lives and of his two worlds by saying that the things and events which belong to the physical world, including his own body, are external, while the workings of his own mind are internal. This antithesis of outer and inner is of course meant to be construed as a metaphor, since minds, not being in space, could not be described as being spatially inside anything else, or as having things going on spatially inside themselves. But relapses from this good intention are common and theorists are found speculating how stimuli, the physical sources of which are yards or miles outside a person's skin, can generate mental responses inside his skull, or how decisions framed inside his cranium can set going movements of his extremities.

Even when 'inner' and 'outer' are construed as metaphors, the problem how a person's mind and body influence one another is notoriously charged with theoretical difficulties. What the mind wills, the legs, arms and the tongue execute; what affects the ear and the eye has something to do with what the mind perceives; grimaces and smiles betray the mind's moods and bodily castigations lead, it is hoped, to moral improvement. But the actual transactions between the episodes of the private history and those of the public history remain mysterious, since by definition they can belong to neither series. They could not be reported among the happenings described in a person's autobiography of his inner life, but nor could they be reported among those described in some one else's biography of that person's overt career. They can be inspected neither by introspection nor by laboratory experiment. They are theoretical shuttlecocks which are forever being bandied from the physiologist back to the psychologist and from the psychologist back to the physiologist.

Underlying this partly metaphorical representation of the bifurcation of a person's two lives there is a seemingly more profound and philosophical assumption. It is assumed that there are two different kinds of existence or status. What exists or happens may have the status of physical existence, or it may have the status of mental existence. Somewhat as the faces of coins are either heads or tails, or somewhat as living creatures are either male or female, so, it is supposed, some existing is physical existing, other existing is mental existing. It is a necessary feature of what has physical existence that it is in space and time; it is a necessary feature of what has mental existence that it is in time but not in space. What has physical existence is composed of matter, or else is a function of matter; what has mental existence consists of consciousness, or else is a function of consciousness.

There is thus a polar opposition between mind and matter, an opposition which is often brought out as follows. Material objects are situated in a common field, known as 'space', and what happens to one body in one part of space is mechanically connected with what happens to other bodies in other parts of space. But mental happenings occur in insulated fields, known as 'minds', and there is, apart maybe from telepathy, no direct causal connection between what happens in one mind and what happens in another. Only through the medium of the public physical world can the mind of one person make a difference to the mind of another. The mind is its own place and in his inner life each of us lives the life of a ghostly Robinson Crusoe. People can see, hear and jolt one another's bodies, but they are irremediably blind and deaf to the workings of one another's minds and inoperative upon them.

What sort of knowledge can be secured of the workings of a mind? On the one side, according to the official theory, a person has direct knowledge of the best imaginable kind of the workings of his own mind. Mental states and processes are (or are normally) conscious states and processes, and the consciousness which irradiates them can engender no illusions and leaves the door open for no doubts. A person's present thinkings, feelings and willings, his perceivings, rememberings and imaginings are intrinsically 'phosphorescent'; their existence and their nature are inevitably betrayed to their owner. The inner life is a stream of consciousness of such a sort that it would be absurd to suggest that the mind whose life is that stream might be unaware of what is passing down it.

True, the evidence adduced recently by Freud seems to show that there exist channels tributary to this stream, which run hidden from their owner. People are actuated by impulses the existence of which they vigorously disavow; some of their thoughts differ from the thoughts which they acknowledge; and some of the actions which they think they will to perform they do not really will. They are thoroughly gulled by some of their own hypocrisies and they successfully ignore facts about their mental lives which on the official theory ought to be patent to them. Holders of the official theory tend, however, to maintain that anyhow in normal circumstances a person must be directly and authentically seized of the present state and workings of his own mind.

Besides being currently supplied with these alleged immediate data of consciousness, a person is also generally supposed to be able to exercise from time to time a special kind of perception, namely inner perception, or introspection. He can take a (non-optical) 'look' at what is passing in his mind. Not only can he view and scrutinize a flower through his sense of sight and listen to and discriminate the notes of a bell through his sense of hearing; he can also reflectively or introspectively watch, without any bodily organ of sense, the current episodes of his inner life. This self-observation is also commonly supposed to be immune from illusion, confusion or doubt. A mind's reports of its own affairs have a certainty superior to the best that is possessed by its reports of matters in the physical world. Sense-perceptions can, but consciousness and introspection cannot, be mistaken or confused.

On the other side, one person has no direct access of any sort to the events of the inner life of another. He cannot do better than make problematic inferences from the observed behaviour of the other person's body to the states of mind which, by analogy from his own conduct, he supposes to be signalised by that behaviour. Direct access to the workings of a mind is the privilege of that mind itself; in default of such privileged access, the workings of one mind are inevitably occult to everyone else. For the supposed arguments from bodily movements similar to their own to mental workings similar to their own would lack any possibility of observational corroboration. Not unnaturally, therefore, an adherent of the official theory finds it difficult to resist this consequence of his premises, that he has no good reason to believe that there do exist minds other than his own. Even if he prefers to believe that to other human bodies there are harnessed minds not unlike his own, he cannot claim to be able to discover their individual characteristics, or the particular things that they undergo and do. Absolute solitude is on this showing the ineluctable destiny of the soul. Only our bodies can meet.

As a necessary corollary of this general scheme there is implicitly prescribed a special way of construing our ordinary concepts of mental powers and operations. The verbs, nouns and adjectives, with which in ordinary life we describe the wits, characters and higher-grade performances of the people with whom we have do, are required to be construed as signifying special episodes in their secret histories, or else as signifying tendencies for such episodes to occur. When someone is described as knowing, believing or guessing something, as hoping, dreading, intending or shirking something, as designing this or being amused at that, these verbs are supposed to denote the occurrence of specific modifications in his (to us) occult stream of consciousness. Only his own privileged access to this stream in direct awareness and introspection could provide authentic testimony that these mental-conduct verbs were correctly or incorrectly applied. The onlooker, be he teacher, critic, biographer or friend, can never assure himself that his comments have any vestige of truth. Yet it was just because we do in fact all know how to make such comments, make them with general correctness and correct them when they turn out to be confused or mistaken, that philosophers found it necessary to construct their theories of the nature and place of minds. Finding mental-conduct concepts being regularly and effectively used, they properly sought to fix their logical geography. But the logical geography officially recommended would entail that there could be no regular or effective use of these mental-conduct concepts in our descriptions of, and prescriptions for, other people's minds.

(2) THE ABSURDITY OF THE OFFICIAL DOCTRINE

Such in outline is the official theory. I shall often speak of it, with deliberate abusiveness, as 'the dogma of the Ghost in the Machine'. I hope to prove that it is entirely false, and false not in detail but in principle. It is not merely an assemblage of particular mistakes. It is one big mistake and a mistake of a special kind. It is, namely, a category-mistake. It represents the facts of mental life as if they belonged to one logical type or category (or range of types or categories), when they actually belong to another. The dogma is therefore a philosopher's myth. In attempting to explode the myth I shall probably be taken to be denying well-known facts about the mental life of human beings, and my plea that I aim at doing nothing more than rectify the logic of mental-conduct concepts will probably be disallowed as mere subterfuge.

I must first indicate what is meant by the phrase 'Category-mistake'. This I do in a series of illustrations.

A foreigner visiting Oxford or Cambridge for the first time is shown a number of colleges, libraries, playing fields, museums, scientific departments and administrative offices. He then asks 'But where is the University? I have seen where the members of the Colleges live, where the Registrar works, where the scientists experiment and the rest. But I have not yet seen the University in which reside and work the members of your University.' It has then to be explained to him that the University is not another collateral institution, some ulterior counterpart to the colleges, laboratories and offices which he has seen. The University is just the way in which all that he has already seen is organized. When they are seen and when their co-ordination is understood, the University has been seen. His mistake lay in his innocent assumption that it was correct to speak of Christ Church, the Bodleian Library, the Ashmolean Museum *and* the University, to speak, that is, as if 'the University' stood for an extra member of the class of which these other units are members. He was mistakenly allocating the University to the same category as that to which the other institutions belong.

The same mistake would be made by a child witnessing the march-past of a division who, having had pointed out to him such and such battalions, batteries, squadrons, etc., asked when the division was going to appear. He would be supposing that a division was a counterpart to the units already seen, partly similar to them and partly unlike them. He would be shown his mistake by being told that in watching the battalions, batteries and squadrons marching past he had been watching the division marching past. The march-past was not a parade of battalions, batteries, squadrons *and* a division; it was a parade of the battalions, batteries and squadrons *of* a division.

One more illustration. A foreigner watching his first game of cricket learns what are the functions of the bowlers, the batsmen, the fielders, the umpires and the scorers. He then says 'But there is no one left on the field to contribute the famous element of team-spirit. I see who does the bowling, the batting and the wicket-keeping; but I do not see whose role it is to exercise *esprit de corps.*' Once more, it would have to be explained that he was looking for the wrong type of thing. Team-spirit is not another cricketing-operation supplementary to all of the other special tasks. It is, roughly, the keenness with which each of the special tasks is performed, and performing a task keenly is not performing two tasks. Certainly exhibiting team-spirit is not the same thing as bowling or catching, but nor is it a third thing such that we can say that the bowler first bowls *and* then exhibits team-spirit or that a fielder is at a given moment *either* catching *or* displaying *esprit de corps*.

These illustrations of category-mistakes have a common feature which must be noticed. The mistakes were made by people who did not know how to wield the concepts *University, division* and *team-spirit*. Their puzzles arose from inability to use certain items in the English vocabularly.

The theoretically interesting category-mistakes are those made by people who are perfectly competent to apply concepts, at least in the situations with which they are familiar, but are still liable in their abstract thinking to allocate those concepts to logical types to which they do not belong. An instance of a mistake of this sort would be the following story. A student of politics has learned the main differences between the British, the French and the American Constitutions, and has learned also the differences and connections between the Cabinet, Parliament, the various Ministries, the Judicature and the Church of England. But he still becomes embarrassed when asked questions about the connections between the Church of England, the Home Office and the British Constitution. For while the Church and the Home Office are institutions, the British Constitution is not another institution in the same sense of that noun. So inter-institutional relations which can be asserted or denied to hold between the Church and the Home Office cannot be asserted or denied to hold between either of them and the British Constitution. 'The British Constitution' is not a term of the same logical type as 'the Home Office' and 'the Church of England'. In a partially similar way, John Doe may be a relative, friend, an enemy or a stranger to Richard Roe; but he cannot be any of these things to the Average Taxpayer. He knows how to talk sense in certain sorts of discussions about the Average Taxpayer, but he is baffled to say why he could not come across him in the street as he can come across Richard Roe.

It is pertinent to our main subject to notice that, so long as the student of politics continues to think of the British Constitution as a counterpart to the other institutions, he will tend to describe it as a mysteriously occult institution; and so long as John Doe continues to think of the Average Taxpayer as a fellow-citizen, he will tend to think of him as an elusive insubstantial man, a ghost who is everywhere yet nowhere.

My destructive purpose is to show that a family of radical category-mistakes is the source of the double-life theory. The representation of a person as a ghost mysteriously ensconced in a machine derives from this argument. Because, as is true, a person's thinking, feeling and purposive doing cannot be described solely in the idioms of physics, chemistry and physiology, therefore they must be described in counterpart idioms. As the human body is a complex organised unit, so the human mind must be another complex organised unit, though one made of a different sort of stuff and with a different sort of structure. Or, again, as the human body, like any other parcel of matter, is a field of causes and effects, so the mind must be another field of causes and effects, though not (Heaven be praised) mechanical causes and effects.

(3) THE ORIGIN OF THE CATEGORY-MISTAKE

One of the chief intellectual origins of what I have yet to prove to be the Cartesian category-mistake seems to be this. When Galileo showed that his methods of scientific discovery were competent to provide a mechanical theory which should cover every occupant of space, Descartes found in himself two conflicting motives. As a man of scientific genius he could not but endorse claims of mechanics, yet as a religious and moral man he could not accept, as Hobbes accepted, the discouraging rider to those claims, namely that human nature differs only in degree of complexity from clockwork. The mental could not be just a variety of the mechanical.

He and subsequent philosophers naturally but erroneously availed themselves of the following escape-route. Since mental-conduct words are not to be construed as signifying the occurrence of mechanical processes, they must be construed as signifying the occurrence of non-mechanical processes; since mechanical laws explain movements in space as the effects of other movements in space, other laws must explain some of the non-spatial workings of minds as the effects of other non-spatial workings of minds. The difference between the human behaviours which we describe as intelligent and those which we describe as unintelligent must be a difference in their causation; so, while some movements of human tongues and limbs are the effects of mechanical causes, others must be the effects of non-mechanical causes, i.e. some issue from movements of particles of matter, others from workings of the mind.

The differences between the physical and the mental were thus represented as differences inside the common framework of the categories of 'thing', 'stuff', 'attribute', 'state', 'process', 'change', 'cause' and 'effect'. Minds are things, but different sorts of things from bodies; mental processes are causes and effects, but different sorts of causes and effects from bodily movements. And so on. Somewhat as the foreigner expected the University to be an extra edifice, rather like a college but also considerably different, so the repudiators of mechanism represented minds as extra centres of causal processes, rather like machines but also considerably different from them. Their theory was a para-mechanical hypothesis.

That this assumption was at the heart of the doctrine is shown by the fact that there was from the beginning felt to be a major theoretical difficulty in explaining how minds can influence and be influenced by bodies. How can a mental process, such as willing, cause spatial movements like the movements of the tongue? How can a physical change in the optic nerve have among its effects a mind's perception of a flash of light? This notorious crux by itself shows the logical mould into which Descartes pressed his theory of the mind. It was the self-same mould into which he and Galileo set their mechanics. Still unwittingly adhering to the grammar of mechanics, he tried to avert disaster by describing minds in what was merely an obverse vocabulary. The workings of minds had to be described by the mere negatives of the specific descriptions given to bodies; they are not in space, they are not motions, they are not modifications of matter, they are not accessible to public observation. Minds are not bits of clockwork, they are just bits of not-clockwork.

As thus represented, minds are not merely ghosts harnessed to machines, they are themselves just spectral machines. Though the human body is an engine, it is not quite an ordinary engine, since some of its workings are governed by another engine inside it—this interior governor-engine being one of a very special sort. It is invisible, inaudible and it has no size or weight. It cannot be taken to bits and the laws it obeys are not those known to ordinary engineers. Nothing is known of how it governs the bodily engine.

A second major crux points the same moral. Since, according to the doctrine, minds belong to the same category as bodies and since bodies are rigidly governed by mechanical laws, it seemed to many theorists to follow that minds must be similarly governed by rigid non-mechanical laws. The physical world is a deterministic system, so the mental world must be a deterministic system. Bodies cannot help the modifications that they undergo, so minds cannot help pursuing the careers fixed for them. *Responsibility, choice, merit* and *demerit* are therefore inapplicable concepts—unless the compromise solution is adopted of saying that the laws governing mental processes, unlike those governing physical processes, have the congenial attribute of being only rather rigid. The problem of the Freedom of the Will was the problem how to reconcile the hypothesis that minds are to be described in terms drawn from the categories of mechanics with the knowledge that higher-grade human conduct is not of a piece with the behaviour of machines.

It is an historical curiosity that it was not noticed that the entire argument was broken-backed. Theorists correctly assumed that any sane man could already recognise the differences between, say, rational and non-rational utterances or between purposive and automatic behaviour. Else there would have been nothing requiring to be salved from mechanism. Yet the explanation given presupposed that one person could in principle never recognise the difference between the rational and the irrational utterances issuing from other human bodies, since he could never get access to the postulated immaterial causes of some of their utterances. Save for the doubtful exception of himself, he could never tell the difference between a man and a Robot. It would have to be conceded, for example, that, for all that we can tell, the inner lives of persons who are classed as idiots or lunatics are as rational as those of anyone else. Perhaps only their overt behaviour is disappointing; that is to say, perhaps 'idiots' are not really idiotic, or 'lunatics' lunatic. Perhaps, too, some of those who are classed as sane are really idiots. According to the theory, external observers could never know how the overt behaviour of others is correlated with their mental powers and processes and so they could never know or even plausibly conjecture whether their applications of mental-conduct concepts to these other people were correct or incorrect. It would then be hazardous or impossible for a man to claim sanity or logical consistency even for himself, since he would be debarred from comparing his own performances with those of others. In short, our characterisations of persons and their performances as intelligent, prudent and virtuous or as stupid, hypocritical and cowardly could never have been made, so the problem of providing a special causal hypothesis to serve as the basis of such diagnoses would never have arisen. The question, 'How do persons differ from machines?' arose just because everyone already knew how to apply mental-conduct concepts before the new causal hypothesis was introduced. This causal hypothesis could not therefore be the source of the criteria used in those applications. Nor, of course, has the causal hypothesis in any degree improved our handling of those criteria. We still distinguish good from bad arithmetic, politic from impolitic conduct and fertile from infertile imaginations in the ways in which Descartes himself distinguished them before and after he speculated how the applicability of these criteria was compatible with the principle of mechanical causation.

He had mistaken the logic of his problem. Instead of asking by what criteria intelligent behaviour is actually distinguished from non-intelligent behaviour, he asked 'Given that the principle of mechanical causation does not tell us the difference, what other causal principle will tell it us?' He realised that the problem was not one of mechanics and assumed that it must therefore be one of some counterpart to mechanics. Not unnaturally psychology is often cast for just this role.

When two terms belong to the same category, it is proper to construct conjunctive propositions embodying them. Thus a purchaser may say that he bought a left-hand glove and a right-hand glove, but not that he bought a left-hand glove, a right-hand glove and a pair of gloves. 'She came home in a flood of tears and a sedan-chair' is a well-known joke based on the absurdity of conjoining terms of different types. It would have been equally ridiculous to construct the disjunction 'She came home either in a flood of tears or else in a sedan-chair'. Now the dogma of the Ghost in the Machine does just this. It maintains that there exist both bodies and minds; that there occur physical processes and mental processes; that there are mechanical causes of corporeal movements and mental causes of corporeal movements. I shall argue that these and other analogous conjunctions are absurd; but, it must be noticed, the argument will not show that either of the illegitimately conjoined propositions is absurd in itself. I am not, for example, denying that there occur mental processes. Doing long division is a mental process and so is making a joke. But I am saying that the phrase 'there occur mental processes' does not mean the same sort of thing as 'there occur physical processes', and, therefore, that it makes no sense to conjoin or disjoin the two.

If my argument is successful, there will follow some interesting consequences. First, the hallowed contrast between Mind and Matter will be dissipated, but dissipated not by either of the equally hallowed absorptions of Mind by Matter or of Matter by Mind, but in quite a different way. For the seeming contrast of the two will be shown to be as illegitimate as would be the contrast of 'she came home in a flood of tears' and 'she came home in a sedan-chair'. The belief that there is a polar opposition between Mind and Matter is the belief that they are terms of the same logical type.

It will also follow that both Idealism and Materialism are answers to an improper question. The 'reduction' of the material world to mental states and processes, as well as the 'reduction' of mental states and processes to physical states and processes, presuppose the legitimacy of the disjunction 'Either there exist minds or there exist bodies (but not both)'. It would be like saying, 'Either she bought a left-hand and a right-hand glove or she bought a pair of gloves (but not both)'.

It is perfectly proper to say, in one logical tone of voice, that there exist minds and to say, in another logical tone of voice, that there exist bodies. But these expressions do not indicate two different species of existence, for 'existence' is not a generic word like 'coloured' or 'sexed'. They indicate two different senses of 'exist', somewhat as 'rising' has different senses in 'the tide is rising', 'hopes are rising', and 'the average age of death is rising'. A man would be thought to be making a poor joke who said that three things are now rising, namely the tide, hopes and the average age of death. It would be just as good or bad a joke to say that there exist prime numbers and Wednesdays and public opinions and navies; or that there exist both minds and bodies. In the succeeding chapters I try to prove that the official theory does rest on a batch of category-mistakes by showing that logically absurd corollaries follow from it. The exhibition of these absurdities will have the constructive effect of bringing out part of the correct logic of mental-conduct concepts.

(4) HISTORICAL NOTE

It would not be true to say that the official theory derives solely from Descartes' theories, or even from a more widespread anxiety about the implications of seventeenth century mechanism. Scholastic and Reformation theology had schooled the intellects of the scientists as well as of the laymen, philosophers and clerics of that age. Stoic-Augustinian theories of the will were embedded in the Calvinist doctrines of sin and grace; Platonic and Aristotelian theories of the intellect shaped the orthodox doctrines of the immortality of the soul. Descartes was reformulating already prevalent theological doctrines of the soul in the new syntax of Galileo. The theologian's privacy of conscience became the philosopher's privacy of consciousness, and what had been the bogy of Predestination reappeared as the bogy of Determinism.

It would also not be true to say that the two-worlds myth did no theoretical good. Myths often do a lot of theoretical good, while they are still new. One benefit bestowed by the para-mechanical myth was that it partly superannuated the then prevalent para-political myth. Minds and their Faculties had previously been described by analogies with political superiors and political subordinates. The idioms used were those of ruling, obeying, collaborating and rebelling. They survived and still survive in many ethical and some epistemological discussions. As, in physics, the new myth of occult Forces was a scientific improvement on the old myth of Final Causes, so, in anthropological and psychological theory, the new myth of hidden operations, impulses and agencies was an improvement on the old myth of dictations, deferences and disobediences.

7

U. T. PLACE

introduction

This now famous essay makes substantially the same point that was made long before by Gassendi in his comments on Descartes' *Meditations*— namely, that no philosopher has shown that the mind must be something distinct from the body or, as Place puts it, that so-called mental states must be states of something other than the body or some part of it, such as the brain. Place does not show that they *are* one and the same; that, he notes, is a question for science, not one to be settled by writing speculative philosophy. His reflections on this ancient question are nevertheless highly significant, for he claims to remove the two fundamental considerations that have seemed to support the supposed dualism of body and mind.

One such consideration, and certainly the one that has had the profoundest effect upon philosophers, is a logical one. It is claimed, correctly, that there is no contradiction whatever in asserting the existence of certain mental states, or what Descartes referred to broadly as "thought," and at the same time denying the existence of any state of the brain or other part of the body or, indeed, as Descartes noted, supposing that the body itself does not even exist. And if we can suppose conscious states to exist independently of the existence of any brain or brain process, then the two can hardly be one and the same. Descartes thought that this reflection proves conclusively the distinctness of mind and matter, for, he said, two things that can be conceived as distinct must in fact be distinct.

But of course that does not follow at all. That thinking can be conceived as distinct from any process in the brain only shows that it is *possible* for them to be distinct; it does not show that they *are* distinct. Or, in terms of one of Place's excellent analogies, the fact that we can imagine clouds in the sky consisting of fleece, rather than tiny water droplets, shows only that it is possible that clouds are composed of fleece. It does not show that they are—for in fact ordinary clouds are, unbeknown to many, actually composed of droplets, not fleece.

The other main consideration that has stood in the way of identifying thought with processes in the brain is what Place calls the "phenomenological fallacy." This consists in supposing that states of consciousness are just what they seem to be. For example, in dreams one "sees" all sorts of things such as, for example, animals. But since no real animals are thus seen, people tend to assume that in such dreams one sees animal-like things, dream images of animals. Or suppose you stare at a bright spot of green light for a time, then close your eyes. You then "see" a green image of the light, commonly called an after-image. Since, however, this is not a real spot of light in the physical world (since your eyes are closed), and since it likewise is not a green spot of light in your brain (since there is nothing at all in your brain that is green and luminous, and you possess no sense organ with which to see such a thing even if it were there), then it is inferred that there must be a *mental*, or nonphysical, green luminous spot, which you are seeing. *Something*, one wants to say, is green and luminous; and if it is not a green light in the physical world, nor a green part of my own brain, then it must be something mental—a green after-image "in the mind."

This kind of reflection has beguiled not only philosophers but psychologists and physiologists as well. The reasoning seems conclusive, and the facts beyond dispute. But everything turns upon the supposition that, in such an experience, there exists something, called an after-image, that is in fact green. The chief merit of Place's essay is to note that, however incontestable this might at first seem, there is in fact no reason at all to affirm it. When one "sees" a green after-image, he does not in fact *see* anything at all, much less does he see anything that is green. The way to express the true state of affairs here is to say that he seems to see something green (which is consistent with saying that he in fact does nothing of the sort), or that he is having an experience—which might very well consist of a process in his own optic nerves and brain—which is rather like the experience he has when he in fact sees a green luminous spot. That describes what we know to be the factual situation. The fallacy is to assume an equivalence between what is thus known and something else that is merely a popular manner of speaking and not something that is known at all—namely, that one must therefore be seeing something, an after-image, that is real and that is green.

U. T. Place studied at Oxford University and is Lecturer in Clinical Psychology at the University of Leeds. The paper that follows was published in 1956.

The Brain and Consciousness*

The thesis that consciousness is a process in the brain is put forward as a reasonable scientific hypothesis, not to be dismissed on logical grounds alone. The conditions under which two sets of observations are treated as observations of the same process, rather than as observations of two independent correlated processes, are discussed. It is suggested that we can identify consciousness with a given pattern of brain activity, if we can explain the subject's introspective observations by reference to the brain processes with which they are correlated. It is argued that the problem of providing a physiological explanation of introspective observations is made to seem more difficult than it really is by the "phenomenological fallacy," the mistaken idea that descriptions of the appearances of things are descriptions of the actual state of affairs in a mysterious internal environment.

INTRODUCTION

The view that there exists a separate class of events, mental events, which cannot be described in terms of the concepts employed by the physical sciences no longer commands the universal and unquestioning acceptance among philosophers and psychologists which it once did. Modern physicalism, however, unlike the materialism of the seventeenth and eighteenth centuries, is behavioristic. Consciousness on this view is either a special type of behavior, "sampling" or "running-back-and-forth" behavior as Tolman has it,[1] or a disposition to behave in a certain way, an itch for example being a temporary propensity to scratch. In the case of cognitive concepts like "knowing," "believing," "understanding," "remembering," and volitional concepts like "wanting" and "intending," there can be little doubt, I think, that an analysis in terms of dispositions to behave is funda-

*U. T. Place, "Is Consciousness a Brain Process?" *British Journal of Psychology*, Vol. XLVII (February 1956). Copyright 1956, British Psychological Society, by permission of Cambridge University Press.

[1]E. C. Tolman, *Purposive Behavior in Animals and Men* (Berkeley: University of California Press, 1932).

mentally sound.[2] On the other hand, there would seem to be an intractable residue of concepts clustering around the notions of consciousness, experience, sensation, and mental imagery, where some sort of inner process story is unavoidable.[3] It is possible, of course, that a satisfactory behavioristic account of this conceptual residuum will ultimately be found. For our present purposes, however, I shall assume that this cannot be done and that statements about pains and twinges, about how things look, sound, and feel, about things dreamed of or pictured in the mind's eye, are statements referring to events and processes which are in some sense private or internal to the individual of whom they are predicated. The question I wish to raise is whether in making this assumption we are inevitably committed to a dualist position in which sensations and mental images form a separate category of processes over and above the physical and physiological processes with which they are known to be correlated. I shall argue that an acceptance of inner processes does not entail dualism and that the thesis that consciousness is a process in the brain cannot be dismissed on logical grounds.

THE "IS" OF DEFINITION AND THE "IS" OF COMPOSITION

I want to stress from the outset that in defending the thesis that consciousness is a process in the brain, I am not trying to argue that when we describe our dreams, fantasies, and sensations we are talking about processes in our brains. That is, I am not claiming that statements about sensations and mental images are reducible to or analyzable into statements about brain processes, in the way in which "cognition statements" are analyzable into statements about behavior. To say that statements about consciousness are statements about brain processes is manifestly false. This is shown (a) by the fact that you can describe your sensations and mental imagery without knowing anything about your brain processes or even that such things exist, (b) by the fact that statements about one's consciousness and statements about one's brain processes are verified in entirely different ways, and (c) by the fact that there is nothing self-contradictory about the statement "X has a pain but there is nothing going on in his brain." What I do want to assert, however, is that the statement "Consciousness is a process in the brain," although not neccessarily true, is not necessarily false. "Consciousness is a process in the brain," on my view is neither self-contradictory nor self-evident; it is a reasonable scientific hypothesis, in the way that the statement "Lightning is a motion of electric charges" is a reasonable scientific hypothesis.

[2]L. Wittgenstein, *Philosophical Investigations* (Oxford: Blackwell, 1953); G. Ryle, *The Concept of Mind* (London: Hutchinson's University Library, 1949).
[3]U. T. Place, "The Concept of Heed," *British Journal of Psychology*, XLV (1954), pp. 243–55.

The all but universally accepted view that an assertion of identity between consciousness and brain processes can be ruled out on logical grounds alone, derives, I suspect, from a failure to distinguish between what we may call the "is" of definition and the "is" of composition. The distinction I have in mind here is the difference between the function of the word "is" in statements like "A square is an equilateral rectangle," "Red is a color," "To understand an instruction is to be able to act appropriately under the appropriate circumstances," and its function in statements like "His table is an old packing case," "Her hat is a bundle of straw tied together with string," "A cloud is a mass of water droplets or other particles in suspension." These two types of "is" statements have one thing in common. In both cases it makes sense to add the qualification "and nothing else." In this they differ from those statements in which the "is" is an "is" of prediction; the statements "Toby is 80 years old and nothing else," "Her hat is red and nothing else" or "Giraffes are tall and nothing else," for example, are nonsense. This logical feature may be described by saying that in both cases both the grammatical and the grammatical predicate are expressions which provide an adequate characterization of the state of affairs to which they both refer.

In another respect, however, the two groups of statements are strikingly different. Statements like "A square is an equilateral rectangle" are necessary statements which are true by definition. Statements like "His table is an old packing case," on the other hand, are contingent statements which have to be verified by observation. In the case of statements like "A square is an equilateral rectangle" or "Red is a color," there is a relationship between the meaning of the expression forming the grammatical predicate and the meaning of the expression forming the grammatical subject, such that whenever the subject expression is applicable the predicate must also be applicable. If you can describe something as red then you must also be able to describe it as colored. In the case of statements like "His table is an old packing case," on the other hand, there is no such relationship between the meanings of the expressions "his table" and "old packing case"; it merely so happens that in this case both expressions are applicable to and at the same time provide an adequate characterization of the same object. Those who contend that the statement "Consciousness is a brain process" is logically untenable base their claim, I suspect, on the mistaken assumption that if the meanings of two statements or expressions are quite unconnected, they cannot both provide an adequate characterization of the same object or state of affairs: if something is a state of consciousness, it cannot be a brain process, since there is nothing self-contradictory in supposing that someone feels a pain when there is nothing happening inside his skull. By the same token we might be led to conclude that a table cannot be an old packing case, since there is nothing self-contradictory in supposing that someone has a table, but is not in possession of an old packing case.

THE LOGICAL INDEPENDENCE
OF EXPRESSIONS AND THE ONTOLOGICAL
INDEPENDENCE OF ENTITIES

There is, of course, an important difference between the table/packing case case and the consciousness/brain process case in that the statement "His table is an old packing case" is a particular proposition which refers only to one particular case, whereas the statement "Consciousness is a process in the brain" is a general or universal proposition applying to all states of consciousness whatever. It is fairly clear, I think, that if we live in a world in which all tables without exception were packing cases, the concepts of "table" and "packing case" in our language would not have their present logically independent status. In such a world a table would be a species of packing case in much the same way that red is a species of color. It seems to be a rule of language that whenever a given variety of object or state of affairs has two characteristics or sets of characteristics, one of which is unique to the variety of object or state of affairs in question, the expression used to refer to the characteristic or set of characteristics which defines the variety of object or state of affairs in question will always entail the expression used to refer to the other characteristic or set of characteristics. If this rule admitted of no exception it would follow that any expression which is logically independent of another expression which uniquely characterizes a given variety of object or state of affairs, must refer to a characteristic or set of characteristics which is not normally or necessarily associated with the object or state of affairs in question. It is because this rule applies almost universally, I suggest, that we are normally justified in arguing from the logical independence of two expressions to the ontological independence of the states of affairs to which they refer. This would explain both the undoubted force of the argument that consciousness and brain processes must be independent entities because the expressions used to refer to them are logically independent and, in general, the curious phenomenon whereby questions about the furniture of the universe are often fought and not infrequently decided merely on a point of logic.

The argument from the logical independence of two expressions to the ontological independence of the entities to which they refer breaks down in the case of brain processes and consciousness, I believe, because this is one of a relatively small number of cases where the rule stated above does not apply. These exceptions are to be found, I suggest, in those cases where the operations which have to be performed in order to verify the presence of the two sets of characteristics inhering in the object or state of affairs in question can seldom if ever be performed simultaneously. A good example here is the case of the cloud and the mass of droplets or other particles in suspension. A cloud is a large semi-transparent mass with a fleecy texture suspended in the atmosphere whose shape is subject to continual and kaleidoscopic change. When observed at close quarters, however, it is found to consist of a mass of tiny particles, usually water droplets, in continuous motion. On the basis of this second observation we conclude that a cloud is a mass of tiny particles and nothing else. But there is no logical connection in our language between a cloud and a mass of tiny particles; there is nothing self-contradictory in talking about a cloud which is not composed of tiny particles in suspension. There is no contradiction involved in supposing that clouds consist of a dense mass of fibrous tissue; indeed, such a consistency seems to be implied by many of the functions performed by clouds in fairy stories and mythology. It is clear from this that the terms "cloud" and "mass of tiny particles in suspension" mean quite different things. Yet we do not conclude from this that there must be two things, the mass of particles in suspension and the cloud. The reason for this, I suggest, is that although the characteristics of being a cloud and being a mass of tiny particles in suspension are invariably associated, we never make the observations necessary to verify the statement "That is a cloud" and those necessary to verify the statement "This is a mass of tiny particles in suspension" at one and the same time. We can observe the microstructure of a cloud only when we are enveloped by it, a condition which effectively prevents us from observing those characteristics which from a distance lead us to describe it as a cloud. Indeed, so disparate are these two experiences that we use different words to describe them. That which is a cloud when we observe it from a distance becomes a fog or mist when we are enveloped by it.

WHEN ARE TWO SETS OF OBSERVATIONS OBSERVATIONS OF THE SAME EVENT?

The example of the cloud and the mass of tiny particles in suspension was chosen because it is one of the few cases of a general proposition involving what I have called the "is" of composition which does not involve us in scientific technicalities. It is useful because it brings out the connection between the ordinary everyday cases of the "is" of composition like the table/packing case example and the more technical cases like "Lightning is a motion of electric charges" where the analogy with the consciousness/brain process case is most marked. The limitation of the cloud/tiny particles in suspension case is that it does not bring out sufficiently clearly the crucial problem of how the identity of the states of affairs referred to by the two expressions is established. In the cloud case the fact that something is a cloud and the fact that something is a mass of tiny particles in suspension are both verified by the normal processes of visual observation. It is arguable, moreover, that the identity of the entities referred to by the two expressions is established by the continuity between the two sets of observations as the observer moves towards or away from the cloud. In the case of brain processes and consciousness there is no such continuity between the two sets of observations involved. A closer introspective scrutiny will never reveal the passage of nerve impulses over a thousand synapses in the way that a closer scrutiny of a cloud will reveal a mass of tiny particles in suspension. The operations required to verify statements about consciousness and statements about brain processes are fundamentally different.

To find a parallel for this feature we must examine other cases where an identity is asserted between something whose occurrence is verified by the ordinary processes of observation and something whose occurrence is established by special scientific procedures. For this purpose I have chosen the case where we say that lightning is a motion of electric charges. As in the case of consciousness, however closely we scrutinize the lightning we shall never be able to observe the electric charges, and just as the operations for determining the nature of one's state of consciousness are radically different from those involved in determining the nature of one's brain processes, so the operations for determining the occurrence of lightning are radically different from those involved in determining the occurrence of a motion of electric charges. What is it, therefore, that leads us to say that the two sets of observations are observations of the same event? It cannot be merely the fact that the two sets of observations are systematically correlated such that whenever there is lightning there is always a motion of electric charges. There are innumerable cases of such correlations where we have no temptation to say that the two sets of observations are observations of the same event. There is a systematic correlation, for example, between the movement of the tides and the stages of the moon, but this does not lead us to say that records of tidal levels are records of the moon's stages or vice versa. We speak rather of a causal connection between two independent events or processes.

The answer here seems to be that we treat the two sets of observations as observations of the same event in those cases where the technical scientific observations set in the context of the appropriate body of scientific theory provide an immediate explanation of the observations made by the man in the street. Thus we conclude that lightning is nothing more than a motion of electric charges, because we know that a motion of electric charges through the atmosphere, such as occurs when lightning is reported, gives rise to the type of visual stimulation which would lead an observer to report a flash of lightning. In the moon/tide case, on the other hand, there is no such direct causal connection between the stages of the moon and the observations made by the man who measures the height of the tide. The causal connection is between the moon and the tides, not between the moon and the measurement of the tides.

THE PHYSIOLOGICAL EXPLANATION
OF INTROSPECTION AND THE
PHENOMENOLOGICAL FALLACY

If this account is correct, it should follow that in order to establish the
identity of consciousness and certain processes in the brain, it would be
necessary to show that the introspective observations reported by the subject can be accounted for in terms of processes which are known to have
occurred in his brain. In the light of this suggestion it is extremely interesting to find that when a physiologist as distinct from a philosopher finds it
difficult to see how consciousness could be a process in the brain, what
worries him is not any supposed self-contradiction involved in such an assumption, but the apparent impossibility of accounting for the reports given
by the subject of his conscious processes in terms of the known properties of
the central nervous system. Sir Charles Sherrington has posed the problem
as follows:

> The chain of events stretching from the sun's radiation entering the eye to, on
> the one hand, the contraction of the pupillary muscles, and on the other, to the
> electrical disturbances in the brain-cortex are all straightforward steps in a
> sequence of physical "causation," such as, thanks to science, are intelligible.
> But in the second serial chain there follows on, or attends, the stage of brain-
> cortex reaction an event or set of events quite inexplicable to us, which both as
> to themselves as to the causal tie between them and what preceded them
> science does not help us; a set of events seemingly incommensurable with any
> of the events leading up to it. The self "sees" the sun; it senses a two-
> dimensional disc of brightness, located in the "sky," this last a field of lesser
> brightness, and overhead shaped as a rather flattened dome, coping the self
> and a hundred other visual things as well. Of hint that this is within the head
> there is none. Vision is saturated with this strange property called "projec-
> tion," the unargued inference that what it sees is at a "distance" from the
> seeing "self." Enough has been said to stress that in the sequence of events a
> step is reached where a physical situation in the brain leads to a psychical,
> which however contains no hint of the brain or any other bodily part. . . . The
> supposition has to be, it would seem, two continuous series of events, one
> physiochemical, the other psychical, and at times interaction between them.[4]

Just as the physiologist is not likely to be impressed by the philosopher's
contention that there is some self-contradiction involved in supposing consciousness to be a brain process, so the philosopher is unlikely to be impressed by the considerations which lead Sherrington to conclude that there
are two sets of events, one physicochemical, the other psychical, Sherrington's argument for all its emotional appeal depends on a fairly simple logical

[4]Sir Charles Sherrington, *The Integrative Action of the Nervous System* (Cambridge: Cambridge University Press, 1947), pp. xx–xxi.

mistake, which is unfortunately all too frequently made by psychologists and physiologists and not infrequently in the past by the philosophers themselves. This logical mistake, which I shall refer to as the "phenomenological fallacy," is the mistake of supposing that when the subject describes his experience, when he describes how things look, sound, smell, taste, or feel to him, he is describing the literal properties of objects and events on a peculiar sort of internal cinema or television screen, usually referred to in the modern psychological literature as the "phenomenal field." If we assume, for example, that when a subject reports a green after-image he is asserting the occurrence inside himself of an object which is literally green, it is clear that we have on our hands an entity for which there is no place in the world of physics. In the case of the green after-image there is no green object in the subject's environment corresponding to the description that he gives. Nor is there anything green in his brain; certainly there is nothing which could have emerged when he reported the appearance of the green after-image. Brain processes are not the sort of things to which color concepts can be properly applied.

The phenomenological fallacy on which this argument is based depends on the mistaken assumption that because our ability to describe things in our environment depends on our consciousness of them, our descriptions of things are primarily descriptions of our conscious experience and only secondarily, indirectly, and inferentially descriptions of the objects and events in our environments. It is assumed that because we recognize things in our environment by their look, sound, smell, taste, and feel, we begin by describing their phenomenal properties, i.e., the properties of the looks, sounds, smells, tastes, and feels which they produce in us, and infer their real properties from their phenomenal properties. In fact, the reverse is the case. We begin by learning to recognize the real properties of things in our environment. We learn to recognize them, of course, by their look, sound, smell, taste, and feel; but this does not mean that we have to learn to describe the look, sound, smell, taste, and feel of things before we can describe the things themselves. Indeed, it is only after we have learned to describe the things in our environment that we can learn to describe our consciousness of them. We describe our consciousness experience not in terms of the mythological "phenomenal properties" which are supposed to inhere in the mythological "objects" in the mythological "phenomenal field," but by reference to the actual physical properties of the concrete physical objects, events, and processes which normally, though not perhaps in the present instance, give rise to the sort of conscious experience which we are trying to describe. In other words when we describe the after-image as green, we are not saying that there is something, the after-image, which is green; we are saying that we are having the sort of experience which we normally have when, and which we have learned to describe as, looking at a green patch of light.

Once we rid ourselves of the phenomenological fallacy we realize that the problem of explaining introspective observations in terms of brain processes is far from insuperable. We realize that there is nothing that the introspecting subject says about his conscious experiences which is inconsistent with anything the physiologist might want to say about the brain processes which cause him to describe the environment and his consciousness of that environment in the way he does. When the subject describes his experience by saying that a light which is in fact stationary, appears to move, all the physiologist or physiological psychologist has to do in order to explain the subject's introspective observations, is to show that the brain process which is causing the subject to describe his experience in this way, is the sort of process which normally occurs when he is observing an actual moving object and which therefore normally causes him to report the movement of an object in his environment. Once the mechanism whereby the individual describes what is going on in his environment has been worked out, all that is required to explain the individual's capacity to make introspective observations is an explanation of his ability to discriminate between those cases where his normal habits of verbal description are appropriate to the stimulus situation and those cases where they are not and an explanation of how and why, in those cases where the appropriateness of his normal descriptive habits is in doubt, he learns to issue his ordinary descriptive protocols preceded by a qualificatory phrase like "it appears," "seems," "looks," "feels," etc.[5]

[5] I am greatly indebted to my fellow-participants in a series of informal discussions on this topic which took place in the Department of Philosophy, University of Adelaide, in particular to Mr. C. B. Martin for his persistent and searching criticism of my earlier attempts to defend the thesis that consciousness is a brain process, to Prof. D. A. T. Gasking, of the University of Melbourne, for clarifying many of the logical issues involved, and to Prof. J. J. C. Smart for moral support and encouragement in what often seemed a lost cause.

III

What Can I Do?

FREEDOM AND FATE

8

A. J. AYER

---

introduction

Many of the problems of metaphysics arise from a clash between two intellectual outlooks. The problem of the relation between mind and matter, and of the nature of a person and his relationship to his body, arose originally from the mingling of ancient mystical traditions with the customary materialism of the Greeks. Similarly, the problem of free will, which is the concern of the next several essays, resulted from the conflict between the Christian supposition of a unique kind of moral responsibility on the part of human beings and the scientific view that all events in the physical world are caused and occur in strict accordance with the so-called laws of nature. It is hard to see how both of these claims could be true, and thus compatible with each other, and it is doubtful whether any philosopher has shown that they are.

A. J. Ayer makes this attempt—that is, he tries to show how, even though every event may be caused and thus, it would seem, unavoidable, nevertheless people should be responsible for those events constituting their own "voluntary" behavior.

Ayer's prose is so pellucid that little commentary is needed for clarification. And his philosophical arguments are very clear, too—up until the last few steps. But there a perceptive reader sees that they begin to fall apart,

and that the problem of free will has been "solved" at the level of behavior
only to re-emerge in exactly the same form at the level of choice.

For what is the problem, as Ayer sees it? And what is its solution?

The problem is that two general theses, both generally believed to be
true, appear incompatible with each other, or such that not both can be true.
The first is that all events, including those that are the motions of our own
bodies, are caused by other events occurring antecedently. The implication
is that, given those antecedent events, their effects—for example, the motions of our own bodies—are unavoidable. The second thesis is that people
are responsible for at least some of their actions. And these theses surely
seem incompatible, for to be responsible for some action seems to presuppose that we could have avoided doing it.

Ayer's proposed solution, consisting of several parts, is not essentially
different from David Hume's, though for modern readers it is easier to understand. William James called this solution "soft determinism," designating
the philosophical view that determinism does not rob us of responsibility.
Among contemporary writers the same view is often called "compatibilism,"
from the claim that the two seemingly incompatible theses that give rise to
the problem are, when examined and analyzed, compatible after all.

Ayer says, first, that freedom is opposed, not to causation, but to constraint. Your actions are not rendered unfree just by the fact that they are,
like any other event, caused. They become unfree only when they are
caused in such a way as to constitute constraint—in other words, when you
are caused to do something against your will or in opposition to your own
choice. When, on the other hand, you act in accordance with your own
choice, then you act freely—for that is exactly what it *means* to act freely.
And in those cases your actions are also caused—for they are caused by your
own choices! Freedom, therefore, is compatible with determinism.

Moreover—and this is a different point—we would in no way preserve
responsibility for our actions if we assumed them to be *uncaused*. For in that
case they would be matters of sheer accident—and the very point in calling
behavior accidental is to relieve one of responsibility for it. We are responsible only for those actions that result from, or are caused by, our own choices,
not those that come about by pure accident, as all of them would if they were
really uncaused. So again, responsibility must be incompatible, not with
determinism, but with the denial of determinism.

Causes do not as such necessitate their effects anyway—which is still
another point. The relationship between causes and their effects is simply
one of constancy of joint occurrence; whenever certain events occur, their
effects occur too, and the latter never occur without the former. But in that
relationship of constancy of conjunction we find no compulsion or necessitation of effects by their causes. Therefore the supposed opposition between
causation and freedom is an illusion to begin with. The two are perfectly

compatible, and the apparent incompatibility is seen, on analysis, not to exist.

Thus Ayer claims, in effect, that the question is not whether our actions are caused, but rather, by *what* they are caused. If caused by some external force over which we have no control, then they are instances of constraint, and we are indeed not responsible for them. But if caused by ourselves, by our own choices, then they are free, and we are responsible for them.

But here an alert reader is certain to ask whether our *choices* are caused. If they are, then how can we be responsible for them? They can hardly be avoided, given the antecedent events that cause them. And if we are not responsible for our choices—if in fact we can never help making just the choices we do make—then how can we be responsible for the actions that flow from them?

This question is very relevant and trenchant, and Ayer does not really answer it. Probably no one ever has or ever will. Some, finding no answer, have concluded that people never are really responsible for what they do. Others have postulated a strange and unique kind of causation of human actions that differs from causation in the physical world, not being in accordance with any of its laws and thus being consistent with the idea of avoidability.

No matter which of these or other possible "answers" one adopts, he, like Ayer, will probably find on his hands some basic question of freedom and responsibility that his theory does *not* resolve.

A. J. Ayer was born in 1910, studied at Oxford, and is Wykeham professor of logic at Oxford University. The essay that follows is reproduced entire.

The Compatibility of Freedom and Necessity*

When I am said to have done something of my own free will it is implied that I could have acted otherwise; and it is only when it is believed that I could have acted otherwise that I am held to be morally responsible for what I have done. For a man is not thought to be morally responsible for an action that it was not in his power to avoid. But if human behaviour is entirely governed by causal laws, it is not clear how any action that is done could ever have been avoided. It may be said of the agent that he would have acted otherwise if the causes of his action had been different, but they being what they were, it seems to follow that he was bound to act as he did. Now it is commonly

*A. J. Ayer, "Freedom and Necessity," in *Philosophical Essays* (London: Macmillan & Co., 1954), by permission of Macmillan London and Basingstoke.

assumed both that men are capable of acting freely, in the sense that is required to make them morally responsible, and that human behaviour is entirely governed by causal laws: and it is the apparent conflict between these two assumptions that gives rise to the philosophical problem of the freedom of the will.

Confronted with this problem, many people will be inclined to agree with Dr. Johnson: 'Sir, we *know* our will is free, and *there's* an end on't'. But, while this does very well for those who accept Dr. Johnson's premiss, it would hardly convince anyone who denied the freedom of the will. Certainly, if we do know that our wills are free, it follows that they are so. But the logical reply to this might be that since our wills are not free, it follows that no one can know that they are: so that if anyone claims, like Dr. Johnson, to know that they are, he must be mistaken. What is evident, indeed, is that people often believe themselves to be acting freely; and it is to this 'feeling' of freedom that some philosophers appeal when they wish, in the supposed interests of morality, to prove that not all human action is causally determined. But if these philosophers are right in their assumption that a man cannot be acting freely if his action is causally determined, then the fact that someone feels free to do, or not to do, a certain action does not prove that he really is so. It may prove that the agent does not himself know what it is that makes him act in one way rather than another: but from the fact that a man is unaware of the causes of his action, it does not follow that no such causes exist.

So much may be allowed to the determinist; but his belief that all human actions are subservient to causal laws still remains to be justified. If, indeed, it is necessary that every event should have a cause, then the rule must apply to human behaviour as much as to anything else. But why should it be supposed that every event must have a cause? The contrary is not unthinkable. Nor is the law of universal causation a necessary presupposition of scientific thought. The scientist may try to discover causal laws, and in many cases he succeeds; but sometimes he has to be content with statistical laws, and sometimes he comes upon events which, in the present state of his knowledge, he is not able to subsume under any law at all. In the case of these events he assumes that if he knew more he would be able to discover some law, whether causal or statistical, which would enable him to account for them. And this assumption cannot be disproved. For however far he may have carried his investigation, it is always open to him to carry it further; and it is always conceivable that if he carried it further he would discover the connection which had hitherto escaped him. Nevertheless, it is also conceivable that the events with which he is concerned are not systematically connected with any others: so that the reason why he does not discover the sort of laws that he requires is simply that they do not obtain.

Now in the case of human conduct the search for explanations has not in fact been altogether fruitless. Certain scientific laws have been established;

and with the help of these laws we do make a number of successful predictions about the ways in which different people will behave. But these predictions do not always cover every detail. We may be able to predict that in
certain circumstances a particular man will be angry, without being able to
prescribe the precise form that the expression of his anger will take. We may
be reasonably sure that he will shout, but not sure how loud his shout will
be, or exactly what words he will use. And it is only a small proportion of
human actions that we are able to forecast even so precisely as this. But that,
it may be said, is because we have not carried our investigations very far.
The science of psychology is still in its infancy and, as it is developed, not
only will more human actions be explained, but the explanations will go into
greater detail. The ideal of complete explanation may never in fact be attained: but it is theoretically attainable. Well, this may be so: and certainly it
is impossible to show a priori that it is not so: but equally it cannot be shown
that it is. This will not, however, discourage the scientist who, in the field of
human behaviour, as elsewhere, will continue to formulate theories and test
them by the facts. And in this he is justified. For since he has no reason a
priori to admit that there is a limit to what he can discover, the fact that he
also cannot be sure that there is no limit does not make it unreasonable for
him to devise theories, nor, having devised them, to try constantly to im-
prove them.

But now suppose it to be claimed that, so far as men's actions are concerned, there is a limit: and that this limit is set by the fact of human
freedom. An obvious objection is that in many cases in which a person feels
himself to be free to do, or not to do, a certain action, we are even now able
to explain, in causal terms, why it is that he acts as he does. But it might be
argued that even if men are sometimes mistaken in believing that they act
freely, it does not follow that they are always so mistaken. For it is not always
the case that when a man believes that he has acted freely we are in fact able
to account for his action in causal terms. A determinist would say that we
should be able to account for it if we had more knowledge of the circumstances, and had been able to discover the appropriate natural laws. But
until those discoveries have been made, this remains only a pious hope. And
may it not be true that, in some cases at least, the reason why we can give no
causal explanation is that no causal explanation is available; and that this is
because the agent's choice was literally free, as he himself felt it to be?

The answer is that this may indeed be true, inasmuch as it is open to
anyone to hold that no explanation is possible until some explanation is
actually found. But even so it does not give the moralist what he wants. For
he is anxious to show that men are capable of acting freely in order to infer
that they can be morally responsible for what they do. But if it is a matter of
pure chance that a man should act in one way rather than another, he may be
free but he can hardly be responsible. And indeed when a man's actions

seem to us quite unpredictable, when, as we say, there is no knowing what he will do, we do not look upon him as a moral agent. We look upon him rather as a lunatic.

To this it may be objected that we are not dealing fairly with the moralist. For when he makes it a condition of my being morally responsible that I should act freely, he does not wish to imply that it is purely a matter of chance that I act as I do. What he wishes to imply is that my actions are the result of my own free choice: and it is because they are the result of my own free choice that I am held to be morally responsible for them.

But now we must ask how it is that I come to make my choice. Either it is an accident that I choose to act as I do or it is not. If it is an accident, then it is merely a matter of chance that I did not choose otherwise; and if it is merely a matter of chance that I did not choose otherwise, it is surely irrational to hold me morally responsible for choosing as I did. But if it is not an accident that I choose to do one thing rather than another, then presumably there is some causal explanation of my choice: and in that case we are led back to determinism.

Again, the objection may be raised that we are not doing justice to the moralist's case. His view is not that it is a matter of chance that I choose to act as I do, but rather that my choice depends upon my character. Nevertheless he holds that I can still be free in the sense that he requires; for it is I who am responsible for my character. But in what way am I responsible for my character? Only, surely, in the sense that there is a causal connection between what I do now and what I have done in the past. It is only this that justifies the statement that I have made myself what I am: and even so this is an over-simplification, since it takes no account of the external influences to which I have been subjected. But, ignoring the external influences, let us assume that it is in fact the case that I have made myself what I am. Then it is still legitimate to ask how it is that I have come to make myself one sort of person rather than another. And if it be answered that it is a matter of my strength of will, we can put the same question in another form by asking how it is that my will has the strength that it has and not some other degree of strength. Once more, either it is an accident or it is not. If it is an accident, then by the same argument as before, I am not morally responsible, and if it is not an accident we are led back to determinism.

Furthermore, to say that my actions proceed from my character or, more colloquially, that I act in character, is to say that my behaviour is consistent and to that extent predictable: and since it is, above all, for the actions that I perform in character that I am held to be morally responsible, it looks as if the admission of moral responsibility, so far from being incompatible with determinism, tends rather to presuppose it. But how can this be so if it is a necessary condition of moral responsibility that the person who is held responsible should have acted freely? It seems that if we are to retain this idea of moral responsibility, we must either show that men can be held responsible for actions which they do not do freely, or else find some way of reconciling determinism with the freedom of the will.

It is no doubt with the object of effecting this reconciliation that some philosophers have defined freedom as the consciousness of necessity. And by so doing they are able to say not only that a man can be acting freely when his action is causally determined, but even that his action must be causally determined for it to be possible for him to be acting freely. Nevertheless this definition has the serious disadvantage that it gives to the word 'freedom' a meaning quite different from any that it ordinarily bears. It is indeed obvious that if we are allowed to give the word 'freedom' any meaning that we please, we can find a meaning that will reconcile it with determinism: but this is no more a solution of our present problem than the fact that the word 'horse' could be arbitrarily used to mean what is ordinarily meant by 'sparrow' is a proof that horses have wings. For suppose that I am compelled by another person to do something 'against my will'. In that case, as the word 'freedom' is ordinarily used, I should not be said to be acting freely: and the fact that I am fully aware of the constraint to which I am subjected makes no difference to the matter. I do not become free by becoming conscious that I am not. It may, indeed, be possible to show that my being aware that my action is causally determined is not incompatible with my acting freely: but it by no means follows that it is in this that my freedom consists. Moreover, I suspect that one of the reasons why people are inclined to define freedom as the consciousness of necessity is that they think that if one is conscious of necessity one may somehow be able to master it. But this is a fallacy. It is like someone's saying that he wishes he could see into the future, because if he did he would know what calamities lay in wait for him and so would be able to avoid them. But if he avoids the calamities then they don't lie in the future and it is not true that he foresees them. And similarly if I am able to master necessity, in the sense of escaping the operation of a necessary law, then the law in question is not necessary. And if the law is not necessary, then neither my freedom nor anything else can consist in my knowing that it is.

Let it be granted, then, that when we speak of reconciling freedom with determinism we are using the word 'freedom' in an ordinary sense. It still remains for us to make this usage clear: and perhaps the best way to make it clear is to show what it is that freedom, in this sense, is contrasted with. Now we began with the assumption that freedom is contrasted with causality: so that a man cannot be said to be acting freely if his action is causally determined. But this assumption has led us into difficulties and I now wish to suggest that is is mistaken. For it is not, I think, causality that freedom is to be contrasted with, but constraint. And while it is true that being constrained to do an action entails being caused to do it, I shall try to show that the converse does not hold. I shall try to show that from the fact that my action is causally determined it does not necessarily follow that I am constrained to do it: and this is equivalent to saying that it does not necessarily follow that I am not free.

If I am constrained, I do not act freely. But in what circumstances can I legitimately be said to be constrained? An obvious instance is the case in which I am compelled by another person to do what he wants. In a case of this sort the compulsion need not be such as to deprive one of the power of choice. It is not required that the other person should have hypnotized me, or that he should make it physically impossible for me to go against his will. It is enough that he should induce me to do what he wants by making it clear to me that, if I do not, he will bring about some situation that I regard as even more undesirable than the consequences of the action that he wishes me to do. Thus, if the man points a pistol at my head I may still choose to disobey him: but this does not prevent its being true that if I do fall in with his wishes he can legitimately be said to have compelled me. And if the circumstances are such that no reasonable person would be expected to choose the other alternative, then the action that I am made to do is not one for which I am held to be morally responsible.

A similar, but still somewhat different, case is that in which another person has obtained an habitual ascendancy over me. Where this is so, there may be no question of my being induced to act as the other person wishes by being confronted with a still more disagreeable alternative: for if I am sufficiently under his influence this special stimulus will not be necessary. Nevertheless I do not act freely, for the reason that I have been deprived of the power of choice. And this means that I have acquired so strong a habit of obedience that I no longer go through any process of deciding whether or not to do what the other person wants. About other matters I may still deliberate; but as regards the fulfilment of this other person's wishes, my own deliberations have ceased to be a causal factor in my behaviour. And it is in this sense that I may be said to be constrained. It is not, however, necessary that such constraint should take the form of subservience to another person. A kleptomaniac is not a free agent, in respect of his stealing, because he does not go through any process of deciding whether or not to steal. Or rather, if he does go through such a process, it is irrelevant to his behaviour. Whatever he resolved to do, he would steal all the same. And it is this that distinguishes him from the ordinary thief.

But now it may be asked whether there is any essential difference between these cases and those in which the agent is commonly thought to be free. No doubt the ordinary thief does go through a process of deciding whether or not to steal, and no doubt it does affect his behaviour. If he resolved to refrain from stealing, he could carry his resolution out. But if it be allowed that his making or not making this resolution is causally determined, then how can he be any more free than the kleptomaniac? It may be true that unlike the kleptomaniac he could refrain from stealing if he chose: but if there is a cause, or set of causes, which necessitate his choosing as he does, how can he be said to have the power of choice? Again, it may be true that no one now compels me to get up and walk across the room: but if my doing so can be causally explained in terms of my history or my environment, or whatever it may be, then how am I any more free than if some other person had compelled me? I do not have the feeling of constraint that I have when a pistol is manifestly pointed at my head; but the chains of causation by which I am bound are no less effective for being invisible.

The answer to this is that the cases I have mentioned as examples of constraint do differ from the others: and they differ just in the ways that I have tried to bring out. If I suffered from a compulsion neurosis, so that I got up and walked across the room, whether I wanted to or not, or if I did so because somebody else compelled me, then I should not be acting freely. But if I do it now, I shall be acting freely, just because these conditions do not obtain; and the fact that my action may nevertheless have a cause is, from this point of view, irrelevant. For it is not when my action has any cause at all, but only when it has a special sort of cause, that it is reckoned not to be free.

But here it may be objected that, even if this distinction corresponds to ordinary usage, it is still very irrational. For why should we distinguish, with regard to a person's freedom, between the operations of one sort of cause and those of another? Do not all causes equally necessitate? And is it not therefore arbitrary to say that a person is free when he is necessitated in one fashion but not when he is necessitated in another?

That all causes equally necessitate is indeed a tautology, if the word 'necessitate' is taken merely as equivalent to 'cause': but if, as the objection requires, it is taken as equivalent to 'constrain' or 'compel', then I do not think that this proposition is true. For all that is needed for one event to be the cause of another is that, in the given circumstances, the event which is said to be the effect would not have occurred if it had not been for the occurrence of the event which is said to be the cause, or *vice versa*, according as causes are interpreted as necessary, or sufficient, conditions: and this fact is usually deducible from some causal law which states that whenever an event of the one kind occurs then, given suitable conditions, an event of the other kind will occur in a certain temporal or spatio-temporal relationship to it. In short, there is an invariable concomitance between the two classes of events; but there is no compulsion, in any but a metaphorical sense. Suppose, for example, that a psycho-analyst is able to account for some aspect of my behaviour by referring it to some lesion that I suffered in my childhood. In that case, it may be said that my childhood experience, together with certain other events, necessitates my behaving as I do. But all that this involves is that it is found to be true in general that when people have had certain experiences as children, they subsequently behave in certain specifiable ways; and my case is just another instance of this general law. It is in this way indeed that my behaviour is explained. But from the fact that my behaviour is capable of being explained, in the sense that it can be subsumed under some natural law, it does not follow that I am acting under constraint.

If this is correct, to say that I could have acted otherwise is to say, first, that I should have acted otherwise if I had so chosen; secondly, that my action was voluntary in the sense in which the actions, say, of the kleptomaniac are not; and thirdly, that nobody compelled me to choose as I did: and these three conditions may very well be fulfilled. When they are fulfilled, I may be said to have acted freely. But this is not to say that it was a matter of chance that I acted as I did, or, in other words, that my action could not be explained. And that my actions should be capable of being explained is all that is required by the postulate of determinism.

If more than this seems to be required it is, I think, because the use of the very word 'determinism' is in some degree misleading. For it tends to suggest that one event is somehow in the power of another, whereas the truth is merely that they are factually correlated. And the same applies to the use, in this context, of the word 'necessity' and even of the the word 'cause' itself. Moreover, there are various reasons for this. One is the tendency to confuse causal with logical necessitation, and so to infer mistakenly that the effect is contained in the cause. Another is the uncritical use of a concept of force which is derived from primitive experiences of pushing and striking. A third is the survival of an animistic conception of causality, in which all causal relationships are modelled on the example of one person's exercising authority over another. As a result we tend to form an imaginative picture of an unhappy effect trying vainly to escape from the clutches of an overmastering cause. But, I repeat, the fact is simply that when an event of one type occurs, an event of another type occurs also, in a certain temporal or spatio-temporal relation to the first. The rest is only metaphor. And it is because of the metaphor, and not because of the fact, that we come to think that there is an antithesis between causality and freedom.

Nevertheless, it may be said, if the postulate of determinism is valid, then the future can be explained in terms of the past: and this means that if one knew enough about the past one would be able to predict the future. But in that case what will happen in the future is already decided. And how then can I be said to be free? What is going to happen is going to happen and nothing that I do can prevent it. If the determinist is right, I am the helpless prisoner of fate.

But what is meant by saying that the future course of events is already decided? If the implication is that some person has arranged it, then the proposition is false. But if all that is meant is that it is possible, in principle, to deduce it from a set of particular facts about the past, together with the appropriate general laws, then, even if this is true, it does not in the least entail that I am the helpless prisoner of fate. It does not even entail that my actions make no difference to the future: for they are causes as well as effects; so that if they were different their consequences would be different also. What it does entail is that my behaviour can be predicted: but to say that my behaviour can be predicted is not to say that I am acting under constraint. It is indeed true that I cannot escape my destiny if this is taken to mean no more than that I shall do what I shall do. But this is a tautology, just as it is a tautology that what is going to happen is going to happen. And such tautologies as these prove nothing whatsoever about the freedom of the will.

9

JOHN HOSPERS

introduction

Hospers' refreshing and now famous treatment of the free-will problem represents a considerable departure from the usual one. Philosophical discussion of this problem is usually purely analytical; that is, philosophers have been content with eliciting the implications of certain ordinary and conventional ways of speaking about people and their behavior, to see to what extent these implications are or are not consistent with each other. Ayer's discussion is a perfect example.

What Hospers does, however, is to show first that the concept of responsibility is not very clear to begin with. Who, he asks, is in any meaningful or philosophical sense responsible for what? What are the conditions for such responsibility anyway? Should we not, perhaps, get rid of this notion altogether, except in those contexts, such as that of the criminal law, where it has a clear and verifiable meaning? Few contemporary philosophers, other than Hospers, have been able to disentangle themselves from prevailing conventional notions sufficiently to raise these fairly basic questions.

But even if we suppose that there is some kind of basic moral responsibility or blameworthiness independently of man-made laws that create it, can we be sure that any human being ever *is* responsible in the sense required?

107

Much human behavior, even of fairly familiar kinds, is caused by factors in
the agent's background that he not only did not create but also may be totally
ignorant of. We have come to accept this in the case of pathological behavior.
Some people act from irrational compulsions, and we call such persons
neurotic, psychotic, disturbed, and so on, precisely to call attention to their
irresponsibility. But are those who are "normal" really different with respect
to the causation of their behavior? All of us enter the world with a certain
hereditary endowment. We all enter adult life, and presumed responsibility,
with a certain background of childhood and adolescence. Do we somehow
find it easier than the "neurotic" to cast these influences aside? Or are we
not, instead, simply luckier in that the formative influences of our lives have
produced the inclination to behave in generally acceptable ways? The person
who is made a thief by the abysmal conditions of his birth and childhood is
responsible neither for those conditions nor for their effects; he is simply
unlucky. Similarly, the person who is made honest and upright and totally
harmless by the more benign conditions of his childhood is responsible
neither for those conditions nor for their effects; he is simply lucky. The two
types of cases differ only in their outcomes, not in any degree of responsibility for those outcomes.

But this view violates the pride and conceit of those whom Hospers calls
lucky and exculpates those he calls unlucky. People who are praised for what
they do like to think that the praise is *deserved*, that it is somehow through
their own *efforts* that they have turned out so well. Indeed, we like to think
that the unlucky ones among us—those who grew up in poverty, for
example—can, *with effort*, overcome and rise above adverse influences.
Many, in fact, seem to have done so.

But, as Hospers notes, this just moves the question of freedom back a
step—from: Could he, given his character, have done otherwise? to: Could
he have made the effort necessary to rise above his own character? To be
sure, one need not act always in accordance with the character that conditions have imposed on him—*provided* he has the strength of character not
to. But we see at once the absurdity of pursuing that familiar line of thought.

Hospers' essay, by forcing attention upon fairly elementary considerations
of psychology, tends to unsettle not only the comfortable compatibilities
philosophers have claimed to find in our ordinary modes of speech, but also
the complacency of those who find little difficulty in assessing praise and
blame.

John Hospers studied at Iowa State University and Columbia and is direc-
tor of the school of philosophical studies at the University of Southern
California. His own commentary on the original version of his paper has not
been included here.

Free Will and Responsibility*

As a preparation for developing my own views on the subject, I want to mention a factor that I think is of enormous importance and relevance: namely, unconscious motivation. There are many actions—not those of an insane person (however the term "insane" be defined), nor of a person ignorant of the effects of his action, nor ignorant of some relevant fact about the situation, nor in any obvious way mentally deranged—for which human beings in general and the courts in particular are inclined to hold the doer responsible, and for which, I would say, he should not be held responsible. The deed may be planned, it may be carried out in cold calculation, it may spring from the agent's character and be continuous with the rest of his behavior, and it may be perfectly true that he could have done differently *if* he had wanted to; nonetheless his behavior was brought about by unconscious conflicts developed in infancy, over which he had no control and of which (without training in psychiatry) he does not even have knowledge. He may even *think* he knows why he acted as he did, he may *think* he has conscious control over his actions, he may even *think* he is fully responsible for them; but he is not. Psychiatric casebooks provide hundreds of examples. The law and common sense, though puzzled sometimes by such cases, are gradually becoming aware that they exist; but at this early stage countless tragic blunders still occur because neither the law nor the public in general is aware of the genesis of criminal actions. The mother blames her daughter for choosing the wrong men as candidates for husbands; but though the daughter thinks she is choosing freely and spends a considerable amount of time "deciding" among them, the identification with her sick father, resulting from Oedipal fantasies in early childhood, prevents her from caring for any but sick men, twenty or thirty years older than herself. Blaming her is beside the point; she cannot help it, and she cannot change it. Countless criminal acts are thought out in great detail; yet the participants are (without their own knowledge) acting out fantasies, fears, and defenses from early childhood, over whose coming and going they have no conscious control.

Now, I am not saying that none of these persons should be in jails or asylums. Often society must be protected against them. Nor am I saying that people should cease the practices of blaming and praising, punishing and rewarding; in general these devices are justified by the results—although very often they have practically no effect; the deeds are done from inner

*John Hospers, "What Means This Freedom?" in *Determinism and Freedom in the Age of Modern Science,* ed. by Sidney Hook (New York: New York University Press, 1958). © 1958 by New York University. Reprinted by permission of the publisher.

compulsion, which is not lessened when the threat of punishment is great. I am only saying that frequently persons we think responsible are not properly to be called so; we mistakenly think them responsible because we assume they are like those in whom no unconscious drive (toward this type of behavior) is present, and that their behavior can be changed by reasoning, exhorting, or threatening.

I

I have said that these persons are not responsible. But what is the criterion for responsibility? Under precisely what conditions is a person to be held morally responsible for an action? Disregarding here those conditions that have to do with a person's *ignorance* of the situation or the effects of his action, let us concentrate on those having to do with his "inner state." There are several criteria that might be suggested:

1. The first idea that comes to mind is that responsibility is determined by the presence or absence of *premeditation*—the opposite of "premeditated" being, presumably, "unthinking" or "impulsive." But this will not do—both because some acts are not premeditated but responsible, and because some are premeditated and not responsible.

Many acts we call responsible can be as unthinking or impulsive as you please. If you rush across the street to help the victim of an automobile collision, you are (at least so we would ordinarily say) acting responsibly, but you did not do so out of premeditation; you saw the accident, you didn't think, you rushed to the scene without hesitation. It was like a reflex action. But you acted responsibly: unlike the knee jerk, the act was the result of past training and past thought about situations of this kind; that is why you ran to help instead of ignoring the incident or running away. When something done originally from conviction or training becomes habitual, it becomes *like* a reflex action. As Aristotle said, virtue should become second nature through habit: a virtuous act should be performed *as if* by instinct; this, far from detracting from its moral worth, testifies to one's mastery of the desired type of behavior; one does not have to make a moral effort each time it is repeated.

There are also premeditated acts for which, I would say, the person is not responsible. Premeditation, especially when it is so exaggerated as to issue in no action at all, can be the result of neurotic disturbance or what we sometimes call an emotional "block," which the person inherits from long-past situations. In Hamlet's revenge on his uncle (I use this example because it is familiar to all of us), there was no lack, but rather a surfeit, of premeditation; his actions were so exquisitely premeditated as to make Freud and Dr. Ernest Jones look more closely to find out what lay behind them. The very premeditation camouflaged unconscious motives of which Hamlet himself was not aware. I think this is an important point, since it seems that the courts often assume that premeditation is a criterion of responsibility. If failure to kill his uncle had been considered a crime, every court in the land would have convicted Hamlet. Again: a woman's decision to stay with her husband in spite of endless "mental cruelty" is, if she is the victim of an unconscious masochistic "will to punishment," one for which she is not responsible; she is the victim and not the agent, no matter how profound her conviction that she is the agent; she is caught in a masochistic web (of complicated genesis) dating back to babyhood, perhaps a repetition of a comparable situation involving her own parents, a repetition-compulsion that, as Freud said, goes "beyond the pleasure principle." Again: a criminal whose crime was carefully planned step by step is usually considered responsible, but as we shall see in later examples, the overwhelming impulse toward it, stemming from an unusually humiliating ego defeat in early childhood, was as compulsive as any can be.

2. Shall we say, then, that a person is not responsible for his act unless he can *defend it with reasons?* I am afraid that this criterion is no better than the previous one. First, intellectuals are usually better at giving reasons than nonintellectuals, and according to this criterion would be more responsible than persons acting from moral conviction not implemented by reasoning; yet it is very doubtful whether we should want to say that the latter are the more responsible. Second, the giving of reasons itself may be suspect. The reasons may be rationalizations camouflaging unconscious motives of which the agent knows nothing. Hamlet gave many reasons for not doing what he felt it was his duty to do: the time was not right, his uncle's soul might go to heaven, etc. His various "reasons" contradicted one another, and if an overpowering compulsion had not been present, the highly intellectual Hamlet would not have been taken in for a moment by these rationalizations. The real reason, the Oedipal conflict that made his uncle's crime the accomplishment of his own deepest desire, binding their fates into one and paralyzing him into inaction, was unconscious and of course unknown to him. One's intelligence and reasoning power do not enable one to escape from unconsciously motivated behavior; it only gives one greater facility in rationalizing that behavior; one's intelligence is simply used in the interests of the neurosis—it is pressed into service to justify with reasons what one does quite independently of the reasons.

If these two criteria are inadequate, let us seek others.

3. Shall we say that a person is responsible for his action unless it is the *result of unconscious forces* of which he knows nothing? Many psychoanalysts would probably accept this criterion. If it is not largely reflected in the language of responsibility as ordinarily used, this may be due to ignorance of fact: most people do not know that there are such things as unconscious motives and unconscious conflicts causing human beings to act.

But it may be that if they did, perhaps they would refrain from holding persons responsible for certain actions.

I do not wish here to quarrel with this criterion of responsibility. I only want to point out the fact that if this criterion is employed a far greater number of actions will be excluded from the domain of responsibility than we might at first suppose. Whether we are neat or untidy, whether we are selfish or unselfish, whether we provoke scenes or avoid them, even whether we can exert our powers of will to change our behavior—all these may, and often do, have their source in our unconscious life.

4. Shall we say that a person is responsible for his act unless it is *compelled?* Here we are reminded of Aristotle's assertion (*Nicomachean Ethics*, Book III) that a person is responsible for his act except for reasons of either ignorance or compulsion. Ignorance is not part of our problem here (unless it is unconsciously induced ignorance of facts previously remembered and selectively forgotten—in which case the forgetting is again compulsive), but compulsion is. How will compulsion do as a criterion? The difficulty is to state just what it means. When we say an act is compelled in a psychological sense, our language is metaphorical—which is not to say that there is no point in it or that, properly interpreted, it is not true. Our actions are compelled in a literal sense if someone has us in chains or is controlling our bodily movements. When we say that the storm compelled us to jettison the cargo of the ship (Aristotle's example), we have a less literal sense of compulsion, for at least it is open to us to go down with the ship. When psychoanalysts say that a man was compelled by unconscious conflicts to wash his hands constantly, this is also not a literal use of "compel"; for nobody forced his hands under the tap. Still, it is a typical example of what psychologists call *compulsive* behavior: it has unconscious causes inaccessible to introspection, and moreover nothing can change it—it is as inevitable for him to do it as it would be if someone were forcing his hands under the tap. In this it is exactly like the action of a powerful external force; it is just as little within one's conscious control.

In its area of application this interpretation of responsibility comes to much the same as the previous one. And this area is very great indeed. For if we cannot be held responsible for the infantile situations (in which we were after all passive victims), then neither, it would seem, can we be held responsible for compulsive actions occurring in adulthood that are inevitable consequences of those infantile situations. And, psychiatrists and psychoanalysts tell us, actions fulfilling this description are characteristic of all people some of the time and some people most of the time. Their occurrence, once the infantile events have taken place, is inevitable, just as the explosion is inevitable once the fuse has been lighted; there is simply more "delayed action" in the psychological explosions than there is in the physical ones.

(I have not used the word "inevitable" here to mean "causally determined," for according to such a definition every event would be inevitable if
one accepted the causal principle in some form or other; and probably nobody except certain philosophers uses "inevitable" in this sense. Rather, I
use "inevitable" in its ordinary sense of "cannot be avoided." To the extent,
therefore, that adult neurotic manifestations *can* be avoided, once the infantile patterns have become set, the assertion that they are inevitable is not
true.)

5. There is still another criterion, which I prefer to the previous ones, by
which a man's responsibility for an act can be measured: the degree to which
that act can (or could have been) *changed by the use of reasons*. Suppose that
the man who washes his hands constantly does so, he says, for hygienic
reasons, believing that if he doesn't do so he will be poisoned by germs. We
now convince him, on the best medical authority, that his belief is groundless. Now, the test of his responsibility is whether the changed belief will
result in changed behavior. If it does not, as with the compulsive hand
washer, he is not acting responsibly, but if it does, he is. It is not the *use* of
reasons, but their *efficacy in changing behavior*, that is being made the
criterion of responsibility. And clearly in neurotic cases no such change
occurs; in fact, this is often made the defining characteristic of neurotic
behavior: it is unchangeable by any rational considerations.

II

I have suggested these criteria to distinguish actions for which we can call
the agent responsible from those for which we cannot. Even persons with
extensive knowledge of psychiatry do not, I think, use any one of these
criteria to the exclusion of the others; a conjunction of two or more may be
used at once. But however they may be combined or selected in actual
application, I believe we can make the distinction along some such lines as
we have suggested.

But is there not still another possible meaning of "responsibility" that we
have not yet mentioned? Even after we have made all the above distinctions,
there remains a question in our minds whether we are, in the final analysis,
responsible for any of our actions at all. The issue may be put this way: How
can anyone be responsible for his actions, since they grow out of his character, which is shaped and molded and made what it is by influences—some
hereditary, but most of them stemming from early parental environment—
that were not of his own making or choosing? This question, I believe, still
troubles many people who would agree to all the distinctions we have just
made but still have the feeling that "this isn't all." They have the uneasy
suspicion that there is a more ultimate sense, a "deeper" sense, in which we
are *not* responsible for our actions, since we are not responsible for the
character out of which those actions spring.

Let us take as an example a criminal who, let us say, strangled several persons and is himself now condemned to die in the electric chair. Jury and public alike hold him fully responsible (at least they utter the words "he is responsible"), for the murders were planned down to the minutest detail, and the defendant tells the jury exactly how he planned them. But now we find out how it all came about; we learn of parents who rejected him from babyhood, of the childhood spent in one foster home after another, where it was always plain to him that he was not wanted; of the constantly frustrated early desire for affection, the hard shell of nonchalance and bitterness that he assumed to cover the painful and humiliating fact of being unwanted, and his subsequent attempts to heal these wounds to his shattered ego through defensive aggression.

> The criminal is the most passive person in this world, helpless as a baby in his motorically inexpressible fury. Not only does he try to wreak revenge on the mother of the earliest period of his babyhood; his criminality is based on the inner feeling of being incapable of making the mother even feel that the child seeks revenge on her. The situation is that of a dwarf trying to annoy a giant who superciliously refuses to see these attempts. . . . Because of his inner feeling of being a dwarf, the criminotic uses, so to speak, dynamite. Of that the giant must take cognizance. True, the "revenge" harms the avenger. He may be legally executed. However, the primary inner aim of forcing the giant to acknowledge the dwarf's fury is fulfilled.[1]

The poor victim is not conscious of the inner forces that exact from him this ghastly toll; he battles, he schemes, he revels in pseudoaggression, he is miserable, but he does not know what works within him to produce these catastrophic acts of crime. His aggressive actions are the wriggling of a worm on a fisherman's hook. And if this is so, it seems difficult to say any longer, "He is responsible." Rather we shall put him behind bars for the protection of society, but we shall no longer flatter our feeling of moral superiority by calling him personally responsible for what he did.

Let us suppose it were established that a man commits murder only if, sometime during the previous week, he has eaten a certain combination of foods—say, tuna fish salad at a meal also including peas, mushroom soup, and blueberry pie. What if we were to track down the factors common to all murders committed in this country during the last twenty years and found this factor present in all of them, and only in them? The example is of course empirically absurd; but may it not be that there is *some* combination of factors that regularly leads to homicide, factors such as are described in general terms in the above quotation? (Indeed the situation in the quotation is less fortunate than in our hypothetical example, for it is easy to avoid certain foods once we have been warned about them, but the situation of the infant is thrust on him; something has already happened to him once and for

---

[1]Edmund Bergler, *The Basic Neurosis* (New York: Grune and Stratton, 1949), p. 305.

all, before he knows it has happened.) When such specific factors are discovered, won't they make it clear that it is foolish and pointless, as well as immoral, to hold human beings responsible for crimes? Or, if one prefers biological to psychological factors, suppose a neurologist is called in to testify at a murder trial and produces X-ray pictures of the brain of the criminal; anyone can see, he argues, that the *cella turcica* was already calcified at the age of nineteen; it should be a flexible bone, growing, enabling the gland to grow. [2] All the defendant's disorders might have resulted from this early calcification. Now, this particular explanation may be empirically false; but who can say that no such factors, far more complex, to be sure, exist?

When we know such things as these, we no longer feel so much tempted to say that the criminal is responsible for his crime; and we tend also (do we not?) to excuse him—not legally (we still confine him to prison) but morally; we no longer call him a monster or hold him personally responsible for what he did. Moreover, we do this in general, not merely in the case of crime: "You must excuse Grandmother for being irritable; she's really quite ill and is suffering some pain all the time." Or: "The dog always bites children after she's had a litter of pups; you can't blame her for it: she's not feeling well, and besides she naturally wants to defend them." Or: "She's nervous and jumpy, but do excuse her: she has a severe glandular disturbance."

Let us note that the more *thoroughly* and *in detail* we know the causal factors leading a person to behave as he does, the more we tend to exempt him from responsibility. When we know nothing of the man except what we see him do, we say he is an ungrateful cad who expects much of other people and does nothing in return, and we are usually indignant. When we learn that his parents were the same way and, having no guilt feelings about this mode of behavior themselves, brought him up to be greedy and avaricious, we see that we could hardly expect him to have developed moral feelings in this direction. When we learn, in addition, that he is not aware of being ungrateful or selfish, but unconsciously represses the memory of events unfavorable to himself, we feel that the situation is unfortunate but "not really his fault." When we know that this behavior of his, which makes others angry, occurs more constantly when he feels tense or insecure, and that he now feels tense and insecure, and that relief from pressure will diminish it, then we tend to "feel sorry for the poor guy" and say he's more to be pitied than censured. We no longer want to say that he is personally responsible; we might rather blame nature or his parents for having given him an unfortunate constitution or temperament.

> In recent years a new form of punishment has been imposed on middle-aged and elderly parents. Their children, now in their twenties, thirties or even forties, present them with a modern grievance: "My analysis proves that *you* are responsible for my neurosis." Overawed by these authoritative statements,

[2]Meyer Levin, *Compulsion* (New York: Simon and Schuster, 1956), p. 403.

the poor tired parents fall easy victims to the newest variations on the scapegoat theory.

In my opinion, this senseless cruelty—which disinters educational sins which had been buried for decades, and uses them as the basis for accusations which the victims cannot answer—is unjustified. Yes, "the truth loves to be centrally located" (Melville), and few parents—since they are human—have been perfect. But granting their mistakes, they acted as *their* neurotic difficulties forced them to act. To turn the tables and declare the children not guilty because of the *impersonal* nature of their own neuroses, while at the same time the parents are *personally* blamed, is worse than illogical; it is profoundly unjust. [3]

And, so it would now appear, neither of the parties is responsible: "they acted as their neurotic difficulties forced them to act." The patients are not responsible for their neurotic manifestations, but then neither are the parents responsible for theirs; and so, of course, for their parents in turn, and theirs before them. It is the twentieth-century version of the family curse, the curse on the House of Atreus.

"But," a critic complains, "it's immoral to exonerate people indiscriminately in this way. I might have thought it fit to excuse somebody because he was born on the other side of the tracks, if I didn't know so many bank presidents who were also born on the other side of the tracks." Now, I submit that the most immoral thing in this situation is the critic's caricature of the conditions of the excuse. Nobody is excused merely because he was born on the other side of the tracks. But if he was born on the other side of the tracks *and* was a highly narcissistic infant to begin with *and* was repudiated or neglected by his parents *and* . . . (here we list a finite number of conditions), and if this complex of factors is *regularly* followed by certain behavior traits in adulthood, and moreover *unavoidably* so—that is, they occur no matter what he or anyone else tries to do—then we excuse him morally and say he is not responsible for his deed. If he is not responsible for A, a series of events occurring in his babyhood, then neither is he responsible for B, a series of things he does in adulthood, provided that B inevitably—that is, unavoidably—follows upon the occurrence of A. And according to psychiatrists and psychoanalysts, this often happens.

But one may still object that so far we have talked only about neurotic behavior. Isn't nonneurotic or normal or not unconsciously motivated (or whatever you want to call it) behavior still within the area of responsibility? There are reasons for answering "No" even here, for the normal person no more than the neurotic one has caused his own character, which makes him what he is. Granted that neurotics are not responsible for their behavior (that part of it which we call neurotic) because it stems from undigested infantile conflicts that they had no part in bringing about, and that are external to

<hr>

[3]Edmund Bergler, *The Superego* (New York: Grune and Stratton, 1952), p. 320.

them just as surely as if their behavior had been forced on them by a
malevolent deity (which is indeed one theory on the subject); but the so-
called normal person is equally the product of causes in which his volition
took no part. And if, unlike the neurotic's, his behavior is changeable by
rational considerations, and if he has the will power to overcome the effects
of an unfortunate early environment, this again is no credit to him; he is just
lucky. If energy is available to him in a form in which it can be mobilized for
constructive purposes, this is no credit to him, for this too is part of his
psychic legacy. Those of us who can discipline ourselves and develop habits
of concentration of purpose tend to blame those who cannot, and call them
lazy and weak-willed; but what we fail to see is that they literally *cannot* do
what we expect; if their psyches were structured like ours, they could, but as
they are burdened with a tyrannical superego (to use psychoanalytic jargon
for the moment), and a weak defenseless ego whose energies are constantly
consumed in fighting endless charges of the superego, they simply cannot do
it, and it is irrational to expect it of them. We cannot with justification blame
them for their inability, any more than we can congratulate ourselves for our
ability. This lesson is hard to learn, for we constantly and naïvely assume that
other people are constructed as we ourselves are.

For example: A child raised under slum conditions, whose parents are
socially ambitious and envy families with money, but who nevertheless
squander the little they have on drink, may simply be unable in later life to
mobilize a drive sufficient to overcome these early conditions. Common
sense would expect that he would develop the virtue of thrift; he would make
quite sure that he would never again endure the grinding poverty he had
experienced as a child. But in fact it is not so: the exact conditions are too
complex to be specified in detail here, but when certain conditions are
fulfilled (concerning the subject's early life), he will always thereafter be a
spendthrift, and no rational considerations will be able to change this. He
will listen to the rational considerations and see the force of these, but they
will not be able to change him, even if he tries; he cannot change his wasteful
habits any more than he can lift the Empire State Building with his bare
hands. We moralize and plead with him to be thrifty, but we do not see how
strong, how utterly overpowering, and how constantly with him, is the
opposite drive, which is so easily manageable with us. But he is possessed by
the all-consuming, all-encompassing urge to make the world see that he
belongs, that he has arrived, that he is just as well off as anyone else, that the
awful humiliations were not real, that they never actually occurred, for isn't
he now able to spend and spend? The humiliation must be blotted out; and
conspicuous, flashy, expensive, and wasteful buying will do this; it shows the
world what the world must know! True, it is only for the moment; true, it is
in the end self-defeating, for wasteful consumption is the best way to bring
poverty back again; but the person with an overpowering drive to mend a

lesion to his narcissism cannot resist the avalanche of that drive with this puny rational consideration. A man with his back against the wall and a gun at his throat doesn't think of what may happen ten years hence. (Consciously, of course, he knows nothing of this drive; all that appears to consciousness is its shattering effects; he knows only that he must keep on spending—not why—and that he is unable to resist.) He hasn't in him the psychic capacity, the energy to stem the tide of a drive that at that moment is all-powerful. We, seated comfortably away from this flood, sit in judgment on him and blame him and exhort him and criticize him; but he, carried along by the flood, cannot do otherwise than he does. He may fight with all the strength of which he is capable, but it is not enough. And we, who are rational enough at least to exonerate a man in a situation of "overpowering impulse" when we recognize it to be one, do not even recognize this as an example of it; and so, in addition to being swept away in the flood that childhood conditions rendered inevitable, he must also endure our lectures, our criticisms, and our moral excoriation.

But, one will say, he could have overcome his spendthrift tendencies; some people do. Quite true: some people do. They are lucky. They have it in them to overcome early deficiencies by exerting great effort, and they are capable of exerting the effort. Some of us, luckier still, can overcome them with but little effort; and a few, the luckiest, haven't the deficiencies to overcome. It's all a matter of luck. The least lucky are those who can't overcome them, even with great effort, and those who haven't the ability to exert the effort.

But, one persists, it isn't a matter simply of luck; it is a matter of effort. Very well then, it's a matter of effort; without exerting the effort you may not overcome the deficiency. But whether or not you are the kind of person who has it in him to exert the effort is a matter of luck.

All this is well known to psychoanalysts. They can predict, from minimal cues that most of us don't notice, whether a person is going to turn out to be lucky or not. "The analyst," they say, "must be able to use the residue of the patient's unconscious guilt so as to remove the symptom or character trait that creates the guilt. The guilt must not only be present, but *available* for use, *mobilizable*. If it is used up (absorbed) in criminal activity, or in an excessive amount of self-damaging tendencies, then it cannot be used for therapeutic purposes, and the prognosis is negative." Not all philosophers will relish the analyst's way of putting the matter, but at least as a physician he can soon detect whether the patient is lucky or unlucky—and he knows that whichever it is, it *isn't the patient's fault.* The patient's conscious volition cannot remedy the deficiency. Even whether he will co-operate with the analyst is really out of the patient's hands: if he continually projects the denying-mother fantasy on the analyst and unconsciously identifies him always with the cruel, harsh forbidder of the nursery, thus frustrating any attempt at impersonal observation, the sessions are useless; yet if it happens that way, he can't help that either. That fatal projection is not under his control; whether it occurs or not depends on how his unconscious identifications have developed since his infancy. He can try, yes—but the ability to try enough for the therapy to have effect is also beyond his control; the capacity to try more than just so much is either there or it isn't—and either way "it's in the lap of the gods."

The position, then, is this: if we *can* overcome the effects of early environment, the ability to do so is itself a product of the early environment. We did not give ourselves this ability; and if we lack it we cannot be blamed for not having it. Sometimes, to be sure, moral exhortation brings out an ability that is there but not being used, and in this lies its *occasional* utility; but very often its use is pointless, because the ability is not there. The only thing that can overcome a desire, as Spinoza said, is a stronger contrary desire; and many times there simply is no wherewithal for producing a stronger contrary desire. Those of us who do have the wherewithal are lucky.

There is one possible practical advantage in remembering this. It may prevent us (unless we are compulsive blamers) from indulging in righteous indignation and committing the sin of spiritual pride, thanking God that we are not as this publican here. And it will protect from our useless moralizings those who are least equipped by nature for enduring them.

As with responsibility, so with deserts. Someone commits a crime and is punished by the state; "he deserved it," we say self-righteously—as if we were moral and he immoral, when in fact we are lucky and he is unlucky—forgetting that there, but for the grace of God and a fortunate early environment, go we. Or, as Clarence Darrow said in his speech for the defense in the Loeb-Leopold case:

> I do not believe that people are in jail because they deserve to be. . . . I know what causes the emotional life. . . . I know it is practically left out of some. Without it they cannot act with the rest. They cannot feel the moral shocks which safeguard others. Is [this man] to blame that his machine is imperfect? Who is to blame? I do not know. I have never in my life been interested so much in fixing blame as I have in relieving people from blame. I am not wise enough to fix it. [4]

[4]Levin, *op. cit.*, pp. 439–40, 469.

10

C. A. CAMPBELL

---

introduction

The problem of free will, as we have indicated, arises from an apparent conflict between certain fundamental beliefs most people share, particularly the belief almost everyone has that he could sometimes act otherwise than he does, on the one hand, and the belief that all events are caused and therefore unavoidable, on the other hand. If this second belief is true, then it is hard to see how the first can be true.

Some philosophers (such as Ayer) have tried to solve this problem by showing that there is really no conflict here. Others (such as Hospers) have declared that, in the light of contemporary science and psychology, the first of these beliefs—that one can sometimes act otherwise than he does—seems to be false, and that the conflict between the two beliefs can therefore be resolved by rejecting this one. The remaining alternative is, of course, to try to show that the second of these two beliefs—that all everts are caused and therefore unavoidable—is at least doubtful. Campbell's essay, which follows, exemplifies this approach.

Campbell puts the problem in terms of moral responsibility, a concept whose validity and applicability to human conduct he does not doubt. For this concept to be valid, however—for anyone to actually be morally responsible for some action—then several things are presupposed; one of these is that he could have done otherwise. Virtually everyone is convinced, Campbell claims, that sometimes his inner act of deciding whether or not to put forth the effort necessary to resist temptation, and rise to the demands of duty, is a free act in precisely the sense that he could have decided otherwise than he did.

The question, therefore, is not whether that is true, for its truth is hardly ever questioned by anyone. The question is, rather, what it means. When you say that you could have decided not to do something that you did, just what are you saying?

Ayer and other compatibilists maintain that you merely mean that you would have decided not to do it, *if* something else had been true—if, for example, you had wanted to, or you had been a different person, or a person of different character, or something of this sort. It is a hypothetical judgment that implicitly contains an *if*-clause. It is like saying: I could have been president, *if* I had been nominated and elected; or, I could have been Moses, *if* I had lived long ago and been sired by Moses' father, and so on—statements that are, of course, in some sense true.

But Campbell maintains that this is not what anyone actually means when he says he could have decided otherwise than he did. What one means, when he believes his decision was really freely made, is that he could have decided otherwise given the very conditions that actually obtained when he made his decision. Campbell declares such a judgment to be not hypothetical but categorical—that is, it does not imply any such if-clause at all.

This essay of Campbell's is quite widely considered to be a decisive refutation of the compatibilist thesis, at least in its familiar formulations. Whether it proves that people have free will or not depends, of course, on whether its presuppositions are true. And the crucial presupposition is whether it ever is true that any agent could have decided otherwise than he actually did. Campbell is probably right in maintaining that most persons do believe this, quite firmly. And he is apparently also right in claiming that they believe it in a categorical, and not merely a hypothetical, sense. And he seems right in claiming that this belief is not compatible with a belief in causal determinism. Still, the belief itself, however widely and firmly held, might in fact be false—just as Hospers has suggested.

C. A. Campbell, who is best known for his philosophical analyses of free will, was Professor of Logic in the University of Glasgow, Scotland, until his retirement in 1961. A small portion of his original lecture, dealing with an obscure concept of freedom that is of little interest, has been dropped from the selection that follows.

The Defense of Free Will*

It is something of a truism that in philosophic enquiry the exact formulation of a problem often takes one a long way on the road to its solution. In the case of the Free Will problem I think there is a rather special need of careful formulation. For there are many sorts of human freedom; and it can easily happen that one wastes a great deal of labour in proving or disproving a freedom which has almost nothing to do with the freedom which is at issue in the traditional problem of Free Will. The abortiveness of so much of the argument for and against Free Will in contemporary philosophical literature seems to me due in the main to insufficient pains being taken over the preliminary definition of the problem. There is, indeed, one outstanding exception, Professor Broad's brilliant inaugural lecture entitled, 'Determinism, Indeterminism, and Libertarianism',[1] in which forty-three pages are devoted to setting out the problem, as against seven to its solution! I confess that the solution does not seem to myself to follow upon the formulation quite as easily as all that:[2] but Professor Broad's eminent example fortifies me in my decision to give here what may seem at first sight a disproportionate amount of time to the business of determining the essential characteristics of the kind of freedom with which the traditional problem is concerned.

Fortunately we can at least make a beginning with a certain amount of confidence. It is not seriously disputable that the kind of freedom in question is the freedom which is commonly recognised to be in some sense a precondition of moral responsibility. Clearly, it is on account of this integral connection with moral responsibility that such exceptional importance has always been felt to attach to the Free Will problem. But in what precise sense is free will a precondition of moral responsibility, and thus a postulate of the moral life in general? This is an exceedingly troublesome question; but until we have satisfied ourselves about the answer to it, we are not in a position to state, let alone decide, the question whether 'Free Will' in its traditional, ethical, significance is a reality.

Our first business, then, is to ask, exactly what kind of freedom is it which is required for moral responsibility? And as to method of procedure in this inquiry, there seems to me to be no real choice. I know of only one method that carries with it any hope of success; viz. the critical comparison of those acts for which, on due reflection, we deem it proper to attribute moral praise or blame to the agents, with those acts for which, on due reflection, we deem such judgments to be improper. The ultimate touchstone, as I see it, can

---

*From C. A. Campbell, *On Selfhood and Godhood* (London: George Allen & Unwin, Ltd., 1957).

[1]Reprinted in *Ethics and the History of Philosophy, Selected Essays.*

[2]I have explained the grounds for my dissent from Broad's final conclusions on pp. 27 ff. of *In Defence of Free Will* (Jackson Son & Co., 1938).

only be our moral consciousness as it manifests itself in our more critical and considered moral judgments. The 'linguistic' approach by way of the analysis of moral *sentences* seems to me, despite its present popularity, to be an almost infallible method for reaching wrong results in the moral field; but I must reserve what I have to say about this for the next lecture.

The first point to note is to that the freedom at issue (as indeed the very name 'Free *Will* Problem' indicates) pertains primarily not to overt acts but to inner acts. The nature of things has decreed that, save the case of one's self, it is only overt acts which one can directly observe. But a very little reflection serves to show that in our moral judgments upon others their overt acts are regarded as significant only in so far as they are the expression of inner acts. We do not consider the acts of a robot to be morally responsible acts; nor do we consider the acts of a man to be so save in so far as they are distinguishable from those of a robot by reflecting an inner life of choice. Similarly, from the other side, if we are satisfied (as we may on occasion be, at least in the case of ourselves) that a person has definitely elected to follow a course which he believes to be wrong, but has been prevented by external circumstances from translating his inner choice into an overt act, we still regard him as morally blameworthy. Moral freedom, then, pertains to *inner* acts.

The next point seems at first sight equally obvious and uncontroversial; but, as we shall see, it has awkward implications if we are in real earnest with it (as almost nobody is). It is the simple point that the act must be one of which the person judged can be regarded as the *sole* author. It seems plain enough that if there are any *other* determinants of the act, external to the self, to that extent the act is not an act which the *self* determines, and to that extent not an act for which the self can be held morally responsible. The self is only part-author of the act, and his moral responsibility can logically extend only to those elements within the act (assuming for the moment that these can be isolated) of which he is the *sole* author.

The awkward implications of this apparent truism will be readily appreciated. For, if we are mindful of the influences exerted by heredity and environment, we may well feel some doubt whether there is any act of will at all of which one can truly say that the self is sole author, sole determinant. No man has a voice in determining the raw material of impulses and capacities that constitute his hereditary endowment, and no man has more than a very partial control of the material and social environment in which he is destined to live his life. Yet it would be manifestly absurd to deny that these two factors do constantly and profoundly affect the nature of a man's choices. That this is so we all of us recognise in our moral judgments when we 'make allowances', as we say, for a bad heredity or a vicious environment, and acknowledge in the victim of them a diminished moral responsibility for evil courses. Evidently we do *try*, in our moral judgments, however crudely, to praise or blame a man only in respect of that of which we can regard him as *wholly* the author. And evidently we do recognise that, for a man to be the author of an act in the full sense required for moral responsibility, it is not enough merely that he 'wills' or 'chooses' the act: since even the most unfortunate victim of heredity or environment does, as a rule, 'will' what he does. It is significant, however, that the ordinary man, though well enough aware of the influence upon choices of heredity and environment, does not feel obliged thereby to give up his assumption that moral predicates *are* somehow applicable. Plainly he still believes that there is *something* for which a man is morally responsible, something of which we can fairly say that he is the sole author. *What is this something?* To that question common-sense is not ready with an explicit answer—though an answer is, I think, implicit in the line which its moral judgments take. I shall do what I can to give an explicit answer later in this lecture. Meantime it must suffice to observe that, if we are to be true to the deliverances of our moral consciousness, it is very difficult to deny that *sole* authorship is a necessary condition of the morally responsible act.

Thirdly we come to a point over which much recent controversy has raged. We may approach it by raising the following question. Granted an act of which the agent is sole author, does this 'sole authorship' suffice to make the act a morally free act? We may be inclined to think that it does, until we contemplate the possibility that an act of which the agent is sole author might conceivably occur as a necessary expression of the agent's nature; the way in which, e. g. some philosophers have supposed the Divine act of creation to occur. This consideration excites a legitimate doubt; for it is far from easy to see how a person can be regarded as a proper subject for moral praise or blame in respect of an act which he *cannot help* performing—even if it be his own 'nature' which necessitates it. Must we not recognise it as a condition of the morally free act that the agent 'could have acted otherwise' than he in fact did? It is true, indeed, that we sometimes praise or blame a man for an act about which we are prepared to say, in the light of our knowledge of his established character, that he 'could no other'. But I think that a little reflection shows that in such cases we are not praising or blaming the man strictly for what he does *now* (or at any rate we ought not to be), but rather for those past acts of his which have generated the firm habit of mind from which his *present* act follows 'necessarily'. In other words, our praise and blame, so far as justified, are really retrospective, being directed not to the agent *qua* performing *this* act, but to the agent *qua* performing those past acts which have built up his present character, and in respect to which we presume that he *could* have acted otherwise, that there really *were* open possibilities before him. These cases, therefore, seem to me to constitute no valid exception to what I must take to be the rule, viz. that a man can be morally praised or blamed for an act only if he could have acted otherwise.

Now philosophers today are fairly well agreed that it is a postulate of the morally responsible act that the agent 'could have acted otherwise' in *some* sense of that phrase. But sharp differences of opinion have arisen over the way in which the phrase ought to be interpreted. There is a strong disposition to water down its apparent meaning by insisting that it is not (as a postulate of moral responsibility) to be understood as a straightforward categorical proposition, but rather as a disguised hypothetical proposition. All that we really require to be assured of, in order to justify our holding X morally responsible for an act, is, we are told, that X could have acted otherwise *if* he had *chosen* otherwise (Moore, Stevenson); or perhaps that X could have acted otherwise *if* he had had a different character, or *if* he had been placed in different circumstances.

I think it is easy to understand, and even, in a measure, to sympathise with, the motives which induce philosophers to offer these counter-interpretations. It is not just the fact that 'X could have acted otherwise', as a bald categorical statement, is incompatible with the universal sway of causal law—though this is, to some philosophers, a serious stone of stumbling. The more widespread objection is that it at least looks as though it were incompatible with that causal continuity of an agent's character with his conduct which is implied when we believe (surely with justice) that we can often tell the sort of thing a man will do from our knowledge of the sort of man he is.

We shall have to make our accounts with that particular difficulty later. At this stage I wish merely to show that neither of the hypothetical propositions suggested—and I think the same could be shown for *any* hypothetical alternative—is an acceptable substitute for the categorical proposition 'X could have acted otherwise' as the presupposition of moral responsibility.

Let us look first at the earlier suggestion—'X could have acted otherwise *if* he had chosen otherwise'. Now clearly there are a great many acts with regard to which we are entirely satisfied that the agent is thus situated. We are often perfectly sure that—for this is all it amounts to—if X had chosen otherwise, the circumstances presented no external obstacle to the translation of that choice into action. For example, we often have no doubt at all that X, who in point of fact told a lie, could have told the truth *if* he had so chosen. But does our confidence on this score allay all legitimate doubts about whether X is really blameworthy? Does it entail that X is free in the sense required for moral responsibility? Surely not. The obvious question immediately arises: 'But *could* X have *chosen* otherwise than he did?' It is doubt about the true answer to *that* question which leads most people to doubt the reality of moral responsibility. Yet on this crucial question the hypothetical proposition which is offered as a sufficient statement of the condition justifying the ascription of moral responsibility gives us no information whatsoever.

Indeed this hypothetical substitute for the categorical 'X could have acted otherwise' seems to me to lack all plausibility unless one contrives to forget why it is, after all, that we ever come to feel fundamental doubts about man's moral responsibility. Such doubts are born, surely, when one becomes aware of certain reputable world-views in religion or philosophy, or of certain reputable scientific beliefs, which in their several ways imply that man's actions are necessitated, and thus could not be otherwise than they in fact are. But clearly a doubt so based is not even touched by the recognition that a man could very often act otherwise *if* he so chose. That proposition is entirely compatible with the necessitarian theories which generate our doubt: indeed it is this very compatibility that has recommended it to some philosophers, who are reluctant to give up either moral responsibility or Determinism. The proposition which we *must* be able to affirm if moral praise or blame of X is to be justified is the categorical proposition that X could have acted otherwise because—not if—he could have chosen otherwise; or, since it is essentially the inner side of the act that matters, the proposition simply that X could have chosen otherwise.

For the second of the alternative formulae suggested we cannot spare more than a few moments. But its inability to meet the demands it is required to meet is almost transparent. 'X could have acted otherwise', as a statement of a precondition of X's moral responsibility, really means (we are told) 'X could have acted otherwise *if* he were differently constituted, or *if* he had been placed in different circumstances'. It seems a sufficient reply to this to point out that the person whose moral responsibility is at issue is X; a specific individual, in a specific set of circumstances. It is totally irrelevant to X's moral responsibility that we should be able to say that some person differently constituted from X, or X in a different set of circumstances, could have done something different from what X did.

Let me, then, briefly sum up the answer at which we have arrived to our question about the kind of freedom required to justify moral responsibility. It is that a man can be said to exercise free will in a morally significant sense only in so far as his chosen act is one of which he is the sole cause or author, and only if—in the straightforward, categorical sense of the phrase—he 'could have chosen otherwise'.

I confess that this answer is in some ways a disconcerting one, disconcerting, because most of us, however objective we are in the actual conduct of our thinking, would *like* to be able to believe that moral responsibility is real: whereas the freedom required for moral responsibility, on the analysis we have given, is certainly far more difficult to establish than the freedom required on the analyses we found ourselves obliged to reject. If, e.g. moral freedom entails only that I could have acted otherwise *if* I had chosen otherwise, there is no real 'problem' about it at all. I am 'free' in the normal case where there is no external obstacle to prevent my translating the alternative choice into action, and not free in other cases. Still less is there a problem if all that moral freedom entails is that I could have acted otherwise *if* I had been a differently constituted person, or been in different circumstances. Clearly I am *always* free in *this* sense of freedom. But, as I have argued, these so-called 'freedoms' fail to give us the pre-conditions of moral responsibility, and hence leave the freedom of the traditional free-will problem, the freedom that people are really concerned about, precisely where it was. . . .

We saw earlier that Common Sense's practice of 'making allowances' in its moral judgments for the influence of heredity and environment indicates Common Sense's conviction, both that a just moral judgment must discount determinants of choice over which the agent has no control, and also (since it still accepts moral judgments as legitimate) that *something* of moral relevance survives which can be regarded as genuinely self-originated. We are now to try to discover what this 'something' is. And I think we may still usefully take Common Sense as our guide. Suppose one asks the ordinary intelligent citizen *why* he deems it proper to make allowances for X, whose heredity and/or environment are unfortunate. He will tend to reply, I think, in some such terms as these: that X has more and stronger temptations to deviate from what is right than Y or Z, who are normally circumstanced, so that he must put forth a *stronger moral effort* if he is to achieve the same level of external conduct. The intended implication seems to be that X is just as morally praiseworthy as Y or Z *if* he exerts an equivalent moral effort, even though he may not thereby achieve an equal success in conforming his will to the 'concrete' demands of duty. And this implies, again, Common Sense's belief that *in moral effort* we have something for which a man is responsible *without qualification*, something that is *not* affected by heredity and environment but depends *solely* upon the self itself.

Now in my opinion Common Sense has here, in principle, hit upon the one and only defensible answer. Here, and here alone, so far as I can see, in the act of deciding whether to put forth or withhold the moral effort required to resist temptation and rise to duty, is to be found an act which is free in the sense required for moral responsibility; an act of which the self is sole author, and of which it is true to say that 'it could be' (or, after the event, 'could have been') 'otherwise'. Such is the thesis which we shall now try to establish.

The species of argument appropriate to the establishment of a thesis of this sort should fall, I think, into two phases. First, there should be a consideration of the evidence of the moral agent's own inner experience. What *is* the act of moral decision, and what does it imply, from the standpoint of the actual participant? Since there is no way of knowing the act of moral decision—or for that matter any other form of activity—except by actual participation in it, the evidence of the subject, or agent, is on an issue of this kind of palmary importance. It can hardly, however, be taken as in itself conclusive. For even if that evidence should be overwhelmingly to the effect that moral decision does have the characteristics required by moral freedom, the question is bound to be raised—and in view of considerations from other quarters pointing in a contrary direction is *rightly* raised—Can we *trust* the evidence of inner experience? That brings us to what will be the second phase of the argument. We shall have to go on to show, if we are to make good our case, that the extraneous considerations so often supposed to be fatal to the belief in moral freedom are in fact innocuous to it.

In the light of what was said in the last lecture about the self's experience of moral decision as a *creative* activity, we may perhaps be absolved from developing the first phase of the argument at any great length. The appeal is throughout to one's own experience in the actual taking of the moral decision in the situation of moral temptation. 'Is it possible', we must ask, 'for anyone so circumstanced to *dis*believe that he could be deciding otherwise?' The answer is surely not in doubt. When we decide to exert moral effort to resist a temptation, we feel quite certain that we *could* withhold the effort; just as, if we decide to withhold the effort and yield to our desires, we feel quite certain that we *could* exert it—otherwise we should not blame ourselves afterwards for having succumbed. It may be, indeed, that this conviction is mere self-delusion. But that is not at the moment our concern. It is enough at present to establish that the act of deciding to exert or to withhold moral effort, as we know it from the inside in actual moral living, belongs to the category of acts which 'could have been otherwise'.

Mutatis mutandis, the same reply is forthcoming if we ask, 'Is it possible for the moral agent in the taking of his decision to *dis*believe that he is the sole author of that decision?' Clearly he cannot disbelieve that it is *he* who takes the decision. That, however, is not in itself sufficient to enable him, on reflection, to regard himself as *solely* responsible for the act. For his 'character' as so far formed might conceivably be a factor in determining it, and no one can suppose that the constitution of his 'character' is uninfluenced by circumstances of heredity and environment with which *he* has nothing to do. But as we pointed out in the last lecture, the very essence of the moral decision as it is experienced is that it is a decision whether or not to *combat* our strongest desire, and our strongest desire *is* the expression in the situation of our character as so far formed. Now clearly our character cannot be a factor in determining the decision whether or not to *oppose* our character. I think we are entitled to say, therefore, that the act of moral decision is one in which the self is for itself not merely 'author' but 'sole author'.

We may pass on, then, to the second phase of our constructive argument; and this will demand more elaborate treatment. Even if a moral agent *qua* making a moral decision in the situation of 'temptation' cannot help believing that he has free will in the sense at issue—a moral freedom between real alternatives, between genuinely open possibilities—are there, nevertheless, objections to a freedom of this kind so cogent that we are bound to distrust the evidence of 'inner experience'?

I begin by drawing attention to a simple point whose significance tends, I think, to be under-estimated. If the phenomenological analysis we have offered is substantially correct, no one while functioning as a moral agent can help believing that he enjoys free will. Theoretically he may be completely convinced by Determinist arguments, but when actually confronted with a personal situation of conflict between duty and desire he is quite certain that it lies with him here and now whether or not he will rise to duty. It follows that if Determinists could produce convincing theoretical arguments against a free will of this kind, the awkward predicament would ensue that a man has to deny as a theoretical being what he has to assert as a practical being. Now I think the Determinist ought to be a good deal more worried about this than he usually is. He seems to imagine that a strong case on general theoretical grounds is enough to prove that the 'practical' belief in free will, even if inescapable for us as practical beings, is mere illusion. But in fact it proves nothing of the sort. There is no reason whatever why a belief that we find ourselves obliged to hold *qua* practical beings should be required to give way before a belief which we find ourselves obliged to hold *qua* theoretical beings; or, for that matter, *vice versa*. All that the theoretical arguments of Determinism can prove, unless they are reinforced by a refutation of the phenomenological analysis that supports Libertarianism, is that there is a radical conflict between the theoretical and the practical sides of man's nature, an antimony at the very heart of the self. And this is a state of affairs with which no one can easily rest satisfied. I think therefore that the Determinist ought to concern himself a great deal more than he does with phenomenological analysis, in order to show, if he can, that the assurance of free will is not really an inexpugnable element in man's practical consciousness. There is just as much obligation upon him, convinced though he may be of the soundness of his theoretical arguments, to expose the errors of the Libertarian's phenomenological analysis, as there is upon us, convinced though we may be of the soundness of the Libertarian's phenomenological analysis, to expose the errors of the Determinist's theoretical arguments.

However, we must at once begin the discharge of our own obligation. The rest of this lecture will be devoted to trying to show that the arguments which seem to carry most weight with Determinists are, to say the least of it, very far from compulsive.

Fortunately a good many of the arguments which at an earlier time in the history of philosophy would have been strongly urged against us make almost no appeal to the bulk of philosophers today, and we may here pass them by. That applies to any criticism of 'open possibilities' based on a metaphysical theory about the nature of the universe as a whole. Nobody today *has* a metaphysical theory about the nature of the universe as a whole! It applies also, with almost equal force, to criticisms based upon the universality of causal law as a supposed postulate of science. There have always been, in my opinion, sound philosophic reasons for doubting the validity, as distinct from the convenience, of the causal postulate in its universal form, but at the present time, when scientists themselves are deeply divided about the need for postulating causality even within their own special field, we shall do better to concentrate our attention upon criticisms which are more confidently advanced. I propose to ignore also, on different grounds, the type of criticism of free will that is sometimes advanced from the side of religion, based upon religious postulates of Divine Omnipotence and Omniscience. So far as I can see, a postulate of human freedom is every bit as necessary to meet certain religious demands (e. g. to make sense of the 'conviction of sin'), as postulates of Divine Omniscience and Omnipotence are to meet certain other religious demands. If so, then it can hardly be argued that religious experience as such tells more strongly against than for the position we are defending; and we may be satisfied, in the present context, to leave the matter there. It will be more profitable to discuss certain arguments which contemporary philosophers do think important, and which recur with a somewhat monotonous regularity in the literature of anti-Libertarianism.

These arguments can, I think, be reduced in principle to no more than two: first, the argument from 'predictability'; second, the argument from the alleged meaninglessness of an act supposed to be the self's act and yet not an expression of the self's character. Contemporary criticism of free will seems to me to consist almost exclusively of variations on these two themes. I shall deal with each in turn.

On the first we touched in passing at an earlier stage. Surely it is beyond question (the critic urges) that when we know a person intimately we can foretell with a high degree of accuracy how he will respond to at least a large number of practical situations. One feels safe in predicting that one's dog-loving friend will not use his boot to repel the little mongrel that comes yapping at his heels; or again that one's wife will not pass with incurious eyes (or indeed pass at all) the new hat-shop in the city. So to behave would not be (as we say) 'in character'. But, so the criticism runs, you with your doctrine of 'genuinely open possibilities', of a free will by which the self can diverge from its own character, remove all rational basis from such prediction. You require us to make the absurd supposition that the success of countless predictions of the sort in the past has been mere matter of chance. If you really believed in your theory, you would not be surprised if tomorrow your friend with the notorious horror of strong drink should suddenly exhibit a passion for whisky and soda, or if your friend whose taste for reading has hitherto been satisfied with the sporting columns of the newspapers should be discovered on a fine Saturday afternoon poring over the works of Hegel. But of course you would be surprised. Social life would be sheer chaos if there were not well-grounded social expectations; and social life is not sheer chaos. Your theory is hopelessly wrecked upon obvious facts.

Now whether or not this criticism holds good against some versions of Libertarian theory I need not here discuss. It is sufficient if I can make it clear that against the version advanced in this lecture, according to which free will is localised in a relatively narrow field of operation, the criticism has no relevance whatsoever.

Let us remind ourselves briefly of the setting within which, on our view, free will functions. There is X, the course which we believe we ought to follow, and Y, the course towards which we feel our desire is strongest. The freedom which we ascribe to the agent is the freedom to put forth or refrain from putting forth the moral effort required to resist the pressure of desire and do what he thinks he ought to do.

But then there is surely an immense range of practical situations— covering by far the greater part of life—in which there is no question of a conflict within the self between what he most desires to do and what he thinks he ought to do? Indeed such conflict is a comparatively rare phenomenon for the majority of men. Yet over that whole vast range there is nothing whatever in our version of Libertarianism to prevent our agreeing that character determines conduct. In the absence, real or supposed, of any 'moral' issue, what a man chooses will be simply that course which, after such reflection as seems called for, he deems most likely to bring him what he most strongly desires; and that is the same as to say the course to which his present character inclines him.

Over by far the greater area of human choices, then, our theory offers no more barrier to successful prediction on the basis of character than any other theory. For where there is no clash of strongest desire with duty, the free will we are defending has no business. There is just nothing for it to do.

But what about the situations—rare enough though they may be—in which there is this clash and in which free will does therefore operate? Does our theory entail that there at any rate, as the critic seems to suppose, 'anything may happen'?

Not by any manner of means. In the first place, and by the very nature of the case, the range of the agent's possible choices is bounded by what he thinks he ought to do on the one hand, and what he most strongly desires on the other. The freedom claimed for him is a freedom of decision to make or withhold the effort required to do what he thinks he ought to do. There is no question of a freedom to act in some 'wild' fashion, out of all relation to his characteristic beliefs and desires. This so-called 'freedom of caprice', so often charged against the Libertarian, is, to put it bluntly, a sheer figment of the critic's imagination, with no *habitat* in serious Libertarian theory. Even in situations where free will does come into play it is perfectly possible, on a view like ours, given the appropriate knowledge of a man's character, to predict within certain limits how he will respond.

But 'probable prediction in such situations can, I think, go further than this. It is obvious that where desire and duty are at odds, the felt 'gap' (as it were) between the two may vary enormously in breadth in different cases.

The moderate drinker and the chronic tippler may each want another glass, and each deem it his duty to abstain, but the felt gap between desire and duty in the case of the former is trivial beside the great gulf which is felt to separate them in the case of the latter. Hence it will take a far harder moral effort for the tippler than for the moderate drinker to achieve the same external result of abstention. So much is a matter of common agreement. And we are entitled, I think, to take it into account in prediction, on the simple principle that the harder the moral effort required to resist desire the less likely it is to occur. Thus in the example taken, most people would predict that the tippler will very probably succumb to his desires, whereas there is a reasonable likelihood that the moderate drinker will make the comparatively slight effort needed to resist them. So long as the prediction does not pretend to more than a measure of probability, there is nothing in our theory which would disallow it.

I claim, therefore, that the view of free will I have been putting forward is consistent with predictability of conduct on the basis of character over a very wide field indeed. And I make the further claim that that field will cover all the situations in life concerning which there is any empirical evidence that successful prediction is possible.

Let us pass on to consider the second main line of criticism. This is, I think, much the more illuminating of the two, if only because it compels the Libertarian to make explicit certain concepts which are indispensable to him, but which, being desperately hard to state clearly, are apt not to be stated at all. The critic's fundamental point might be stated somewhat as follows:

'Free will as you describe it is completely unintelligible. On your own showing no *reason* can be given, because there just *is* no reason, why a man decides to exert rather than to wihhold moral effort, or *vice versa*. But such an act—or more properly, such an "occurrence"—it is nonsense to speak of as an act of a *self*. If there is nothing in the self's character to which it is, even in principle, in any way traceable, the self has nothing to do with it. Your so-called "freedom", therefore, so far from supporting the self's moral responsibility, destroys it as surely as the crudest Determinism could do'.

If we are to discuss this criticism usefully, it is important, I think, to begin by getting clear about two different senses of the word 'intelligible'.

If, in the first place, we mean by an 'intelligible' act one whose occurrence is in principle capable of being inferred, since it follows necessarily from something (though we may not know in fact from what), then it is certainly true that the Libertarian's free will is unintelligible. But that is only saying, is it not, that the Libertarian's 'free' act is not an act which follows necessarily from something! This can hardly rank as a *criticism* of Libertarianism. It is just a description of it. That there can be nothing unintelligible in *this* sense is precisely what the Determinist has got to *prove*.

Yet it is surprising how often the critic of Libertarianism involves himself in this circular mode of argument. Repeatedly it is urged against the Libertarian, with a great air of triumph, that on his view he can't say *why* I now decide to rise to duty, or now decide to follow my strongest desire in defiance of duty. Of course he can't. If he could he wouldn't *be* a Libertarian. To 'account for' a 'free' act is a contradiction in terms. A free will is *ex hypothesi* the sort of thing of which the request for an *explanation* is absurd. The assumption that an explanation must be in principle possible for the act of moral decision deserves to rank as a classic example of the ancient fallacy of 'begging the question'.

But the critic usually has in mind another sense of the word 'unintelligible'. He is apt to take it for granted that an act which is unintelligible in the *above* sense (as the morally free act of the Libertarian undoubtedly is) is unintelligible in the *further* sense that we can attach no meaning to it. And this is an altogether more serious matter. If it could really be shown that the Libertarian's 'free will' were unintelligible in this sense of being meaningless, that, for myself at any rate, would be the end of the affair. Libertarianism would have been conclusively refuted.

But it seems to me manifest that this can *not* be shown. The critic has allowed himself, I submit, to become the victim of a widely accepted but fundamentally vicious assumption. He has assumed that whatever is meaningful must exhibit its meaningfulness to those who view it from the standpoint of external observation. Now if one chooses thus to limit one's self to the role of external observer, it is, I think, perfectly true that one can attach no meaning to an act which is the act of something we call a 'self' and yet follows from nothing in that self's character. But then *why should we* so limit ourselves, when what is under consideration is a subjective activity? For the apprehension of subjective acts there is *another* standpoint available, that of *inner experience*, of the practical consciousness in its actual functioning. If our free will should turn out to be something to which we can attach a meaning from *this* standpoint, no more is required. And no more ought to be expected. For I must repeat that only from the inner standpoint of living experience *could* anything of the nature of 'activity' be directly grasped. Observation from without is in the nature of the case impotent to apprehend the active *qua* active. We can from without observe sequences of states. If into these we read activity (as we sometimes do), this can only be on the basis of what we discern in ourselves from the inner standpoint. It follows that if anyone insists upon taking his criterion of the meaningful simply from the standpoint of external observation, he is really deciding in advance of the evidence that the notion of activity, and *a fortiori* the notion of a free will, is 'meaningless'. He looks for the free act through a medium which is in the nature of the case incapable of revealing it, and then, because inevitably he doesn't find it, he declares that it doesn't exist!

But if, as we surely ought in this context, we adopt the inner standpoint, then (I am suggesting) things appear in a totally different light. From the inner standpoint, it seems to me plain, there is no difficulty whatever in attaching meaning to an act which is the self's act and which nevertheless does not follow from the self's character. So much I claim has been established by the phenomenological analysis, in this and the previous lecture, of the act of moral decision in face of moral temptation. It is thrown into particularly clear relief where the moral decision is to make the moral effort required to rise to duty. For the very function of moral effort, as it appears to the agent engaged in the act, is to enable the self to act against the line of least resistance, against the line to which his character as so far formed most strongly inclines him. But if the self is thus conscious here of *combating* his formed character, he surely cannot possibly suppose that the act, although his own act, *issues from* his formed character? I submit, therefore, that the self knows very well indeed—from the inner standpoint—what is meant by an act which is the *self's* act and which nevertheless does not follow from the self's *character*.

What this implies—and it seems to me to be an implication of cardinal importance for any theory of the self that aims at being more than superficial—is that the nature of the self is for itself something more than just its character as so far formed. The 'nature' of the self and what we commonly call the 'character' of the self are by no means the same thing, and it is utterly vital that they should not be confused. The 'nature' of the self comprehends, but is not without remainder reducible to, its 'character'; it must, if we are to be true to the testimony of our experience of it, be taken as including *also* the authentic creative power of fashioning and re-fashioning 'character'.

The misguided, and as a rule quite uncritical, belittlement, of the evidence offered by inner experience has, I am convinced, been responsible for more bad argument by the opponents of Free Will than has any other single factor. How often, for example, do we find the Determinist critic saying, in effect, '*Either* the act follows necessarily upon precedent states, *or* it is a mere matter of chance and accordingly of no moral significance'. The disjunction is invalid, for it does not exhaust the possible alternatives. It seems to the critic to do so only because he *will* limit himself to the standpoint which is proper, and indeed alone possible, in dealing with the physical world, the standpoint of the external observer. If only he would allow himself to assume the standpoint which is not merely proper for, but necessary to, the apprehension of subjective activity, the inner standpoint of the practical consciousness in its actual functioning, he would find himself obliged to recognise the falsity of his disjunction. Reflection upon the act of moral decision as apprehended from the inner standpoint would force him to recognise a *third* possibility, as remote from chance as from necessity, that, namely, of *creative activity*, in which (as I have ventured to express it) nothing determines the act save the agent's doing of it.

There we must leave the matter. But as this lecture has been, I know, somewhat densely packed, it may be helpful if I conclude by reminding you, in bald summary, of the main things I have been trying to say. Let me set them out in so many successive theses.

1. The freedom which is at issue in the traditional Free Will problem is the freedom which is presupposed in moral responsibility.

2. Critical reflection upon carefully considered attributions of moral responsibility reveals that the only freedom that will do is a freedom which pertains to inner acts of choice, and that these acts must be acts (a) of which the self is *sole* author, and (b) which the self could have performed otherwise.

3. From phenomenological analysis of the situation of moral temptation we find that the self as engaged in this situation is inescapably convinced that it possesses a freedom of precisely the specified kind, located in the decision to exert or withhold the moral effort needed to rise to duty where the pressure of its desiring nature is felt to urge it in a contrary direction.

Passing to the question of the *reality* of this moral freedom which the moral agent believes himself to possess, we argued:

4. Of the two types of Determinist criticism which seem to have most influence today, that based on the predictability of much human behaviour fails to touch a Libertarianism which confines the area of free will as above indicated. Libertarianism so understood is compatible with all the predictability that the empirical facts warrant. And:

5. The second main type of criticism, which alleges the 'meaninglessness' of an act which is the self's act and which is yet not determined by the self's character, is based on a failure to appreciate that the standpoint of inner experience is not only legitimate but indispensable where what is at issue is the reality and nature of a subjective activity. The creative act of moral decision is inevitably meaningless to the mere external observer; but from the inner standpoint it is as real, and as significant, as anything in human experience.

11

GILBERT RYLE

---

introduction

The problem of fatalism is similar to, but distinct from, the problem of free will, as these are understood in modern philosophy. The problem of free will, as we have seen, is that of trying to reconcile the generally accepted belief that all events are causally determined with the equally accepted view that people sometimes act freely, in the sense that they could have avoided doing what they actually did. The problem of fatalism, on the other hand, is that of trying to reconcile the generally accepted belief that all statements are either true or are false with the view that, in the sense just described, people sometimes act freely.

The fatalist thesis has nothing to do with cause and effect; it has to do, instead, with true and false. And it emerges from the following straightforward reflection: In the case of every event that actually happens, including every action you perform, it is true forever after that it did happen, and it was true forever before that it was going to happen. But if it was always true that it was going to happen, how could it have been avoided? If it was true a hundred years ago that you were going to perform yesterday the very actions you did perform, and no others, and that you were going to perform tomorrow the very actions that you will perform, and no others, then how could you have avoided doing yesterday the things you did then? And how can you consider avoidable the actions of tomorrow?

Gilbert Ryle's method of dealing with this problem is to talk *about* it, from a variety of viewpoints, in the effort to expose every subtlety and every type of confusion that can arise from it. We have already seen how he applies the same method to the mind-body problem. Ryle's conviction is that when a philosophical problem is entirely unraveled, or some philosophical thesis is minutely dissected, then we can see for ourselves in what direction the truth lies without being taken in by subtle dialectic. He does not, then, really *rebut* philosophical arguments with alternative arguments, but instead he tries to elicit the absurdities in the presuppositions of this or that philosophical theory.

Here he insists that what we are concerned with is predictions or guesses and not, in the ordinary sense, with statements. We sometimes guess what is going to happen, or hazard predictions, but these are not quite the same as solemn statements that already have the properties of *true* or *false* inhering in them. A guess can be lucky, or turn out to be correct, without being, strictly speaking, true when hazarded. Similarly, a prediction can be fulfilled without being, strictly speaking, already true when first made. Furthermore, the correctness or incorrectness of such an utterance about the future does not by itself influence that future. If I guess that something is going to happen, and then it does, then my guess is shown to have been correct—but its correctness is not what brought about the event that showed it to have been right. If a man falls dead from a bullet wound, what brings about his death is the wound, and not any prediction that he was going to die in that fashion. I can command someone to shoot, and thus bring about a shooting; but my merely guessing or predicting that something like that is going to happen does not bring it about. On the contrary, the occurrence of the event brings it about that the prediction is fulfilled.

Although Ryle's observations on this question are indisputable, a very perceptive reader will note that he has not really solved the problem. He has given us a great array of good reasons why we should not be fatalists. But the *problem* was that of reconciling two generally held beliefs—namely, (a) that every statement, and hence every prediction or guess, is either true or false, and (b) that our actions are sometimes freely performed, in the sense that we could have avoided doing some of the things that we did. Ryle in effect has rejected the first of these beliefs, declaring that some statements about the future, certain guesses and predictions, are not either true or false when made. They become fulfilled, and are thus forever afterward true, or fail to become fulfilled, and are thus forever afterward false, having been, antecedently, neither. This suggestion, whether or not it is correct, amounts to rejecting one of the presuppositions upon which the thesis of fatalism rests—but without really showing why it should be rejected.

Gilbert Ryle is the author of an earlier selection in this volume. His discussions of certain technicalities that have little bearing on the central point have been omitted.

The Refutation of Fatalism*

At a certain moment yesterday evening I coughed and at a certain moment yesterday evening I went to bed. It was therefore true on Saturday that on Sunday I would cough at the one moment and go to bed at the other. Indeed, it was true a thousand years ago that at certain moments on a certain Sunday a thousand years later I should cough and go to bed. But if it was true beforehand—forever beforehand—that I was to cough and go to bed at those two moments on Sunday, 25 January 1953, then it was impossible for me not to do so. There would be a contradiction in the joint assertion that it was true that I would do something at a certain time and that I did not do it. This argument is perfectly general. Whatever anyone ever does, whatever happens anywhere to anything, could not *not* be done or happen, if it was true beforehand that it was going to be done or was going to happen. So everything, including everything that we do, has been definitively booked from any earlier date you like to choose. Whatever is, was to be. So nothing that does occur could have been helped and nothing that has not actually been done could possibly have been done.

This point, that for whatever takes place it was antecedently true that it was going to take place, is sometimes picturesquely expressed by saying that the Book of Destiny has been written up in full from the beginning of time. A thing's actually taking place is, so to speak, merely the turning up of a passage that has for all time been written. This picture has led some fatalists to suppose that God, if there is one, or, we ourselves, if suitably favoured, may have access to this book and read ahead. But this is a fanciful embellishment upon what in itself is a severe and seemingly rigorous argument. We may call it 'the fatalist argument'.

Now the conclusion of this argument from antecedent truth, namely that nothing can be helped, goes directly counter to the piece of common knowledge that some things are our own fault, that some threatening disasters can be foreseen and averted, and that there is plenty of room for precautions, planning and weighing alternatives. Even when we say nowadays of someone that he is born to be hanged or not born to be drowned, we say it as a humorous archaism. We really think that it depends very much on himself whether he is hanged or not, and that his chances of drowning are greater if he refuses to learn to swim. Yet even we are not altogether proof against the fatalist view of things. In a battle I may well come to the half-belief that either there exists somewhere behind the enemy lines a bullet with my name on it, or there does not, so that taking cover is either of no avail or else unnecessary. In card-games and at the roulette-table it is easy to subside into

*From Gilbert Ryle, " 'It Was to Be,' " in *Dilemmas*. Copyright 1954. Reprinted by permission of Cambridge University Press.

the frame of mind of fancying that our fortunes are in some way prearranged, well though we know that it is silly to fancy this.

But how can we deny that whatever happens was booked to happen from all eternity? What is wrong with the argument from antecedent truth to the inevitability of what the antecedent truths are antecedently true about? For it certainly is logically impossible for a prophecy to be true and yet the event prophesied not to come about.

We should notice first of all that the premiss of the argument does not require that anyone, even God, *knows* any of these antecedent truths, or to put it picturesquely, that the Book of Destiny has been written by anybody or could be perused by anybody. This is just what distinguishes the pure fatalist argument from the mixed theological argument for predestination. This latter argument does turn on the supposition that God at least has foreknowledge of what is to take place, and perhaps also preordains it. But the pure fatalist argument turns only on the principle that it was true that a given thing would happen, before it did happen, i.e. that what is, was to be; not that it was known by anyone that it was to be. Yet even when we try hard to bear this point in mind, it is very easy inadvertently to reinterpret this initial principle into the supposition that before the thing happened it was known by someone that it was booked to happen. For there is something intolerably vacuous in the idea of the eternal but unsupported pre-existence of truths in the future tense. When we say 'a thousand years ago it was true that I should now be saying what I am', it is so difficult to give any body to this 'it' of which we say that it was then true, that we unwittingly fill it out with the familiar body of an expectation which someone once entertained, or of a piece of foreknowledge which someone once possessed. Yet to do this is to convert a principle which was worrying because, in a way, totally truistic, into a supposition which is unworrying because quasi-historical, entirely without evidence and most likely just false.

Very often, though certainly not always, when we say 'it was true that. . .' or 'it is false that. . .' we are commenting on some actual pronouncement made or opinion held by some identifiable person. Sometimes we are commenting in a more general way on a thing which some people, unidentified and perhaps unidentifiable, have believed or now believe. We can comment on the belief in the Evil Eye without being able to name anyone who held it; we know that plenty of people did hold it. Thus we can say 'it was true' or 'it is false' in passing verdicts upon the pronouncements both of named and of nameless authors. But in the premiss of the fatalist argument, namely that it was true before something happened that it would happen, there is no implication of anyone, named or unnamed, having made that prediction.

There remains a third thing that might be meant by 'it was true a thousand years ago that a thousand years later these things would be being said in this place', namely that *if* anybody had made a prediction to this effect, though doubtless nobody did, he would have been right. It is not a case of an actual prediction having come true but of a conceivable prediction having come true. The event has not made an actual prophecy come true. It has made a might-have-been prophecy come true.

Or can we say even this? A target can be hit by an actual bullet, but can it be hit by a might-have-been bullet? Or should we rather say only that it could have been hit by a might-have-been bullet? The historical-sounding phrases 'came true', 'made true' and 'was fulfilled' apply well enough to predictions actually made, but there is a detectable twist, which may be an illegitimate twist, in saying that a might-have-been prediction did come true or was made true by the event. If an unbacked horse wins a race, we can say that it would have won money for its backers, if only there had been any. But we cannot say that it did win money for its backers, if only there had been any. There is no answer to the question 'How much money did it win for them?' Correspondingly, we cannot with a clear conscience say of an event that it has fulfilled the predictions of it which could have been made, but only that it would have fulfilled any predictions of it which might have been made. There is no answer to the question 'Within what limits of precision were these might-have-been predictions correct about the time and the loudness of my cough?'

Let us consider the notions of truth and falsity. In characterizing somebody's statement, for example a statement in the future tense, as true or as false, we usually though not always, mean to convey rather more than that what was forecast did or did not take place. There is something of a slur in 'false' and something honorific in 'true', some suggestion of the insincerity or sincerity of its author, or some suggestion of his rashness or cautiousness as an investigator. This is brought out by our reluctance to characterize either as true or as false pure and avowed guesses. If you make a guess at the winner of the race, it will turn out right or wrong, correct or incorrect, but hardly true or false. These epithets are inappropriate to avowed guesses, since the one epithet pays an extra tribute, the other conveys an extra adverse criticism of the maker of the guess, neither of which can he merit. In guessing there is no place for sincerity or insincerity, or for caution or rashness in investigation. To make a guess is not to give an assurance and it is not to declare the result of an investigation. Guessers are neither reliable nor unreliable.

Doubtless we sometimes use 'true' without intending any connotation of trustworthiness and, much less often, 'false' without any connotation of trust misplaced. But, for safety's sake, let us reword the fatalist argument in terms of these thinner words, 'correct' and 'incorrect'. It would now run as follows. For any event that takes place, an antecedent guess, if anyone had made one, that it was going to take place, would have been correct, and an antecedent guess to the contrary, if anyone had made it, would have been incorrect. This formulation already sounds less alarming than the original formulation. The word 'guess' cuts out the covert threat of foreknowledge, or of there being budgets of antecedent forecasts, all meriting confidence before the event. What, now, of the notion of guesses in the future tense being correct or incorrect?

Antecedently to the running of most horse-races, some people guess that one horse will win, some that another will. Very often every horse has its backers. If, then, the race is run and won, then some of the backers will have guessed correctly and the rest will have guessed incorrectly. To say that someone's guess that Eclipse would win was correct is to say no more than that he guessed that Eclipse would win and Eclipse did win. But can we say in retrospect that his guess, which he made before the race, was already correct before the race? He made the correct guess two days ago, but was his guess correct during those two days? It certainly was not incorrect during those two days, but it does not follow, though it might seem to follow, that it was correct during those two days. Perhaps we feel unsure which we ought to say, whether that his guess was correct during those two days, though no one could know it to be so, or only that, as it turned out, it was during those two days going to prove correct, i.e. that the victory which did, in the event, make it correct had not yet happened. A prophecy is not fulfilled until the event forecast has happened. Just here is where 'correct' resembles 'fulfilled' and differs importantly from 'true'. The honorific connotations of 'true' can certainly attach to a person's forecasts from the moment at which they are made, so that if these forecasts turn out incorrect, while we withdraw the word 'true', we do not necessarily withdraw the testimonials which it carried. The establishment of incorrectness certainly cancels 'true' but not, as a rule, so fiercely as to incline us to say 'false'.

The words 'true' and 'false' and the words 'correct' and 'incorrect' are adjectives, and this grammatical fact tempts us to suppose that trueness and falseness, correctness and incorrectness, and even, perhaps, fulfilledness and unfulfilledness must be qualities or properties resident in the propositions which they characterize. As sugar is sweet and white from the moment it comes into existence to the moment when it goes out of existence, so we are tempted to infer, by parity of reasoning, that the trueness or correctness of predictions and guesses must be features or properties which belong all the time to their possessors, whether we can detect their presence in them or not. But if we consider that 'deceased', 'lamented' and 'extinct' are also adjectives, and yet certainly do not apply to people or mastodons while they exist, but only after they have ceased to exist, we may feel more cordial towards the idea that 'correct' is in a partly similar way a merely obituary and valedictory epithet, as 'fulfilled' more patently is. It is more like a verdict than a description. So when I tell you that if anyone had guessed that Eclipse would win today's race his guess would have turned out correct, I give you

no more information about the past than is given by the evening newspaper
which tells you that Eclipse won the race.

I want now to turn to the fatalist conclusion, namely that since whatever is
was to be, therefore nothing can be helped. The argument seems to compel
us to say that since the antecedent truth requires the event of which it is the
true forecast, therefore this event is in some disastrous way fettered to or
driven by or bequeathed by that antecedent truth—as if my coughing last
night was made or obliged to occur by the antecedent truth that it was going
to occur, perhaps in something like the way in which gunfire makes the
windows rattle a moment or two after the discharge. What sort of necessity
would this be?

To bring this out let us by way of contrast suppose that someone produced
the strictly parallel argument, that for everything that happens, it is true for
ever *afterwards* that it happened.

I coughed last night, so it is true today and will be true a thousand years
hence that I coughed last night. But these posterior truths in the past tense,
could not be true without my having coughed. Therefore my coughing was
necessitated or obliged to have happened by the truth of these posterior
chronicles of it. Clearly something which disturbed us in the original form of
the argument is missing in this new form. We cheerfully grant that the
occurrence of an event involves and is involved by the truth of subsequent
records, actual or conceivable, to the effect that it occurred. For it does not
even seem to render the occurrence a product or effect of these truths about
it. On the contrary, in this case we are quite clear that it is the occurrence
which makes the posterior truths about it true, not the posterior truths
which make the occurrence occur. These posterior truths are shadows cast
by the events, not the events shadows cast by these truths about them, since
these belong to the posterity, not to the ancestry of the events.

Why does the fact that a posterior truth about an occurrence requires that
occurrence not worry us in the way in which the fact that an anterior truth
about an occurrence requires that occurrence does worry us? Why does the
slogan 'Whatever is, always was to be' seem to imply that nothing can be
helped, where the obverse slogan 'Whatever is, will always have been' does
not seem to imply this? We are not exercised by the notorious fact that when
the horse has already escaped it is too late to shut the stable door. We are
sometimes exercised by the idea that as the horse is either going to escape or
not going to escape, to shut the stable door beforehand is either unavailing
or unnecessary. A large part of the reason is that in thinking of a predecessor
making its successor necessary we unwittingly assimilate the necessitation to
causal necessitation. Gunfire makes windows rattle a few seconds later, but
rattling windows do not make gunfire happen a few seconds earlier, even
though they may be perfect evidence that gunfire did happen a few seconds
earlier. We slide, that is, into thinking of the anterior truths as *causes* of the

happenings about which they were true, where the mere matter of their relative dates saves us from thinking of happenings as the effects of those truths about them which are posterior to them. Events cannot be the effects of their successors, any more than we can be the offspring of our posterity.

So let us look more suspiciously at the notions of *necessitating, making, obliging, requiring* and *involving* on which the argument turns. How is the notion of *requiring* or *involving* that we have been working with related to the notion of *causing*?

It is quite true that a backer cannot guess correctly that Eclipse will win without Eclipse winning and still it is quite false that his guessing made or caused Eclipse to win. To say that his guess that Eclipse would win was correct does logically involve or require that Eclipse won. To assert the one and deny the other would be to contradict oneself. To say that the backer guessed correctly is just to say that the horse which he guessed would win, did win. The one assertion cannot be true without the other assertion being true. But in this way in which one truth may require or involve another truth, an event cannot be one of the implications of a truth. Events can be effects, but they cannot be implications. Truths can be consequences of other truths, but they cannot be causes of effects or effects of causes.

In much the same way, the truth that someone revoked involves the truth that he had in his hand at least one card of the suit led. But he was not forced or coerced into having a card of that suit in his hand by the fact that he revoked. He could not both have revoked and not had a card of that suit in his hand, but this 'could not' does not connote any kind of duress. A proposition can imply another proposition, but it cannot thrust a card into a player's hand. The questions, what makes things happen, what prevents them from happening, and whether we can help them or not, are entirely unaffected by the logical truism that a statement to the effect that something happens, is correct if and only if it happens. Lots of things could have prevented Eclipse from winning the race; lots of other things could have made his lead a longer one. But one thing had no influence on the race at all, namely the fact that if anyone guessed that he would win, he guessed correctly.

We are now in a position to separate out one unquestionable and very dull true proposition from another exciting but entirely false proposition, both of which seem to be conveyed by the slogan 'What is, always was to be'. It is an unquestionable and very dull truth that for anything that happens, if anyone had at any previous time made the guess that it would happen, his guess would have turned out correct. The twin facts that the event could not take place without such a guess turning out correct and that such a guess could not turn out correct without the event taking place tell us nothing whatsoever about how the event was caused, whether it could have been prevented, or even whether it could have been predicted with certainty or probability from what had happened before. The menacing statement that what is was to be, construed in one way, tells us only the trite truth that if it is true to say (*a*) that something happened, then it is also true to say (*b*) that that original statement (*a*) is true, no matter when this latter comment (*b*) on the former statement (*a*) may be made.

The exciting but false proposition that the slogan seems to force upon us is that whatever happens is inevitable or doomed, and, what makes it sound even worse, *logically* inevitable or *logically* doomed—somewhat as it is logically inevitable that the immediate successor of any even number is an odd number. So what does 'inevitable' mean? An avalanche may be, for all practical purposes, unavoidable. A mountaineer in the direct path of an avalanche can himself do nothing to stop the avalanche or get himself out of its way, though a providential earthquake might conceivably divert the avalanche or a helicopter might conceivably lift him out of danger. His position is much worse, but only much worse, than that of a cyclist half a mile ahead of a lumbering steam-roller. It is extremely unlikely that the steam-roller will catch up with him at all, and even if it does so it is extremely likely that its driver will halt or that the cyclist himself will move off in good time. But these differences between the plights of the mountaineer and the cyclist are differences of degree only. The avalanche is practically unavoidable, but it is not logically inevitable. Only conclusions can be logically inevitable, given the premises, and an avalanche is not a conclusion. The fatalist doctrine, by contrast, is that everything is absolutely and logically inevitable in a way in which the avalanche is not absolutely or logically inevitable; that we are all absolutely and logically powerless where even the hapless mountaineer is only in a desperate plight and the cyclist is in no real danger at all; that everything is fettered by the Law of Contradiction to taking the course it does take, as odd numbers are bound to succeed even numbers. What sort of fetters are these purely logical fetters?

Certainly there are infinitely many cases of one truth making necessary the truth of another proposition. The truth that today is Monday makes necessary the truth of the proposition that tomorrow is Tuesday. It cannot be Monday today without tomorrow being Tuesday. A person who said 'It is Monday today but not Tuesday tomorrow' would be taking away with his left hand what he was giving with his right hand. But in the way in which some truths carry other truths with them or make them necessary, events themselves cannot be made necessary by truths. Things and events may be the topics of premisses and conclusions, but they cannot themselves be premisses or conclusions. You may preface a statement by the word 'therefore', but you cannot pin either a 'therefore' or a 'perhaps not' on to a person or an avalanche. It is a partial parallel to say that while a sentence may contain or may be without a split infinitive, a road accident cannot either contain or lack a split infinitive, even though it is what a lot of sentences, with or without split infinitives in them, are about. It is true that an avalanche may be practically inescapable and the conclusion of an argument may be logically inescapable, but the avalanche has not got—nor does it lack—the inescapability of the conclusion of an argument. The fatalist theory tries to endue happenings with the inescapability of the conclusions of valid arguments. Our familiarity with the practical inescapability of some things, like some avalanches, helps us to yield to the view that really everything that happens is inescapable, only not now in the way in which some avalanches are inescapable and others not, but in the way in which logical consequences are inescapable, given their premises. The fatalist has tried to characterize happenings by predicates which are proper only to conclusions of arguments. He tried to flag my cough with a Q.E.D. . . .

Now for some general morals which can be drawn from the existence of this dilemma and from attempts to resolve it. It arose out of two seemingly innocent and unquestionable propositions, propositions which are so well embedded in what I may vaguely call 'common knowledge' that we should hardly wish to give them the grand title of 'theories'. These two propositions were, first, that some statements in the future tense are or come true, and, second, that we often can and sometimes should secure that certain things do happen and that certain other things do not happen. Neither of these innocent-seeming propositions is as yet a philosopher's speculation, or even a scientist's hypothesis or a theologian's doctrine. They are just platitudes. We should, however, notice that it would not very often occur to anyone to state these platitudes. People say of this particular prediction that it was fulfilled and of that particular guess that it turned out correct. To say that some statements in the future tense are true is a generalization of these particular concrete comments. But it is a generalization which there is not usually any point in propounding. Similarly people say of particular offences that they ought not to have been committed and of particular catastrophes that they could or could not have been prevented. It is relatively rare to stand back and say in general terms that people sometimes do wrong and that mishaps are sometimes our own fault. None the less, there are occasions, long before philosophical or scientific speculations begin, on which people do deliver generalities of these sorts. It is part of the business of the teacher and the preacher, of the judge and the doctor, of Solon and Æsop, to say general things, with concrete examples of which everyone is entirely familiar. In one way the generality is not and cannot be news to anyone that everyday has its yesterday and every day has its tomorrow; and yet, in another way, this can be a sort of news. There was the first occasion on which this generality was presented to us, and very surprising it was—despite the fact that on every day since infancy we had thought about its particular yesterday and its particular tomorrow. There is, anyhow at the start, an important sort of unfamiliarity about such generalizations of the totally familiar. We do not yet know how we should and how we should not operate with them, although we know quite well how to operate with the daily particularities of which they are the generalizations. We make no foot-faults on Monday morning with 'will be' and 'was'; but when required to deal in the general case with the notions of *the future* and *the past*, we are no longer sure of our feet.

The two platitudes from which the trouble arose are not in direct conflict with one another. It is real or seeming deductions from the one which quarrel with the other, or else with real or seeming deductions from it. They are not rivals such that before these deductions had been noticed anyone would want to say 'I accept the proposition that some statements in the future tense are fulfilled, so naturally I reject the proposition that some things need not and should not have happened'. It is because the former proposition seems indirectly to entail that what is was from all eternity going to be and because this, in its turn, seems to entail that nothing is anybody's fault, that some thinkers have felt forced to make a choice between the two platitudes. Aristotle, for example, rejected, with reservations, the platitude that statements in the future tense are true or false. Certain Stoics rejected the platitude that we are responsible for some things that happen. If we accept both platitudes, it is because we think that the fatalist deductions from 'it was true. . .' are fallacious or else that certain deductions drawn from 'some things are our fault' are fallacious, or both. . . .

12

DIODORUS CRONUS

introduction

This terse paper by Cronus is a conundrum, of a kind much enjoyed by philosophers of a certain strange turn of mind. What the author does is postulate certain presuppositions that are almost universally held by philosophers and elicit from them an unwelcome and even irritating conclusion—in this case, the fatalistic thesis that no one can ever perform any actions other than those that he does. That inference here is merely implied; all that is actually asserted is that a certain Stilpo is unable to do at the time referred to anything except what he does: his ability to do anything else is ruled out. But considerations of exactly the same kind can then be applied to the actions of any person at any time—no one is able ever to do anything except what he actually does. And this is exactly the thesis of fatalism.

The argument is extremely logical and precise, and as soon as one begins to see its unwelcome outcome and tries to avoid it, he finds his path blocked. The author forces us, step by step, to his conclusion. If an agent—any agent—performs a given act at a given time, then it is certainly true that he then performs that act. His performing it renders true the statement that he performs it. It is forever afterward true that he then performed it; it is true while he is performing it that he then performs it; and it always was true that

147

he was then going to perform it. After you have done something, then it is, often regrettably, too late to undo it. And while you are actually doing something—passing through a doorway, for instance—then it is too late for you to refrain from doing exactly that at that moment. And—here is the crucial step—even *before* you do something, then you are unable to avoid it, *provided* it is "already true" that you are going to do exactly that at exactly that moment.

Some people, particularly those unaccustomed to rigorous thought, want to say that it is never really true that something happens *until it actually happens*. Until you actually walk through a given doorway, for example, then it is neither true nor false that you are going to do so. It will become true, just in case you go through the door then, and remain true for the rest of eternity, or it will become false, just in case you avoid going through the door then, and remain false for the rest of eternity. And until then it will be neither.

Most philosophers, however, have rejected this position—for three reasons: *First*, it constitutes a rejection of one of the most firmly held presuppositions of rational thought, the law of excluded middle, which is that every meaningful assertion is either true or false, there being no "middle" ground between them. *Second*, the suggestion is arbitrary and question-begging, there being no reason whatever to hold that statements in the future tense differ so radically from statements in the past tense, except to avoid the fatalistic inference. *Third*, no one really believes that statements about the future have this strange characteristic of being neither true nor false anyway. Everyone knows, for example, that he will someday die, that the sun will rise to commence another day, that an eclipse of the sun will occur again, and so on, all of which are statements about future events. And not only are such statements about the future believed by everyone to be true, but sometimes they can be made with great precision— predictions of certain eclipses, for example.

One can, then, wiggle out of fatalism by denying the law of excluded middle, but not without incurring the charge of being philosophically arbitrary and even irrational. And it is not easy to see any other way to wiggle out of it. Most people, to be sure, are content simply with *denying* the thesis of fatalism, which they have every right to do. But that is no more than the right to be irrational. Cronus' challenge is to offer a *reason* for rejecting it. And it is not enough to assert that statements about the future are neither true nor false, if your whole reason is that otherwise the thesis of fatalism would be true. For this is only equivalent to saying you do not wish to be a fatalist. That is your privilege, but hardly an argument.

Diodorus Cronus is a metaphysician and beekeeper who lives in Trumansburg, N.Y. This selection, first published in 1965, is reproduced entire.

The Necessity of Everything
That One Does*

We shall here be concerned with statements of the form '*M* does *A* at *t* ', wherein *M* designates a specific person, *A* a specific action and *t* a specific time. We shall refer to these as R-statements. Thus, 'Someone raised his hand at noon last Tuesday', 'Stilpo raised his hand', and 'Stilpo did something at noon last Tuesday' are none of them R-statements; but 'Stilpo raised his right hand at noon last Tuesday' is an R-statement.

Let us assume that it sometimes at least makes sense to speak of an agent's being able to render an R-statement true, as distinguished, for example, from simply *discovering* that it is true; and similarly, that it sometimes makes sense to speak of his being able to render an R-statement false. Thus, Stilpo could render it true that he is running at a certain time simply by running at that time, and this would be something quite different from his then merely discovering—observing, noting, etc.—that he is running. He could, of course, render the same statement false in a variety of ways—by standing still, for instance, or by lying down, and so on. We, on the other hand, could not in any similar way render *that* R-statement true. We could only discover by some means that it is true, or that it is false—by looking at Stilpo at the time in question, for instance, to *see* whether he is then running.

Further, let us assume that it sometimes at least makes sense to speak of *asking* someone to render an R-statement true. This, of course, is only an application of the general principle that, in the case of something that someone is able to do, it sometimes makes sense to ask him to do it. To illustrate, suppose that Crates has a bet with Metrocles that Stilpo will pass through the Diomean Gate at noon on the following day (call that day D). Now it surely seems to make sense that Crates might ask, and perhaps even bribe, Stilpo to do just that—to pick just that time to pass through the gate—and thus render true the R-statement 'Stilpo passes through the Diomean Gate at noon on day D'. That a request or even a bribe would not be out of place in such circumstances suggests both that it sometimes makes sense to speak of an agent's rendering an R-statement true, and that it sometimes makes sense to ask someone—namely, the agent referred to in such a statement—to do it.

Now it is easy enough to state, in general terms, what one has to do in order to render a given R-statement true. He has to do *precisely* what the statement in question says he does, at precisely the time the statement says he does it. The *only* way Stilpo can render it true that he passes through the Diomean Gate at a specific time is to pass through the gate at just that time. Similarly, the *only* way he can render it false is to refrain from passing

*Diodorus Cronus, "Time, Truth and Ability," *Analysis*, Vol. 25, 1965.

through the gate at just that time. For someone to be *able* to render an R-statement true, then, consists simply of his being able to do something which is *logically* both necessary and sufficient for the truth of the statement to the effect that he does the thing in question at the time in question. Nothing else suffices, and this will need to be borne in mind.

Finally, we shall assume that, in case one speaks truly in uttering a particular R-statement at a particular time, then one also speaks truly in uttering the same R-statement at any other time. If, for example, one were to speak truly in saying that Stilpo is running at noon on a given Tuesday, one would also speak truly if one said the same thing again a week later, or at any other time. This, of course, is only an application of the orthodox assumption that complete statements, or the utterances of them, are not converted from true to false, or from false to true, just by the passage of time. There are some statements, to be sure, like 'Stilpo is running', which are not, as they stand, true every time they are uttered, since it is not always the case that Stilpo is running. But that is not an R-statement. If one adds to it an explicit reference to the time at which Stilpo is alleged to be running—say, at noon on a given Tuesday—then it becomes an R-statement. It also thereby becomes a statement that is true every time it is uttered, in case it is true at all, for one can on Wednesday still say truly that Stilpo was running at noon on the day preceding, in case he was, even though Stilpo may in the meantime have stopped running. This assumption, it should be noted, does not imply that *truth* and *falsity* are 'properties' of 'propositions' that might be gained or lost through the passage of time, nor does it imply that they are not. Some say that they are, others that they are not, and still others that such a notion is meaningless to begin with; but we, at least, prefer to take no stand on that somewhat metaphysical point.

Now let us consider three times, t_1, t_2 and t_3, all of them being *past*, and t_1 being earlier than t_2 which is earlier than t_3. Consider, then, the R-statement (S):

Stilpo walks through the Diomean Gate at t_2

and assume that statement, tenselessly expressed so as to avoid ambiguity in what follows, to be *true*. What we want to consider is: which, if any, of the following, which are not R-statements but are statements concerning Stilpo's abilities, are also true?

1. Stilpo was at t_3 able to render S false.

2. Stilpo was at t_3 able to render S true.

3. Stilpo was at t_1 able to render S false.

4. Stilpo was at t_1 able to render S true.

5. Stilpo was at t_2 able to render S false.

6. Stilpo was at t_2 able to render S true.

Now the first of these is quite evidently false. If, as assumed, it is true that Stilpo was walking through the gate at t_2, then there is absolutely nothing he (or anyone) was able to do at t_3 which could render that statement false. It was, it would seem natural to say, by that time *too late* for that. He was perhaps able at t_3 to refrain from passing through the gate again, of course, and he was perhaps able to regret that he had walked through it, to wish he had not, and so on, but his doing any of those things would not have the least tendency to render S false. Or we might think that he was at t_3 able to find conclusive evidence that he had *not* walked through the gate; but that is not in fact anything that he was able to do, for he had already walked through the gate, and hence there was at t_3 no conclusive evidence to the contrary that he could possibly find.

The second statement seems also to be clearly false. S is, we said, true. So if anyone were, at t_2 (or any other time), to assert S, he would then be speaking truly. No sense, then, can be made of Stilpo's subsequently undertaking to *render* it true. It is in this case not only too late for him to do anything about that; it is also superfluous. What he wants to do—to render S true—he has already done.

The truth or falsity of the third statement is not quite so obvious, but it certainly appears to be false, and for the same kind of reason that (1) is false. That is, if it is true that Stilpo was walking through the gate at t_2, then it is difficult to see what he (or anyone) was able to do at t_1 which might render that statement false. Analogously to the foregoing remarks one might say, though it seems less natural to do so, that it was at that time *"too early"* for that. Stilpo was perhaps able at t_1 to refrain from then and there walking through the gate, to be sure, and perhaps he did then refrain, but that does not in the least affect the truth of S, which says nothing about what he was doing at t_1. Or we might think that he was, at t_1 able to find some conclusive evidence or indication that he was not going to walk through the gate at t_2, but that again is not anything he was able to do; for he did walk through the gate at t_2, and hence there was at t_1 no conclusive indication to the contrary that he could possibly have found.

To have been able at t_1 to render S false, Stilpo would have to have been able at t_1 to do something that would have been *logically* sufficient for the falsity of S. But nothing that he might have done at t_1 has the least logical relevance to the truth or falsity of S. We might, to be sure, suppose that he was able at t_1 firmly to resolve not to walk through the gate at t_2, but his making such a resolve would not be sufficient for the falsity of S. In fact, it has no logical relevance to S, which is, in any case, true.

Perhaps, then, Stilpo was able at t_1 to do something which would have been causally or physically sufficient for the falsity of S—to commit suicide, for example. Actually, this suggestion is irrelevent, for we have said that one renders an R-statement false only by doing something that is *logically* sufficient for its falsity. But even if it were relevant, it would not do. What is behind this suggestion is, obviously, that it is physically impossible that

Stilpo should be walking through the gate at t_2 in case he killed himself at t_1. This is of course true—but if so, then it is *also* true that it was physically impossible that Stilpo should have killed himself at t_1 in case he was walking through the gate at t_2—and we have said from the start that he *was* then walking through the gate. The only conclusion, then, is that (3) is false, even on this enlarged and still irrelevant conception of what is involved in rendering an R-statement false.

The fourth statement appears false for reasons similar to those given for the falsity of (2). Namely, that S is true, or such that if anyone had uttered S at t_1 he would then have spoken truly. No sense, then, can be made of Stilpo's being able to do something at t_1 to *render* it true. There would have been no point, for example, in his passing through the gate at t_1, for that would certainly not by itself render it true that he was still passing through the gate at t_2. Similarly, it would not have been enough for him simply to have resolved at t_1 to pass through the gate at t_2, for that would have been entirely compatible with the falsity of S, which in any case neither says nor implies anything whatsoever about Stilpo's resolutions. Men do not always act upon their resolves anyway, and there is in any case no logical necessity in their doing so. Besides, anything Stilpo might do at t_1 would be superfluous, even if it were not pointless, for one can no more render true a statement that is true than he can render hard a piece of clay that is hard. He can only verify that it *is* true, and this, we have seen, is something quite different. Anything Stilpo does at t_1, or is able to do then, is entirely wasted.

The fifth statement likewise appears to be false. If, as we are assuming, it is true that Stilpo was passing through the gate at t_2, then it is quite impossible to see what he might be able then and there to do, in addition to passing through the gate, which would, if done, render that statement false. Indeed, it is logically impossible that there should be any such supplementary action, for no matter what it was, it would have no tendency to render S false. Even if Stilpo were to declare, most gravely and emphatically, that he was not passing through the gate, this would not render it false that he was—it would only render him a liar. A condition logically sufficient for the truth of S—namely, Stilpo's walking through the gate—already obtains at t_2, and can by no means be conjoined with another condition logically sufficient for the falsity of that statement. Now Stilpo might, to be sure, suddenly *stop* walking through the gate, which we can for now assume that he is able to do, but this would not in the least alter the truth of S. On the contrary, unless he were walking through the gate at t_2, and unless, accordingly, S were true, he could not then *stop* walking. His ceasing to walk would only render it false that he was walking shortly after t_2; and this is hardly inconsistent with S.

The sixth statement, finally, appears, unlike the others, to be quite evidently true in one seemingly trivial sense, but nonsensical in another. The sense in which it is true is simply this: that if S is true, then it follows that

Stilpo was able to be walking through the gate at t₂, that being, in fact, precisely what he was doing. It is not clear, however, what sense can be attached to his being able to render true what is true, just as it is not clear what sense could be made of someone's rendering hard some clay that is already hard.

If a piece of clay is hard we cannot sensibly ask anyone to *render* it hard. Similarly, if Stilpo is walking through the gate we cannot sensibly ask him to render it true that he is walking through the gate. We cannot sensibly ask him to *be* walking through the gate, for he is already doing that, and our request would be otiose and absurd, like asking a man who is sitting to be sitting, or one who is talking to be talking. We cannot ask him to *continue* walking through the gate, for that would not be to the point. It would, if done, only render it true that he was still walking through the gate at some time *after* t₂, which is not what we are after. And obviously, there is nothing else we could ask him to do which is anywhere to the point.

The only conclusion we can draw is that, of the six statements before us, those that make clear sense are all false, and the only one that is true makes only trivial and dubious sense. More generally, we can say that while it might, as we assumed at the beginning, make sense to speak of being able to render an R-statement true, or being able to render such a statement false, men can in fact only render true those R-statements that are true, and can only render false those that are false, and that these latter two conceptions themselves make very dubious sense.

IV

Where Am I?

THE WORLD AND TIME

13

ST. AUGUSTINE

introduction

St. Augustine, besides being a great theologian and church father, was a remarkable philosopher. Deeply influenced by the tradition of Platonism before his conversion to Christianity, he was largely responsible for transmitting it, through the Church, to every generation since.

The following passages from the eleventh book of his *Confessions* beautifully illustrate the metaphysical puzzlement that arises in every truly philosophical mind. The question of what God might have been doing before he created the world leads the theologian straight into the metaphysics of time. What is it? How can it exist at all? How can it be measured? What is its relation to eternity? and to motion?

St. Augustine's puzzlement over these questions is of exactly the sort that anyone might feel, and he is never able really to resolve it. We speak, for example, of times that are longer and shorter—of a long period of years, for example, or of the short time needed to pronounce a syllable. But how can any future time be long or short, when no such time actually exists? To say of anything that it is future, is to say that it does not yet exist. How, then, can it have size? And if this is somehow possible, then how can it be measured, when we, who would measure it, are so clearly confined to the present? Similarly for past times. How can they be long or short, when they do not exist and never will?

If we say that past times were once present, and could then, while present, be measured, we have to take account of the fact that no large amount of time can ever have been present. All that is present is the briefest imaginable moment. And if we consider that moment to be but a part of a larger interval, some of it extending into the future and some of it into the past, then our original problem comes back to us: That which is past or future does not really exist, and what does not exist can in no way be a part of what does. What is past did once exist, and what is future will exist; but by the time we have measured the former, and declared it to be part of the present, it has ceased, and the latter cannot be measured and declared to be a part of anything until it has become real. The only thing in time that actually exists is, in fact, the present, and this is not only too small to be measured, it also ceases to exist the very instant after it has come into being, and is therefore too elusive to measure or do anything with at all.

At the bottom of this mystery of time, which seemed to St. Augustine the deepest of all metaphysical mysteries, is the presumption that time *moves* — from the future into the present and then into an endless and ever growing past. To say that it moves from the future however, is to imply that it already *is* the future, which amounts to saying that it *is not*—that as yet it has no reality at all. Similar reflections apply to times past. And anyway, how can time be moving, when to speak of anything as moving is to presuppose a time within which it moves? Shall we say, then, that time does *not* move? But what could be more obvious than that times future—tomorrow, for example—will become present, and then be added forever to the past, never to be revived? And what is that, if not to say that time is moving?

Every answer to such questions seems simply to raise new questions. Suppose, for example, we say that time is nothing but the regular motions of the sun and the moon and the heavens. These we understand, at least in a general way; so if time is identical with them, then we can just talk about these motions, with less mystery. But what, St. Augustine wonders, if those motions should cease—what if the sun stood still, and the moon and the heavens too? In modern terms, what if the earth ceased its rotation— something that is not likely to happen, of course, but is perfectly easy to imagine. Would time then cease? If so, for how long? For as long as those motions ceased? But that is to speak of the passage of time! Moreover, while time should in that sense stand still, can we not imagine a potter's wheel turning? And might it not turn faster or slower? And does this not clearly show that the passage of time is quite independent of the motions of the heavenly bodies and, indeed, of every other motion? For even if *all* motion should cease, we would have to suppose it to cease *for a certain length of time*; for otherwise we can give no meaning to the idea of its *ceasing*. But that is surely to suppose that, while motion might cease, time would not.

What, furthermore, are the units into which time is measured? Are they hours, days, weeks, years, and intervals of this sort? But we do not really know what any such length of time is. Suppose we say, for example, that a day is the interval of time between two successive sunrises. What, then, if the sun should complete its circuit of the heavens more rapidly than heretofore? What if, for example, (in modern terms) the speed of the earth's rotation should double? Would the sun not then rise twice a day? Or if not, then wouldn't the interval we were calling "one day" be only half as long as before? Then how long, really, is such an interval? Or do we perhaps not really know what we are saying when we speak thus?

Time, St. Augustine says, is one thing, and the motion of bodies is another; and however closely they may be related, we do not really know what time is. If no one asks, then we feel that we know, but as soon as we try to express our knowledge in words, we fall helpless and realize that we do not know.

St. Augustine, the Bishop of Hippo, died in A.D. 430 at the age of 76. He bore much of the responsibility of transmitting to the Middle Ages, through his theological and philosophical writings, the philosophical and cultural ideals of antiquity.

The Paradoxes of Time*

See, I answer him that asketh, "What did God before He *made heaven and earth?*" I answer not as one is said to have done merrily, (eluding the pressure of the question,) "He was preparing hell (saith he) for pryers into mysteries." It is one thing to answer enquiries, another to make sport of enquirers. So I answer not; for rather had I answer, "I know not," what I know not, that so as to raise a laugh at him who asketh deep things and gain praise for one who answereth false things. But I say that Thou, our God, art the Creator of every creature: and if by the name "heaven and earth," every creature be understood; I boldly say, "that before God made heaven and earth, He did not make anything." For if He made, what did He make but a creature? And would I knew whatsoever I desire to know to my profit, as I know, that no creature was made, before there was made any creature.

But if any excursive brain rove over the images of forepassed times, and wonder that Thou the God Almighty and All-creating and All-supporting, Maker of heaven and earth, didst for innumerable ages forbear from so great a work, before Thou wouldest make it; let him awake and consider, that he wonders at false conceits. For whence could innumerable ages pass by, which Thou madest not, Thou the Author and Creator of all ages? or what

*From St. Augustine, *Confessions*, trans. E. B. Pusey. An Everyman's Library Edition. Published in the United States by E. P. Dutton & Co., Inc., and reprinted by their permission.

times should there be, which were not made by Thee? or how should they pass by, if they never were? Seeing then Thou art the Creator of all times, if any time was before Thou *madest heaven and earth*, why say they that Thou didst forego working? For that very time didst Thou make, nor could time pass by, before Thou madest those times. But if before *heaven and earth* there was no time, why is it demanded, what Thou then didst? For there was no "then," when there was no time.

Nor dost Thou by time, precede time: else shouldest Thou not precede all times. But Thou precedest all things past, by the sublimity of an everpresent eternity; and surpassest all future because they are future, and when they come, they shall be past; *but Thou art the Same, and Thy years fail not*. Thy years neither come nor go; whereas ours both come and go, that they all may come. Thy years stand together, because they do stand; nor are departing thrust out by coming years, for they pass not away; but ours shall all be, when they shall no more be. Thy years are one day; and Thy day is not daily, but To-day, seeing Thy To-day gives not place unto to-morrow, for neither doth it replace yesterday. Thy To-day, is Eternity; therefore didst Thou beget the Coeternal, to whom Thou saidst, *This day have I begotten Thee*. Thou hast made all things; and before all times Thou art: neither in any time was time not.

At no time then hadst Thou not made any thing, because time itself Thou madest. And no times are coeternal with Thee, because Thou abidest; but if they abode, they should not be times. For what is time? Who can readily and briefly explain this? Who can even in thought comprehend it, so as to utter a word about it? But what in discourse do we mention more familiarly and knowingly, than time? And, we understand, when we speak of it; we understand also, when we hear it spoken of by another. What then is time? If no one asks me, I know: if I wish to explain it to one that asketh, I know not: yet I say boldly, that I know, that if nothing passed away, time past were not; and if nothing were coming, a time to come were not; and if nothing were, time present were not. Those two times then, past and to come, how are they, seeing the past now is not, and that to come is not yet? But the present, should it always be present, and never pass into time past, verily it should not be time, but eternity. If time present (if it is to be time) only cometh into existence, because it passeth into time past, how can we say that either this is, whose cause of being is, that it shall not be; so, namely, that we cannot truly say that time is, but because it is tending not to be?

And yet we say, "a long time" and "a short time;" still, only of time past or to come. A long time past (for example) we call an hundred years since; and a long time to come, an hundred years hence. But a short time past, we call (suppose) ten days since; and a short time to come, ten days hence. But in what sense is that long or short, which is not? For the past, is not now; and the future, is not yet. Let us not then say, "it is long;" but of the past, "it hath been long;" and of the future, "it will be long." O my Lord, my Light, shall not here also Thy Truth mock at man? For that past time which was long, was it long when it was now past, or when it was yet present? For then might it be long, when there was, what could be long; but when past, it was no longer; wherefore neither could that be long, which was not at all. Let us not then say, "time past hath been long:" for we shall not find, what hath been long, seeing that since it was past, it is no more; but let us say, "that present time was long;" because, when it was present, it was long. For it had not yet passed away, so as not to be; and therefore there was, what could be long; but after it was past, that ceased also to be long, which ceased to be.

Let us see then, thou soul of man, whether present time can be long: for to thee it is given to feel and to measure length of time. What wilt thou answer me? Are an hundred years, when present, a long time? See first, whether an hundred years can be present. For if the first of these years be now current, it is present, but the other ninety and nine are to come, and therefore are not yet, but if the second year be current, one is now past, another present, the rest to come. And so if we assume any middle year of this hundred to be present, all before it, are past; all after it, to come; wherefore an hundred years cannot be present. But see at least whether that one which is now current, itself is present; for if the current month be its first, the rest are to come; if the second, the first is already past, and the rest are not yet. Therefore, neither is the year now current present; and if not present as a whole, then is not the year present. For twelve months are a year; of which whatever be the current month is present; the rest past, or to come. Although neither is that current month present; but one day only; the rest being to come, if it be the first; past, if the last; if any of the middle, then amid past and to come.

See how the present time, which alone we found could be called long, is abridged to the length scarce of one day. But let us examine that also; because neither is one day present as a whole. For it is made up of four and twenty hours of night and day: of which, the first hath the rest to come; the last hath them past; and any of the middle hath those before it past, those behind it to come. Yea, that one hour passeth away in flying particles. Whatsoever of it hath flown away, is past; whatsoever remaineth, is to come. If an instant of time be conceived, which cannot be divided into the smallest particles of moments, that alone is it, which may be called present. Which yet flies with such speed from future to past, as not to be lengthened out with the least stay. For if it be, it is divided into past and future. The present hath no space. Where then is the time, which we may call long? Is it to come? Of it we do not say, "it is long;" because it is not yet, so as to be long; but we say, "it will be long." When therefore will it be? For if even then, when it is yet to come, it shall not be long, (because what can be long, as yet is not,) and so it shall then be long, when from future which as yet is not, it shall begin now to be, and have become present, that so there should exist what may be long; then does time present cry out in the words above, that it cannot be long.

And yet, Lord, we perceive intervals of times, and compare them, and say, some are shorter, and others longer. We measure also, how much longer or shorter this time is than that; and we answer, "This is double, or treble; and that, but once, or only just so much as that." But we measure times as they are passing, by perceiving them; but past, which now are not, or the future, which are not yet, who can measure? unless a man shall presume to say, that can be measured, which is not. When then time is passing, it may be perceived and measured; but when it is past, it cannot, because it is not.

I ask, Father, I affirm not: O my God, rule and guide me. "Who will tell me that there are not three times, (as we learned when boys, and taught boys,) past, present, and future; but present only, because those two are not? Or are they also; and when from future it becometh present, doth it come out of some secret place; and so, when retiring, from present it becometh past? For where did they, who foretold things to come, see them, if as yet they be not? For that which is not, cannot be seen. And they who relate things past, could not relate them, if in mind they did not discern them, and if they were not, they could no way be discerned. Things then past and to come are."

Permit me, Lord, to seek further. O my hope, let not my purpose be confounded. For if times past and to come be, I would know where they be. Which yet if I cannot, yet I know, wherever they be, they are not there as future, or past, but present. For if there also they be future, they are not yet there; if there also they be past, they are no longer there. Wheresoever then is whatsoever is, it is only as present. Although when past facts are related, there are drawn out of the memory, not the things themselves which are past, but words which, conceived by the images of the things, they, in passing, have through the senses left as traces in the mind. Thus my childhood, which now is not, is in time past, which now is not: but now when I recall its image, and tell of it, I behold it in the present because it is still in my memory. Whether there be a like cause of foretelling things to come also; that of things which as yet are not, the images may be perceived before, already existing, I confess, O my God, I know not. This indeed I know, that we generally think before on our future actions, and that that forethinking is present, but the action whereof we forethink is not yet, because it is to come. Which, when we have set upon, and have begun to do what we were forethinking, then shall that action be; because then it is no longer future, but present.

Which way soever then this secret fore-perceiving of things to come be; that only can be seen, which is. But what now is, is not future, but present. When then things to come are said to be seen, it is not themselves which as yet are not, (that is, which are to be,) but their causes perchance or signs are seen, which already are. Therefore they are not future but present to those who now see that, from which the future, being fore-conceived in the mind, is foretold. Which fore-conceptions again now are; and those who foretel those things, do behold the conceptions present before them. Let now the numerous variety of things furnish me some example. I behold the day-break, I foreshew, that the sun is about to rise. What I behold, is present; what I foresignify, to come; not the sun, which already is; but the sunrising, which is not yet. And yet did I not in my mind imagine the sun-rising itself, (as now while I speak of it,) I could not foretel it. But neither is that day-break which I discern in the sky, the sun-rising, although it goes before it; nor that imagination of my mind; which two are seen now present, that the other which is to be may be foretold. Future things then are not yet: and if they be not yet, they are not: and if they are not, they cannot be seen; yet foretold they may be from things present, which are already, and are seen.

Thou then, Ruler of Thy creation, by what way dost Thou teach souls things to come? For Thou didst teach Thy Prophets. By what way dost Thou, to whom nothing is to come, teach things to come; or rather of the future, dost teach things present? For, what is not, neither can it be taught. Too far is this way out of my ken: *it is too mighty for me, I cannot attain unto it*; but from Thee I can, when Thou shalt vouchsafe it, O sweet light of my hidden eyes.

What now is clear and plain is, that neither things to come nor past are. Nor is it properly said, "there be three times, past, present, and to come:" yet perchance it might be properly said, "there be three times; a present of things past, a present of things present, and a present of things future." For these three do exist in some sort, in the soul, but otherwhere do I not see them; present of things past, memory; present of things present, sight; present of things future, expectation. If thus we be permitted to speak, I see three times, and I confess there are three. Let it be said too, "there be three times, past, present, and to come:" in our incorrect way. See, I object not, nor gainsay, nor find fault, if what is so said be but understood, that neither what is to be, now is, nor what is past. For but few things are there, which we speak properly, most things improperly; still the things intended are understood.

I said then even now, we measure times as they pass, in order to be able to say, this time is twice so much as that one; or, this is just so much as that; and so of any other parts of time, which be measurable. Wherefore, as I said, we measure times as they pass. And if any should ask me, "How knowest thou?" I might answer, "I know, that we do measure, nor can we measure things that are not; and things past and to come, are not." But time present how do we measure, seeing it hath no space? It is measured while passing, but when it shall have passed, it is not measured; for there will be nothing to be measured. But whence, by what way, and whither passes it while it is a measuring? whence, but from the future? Which way, but through the present? whither, but into the past? From that therefore, which is not yet, through that, which hath no space, into that which now is not. Yet what do we measure, if not time in some space? For we do not say, single, and double, and triple, and equal, or any other like way that we speak of time, except of spaces of times. In what space then do we measure time passing? In the future, whence it passeth through? But what is not yet, we measure not. Or in the present, by which it passes? but no space, we do not measure: or in the past, to which it passes? But neither do we measure that, which now is not. . . .

I heard once from a learned man, that the motions of the sun, moon, and stars, constituted time, and I assented not. For why should not the motions of all bodies rather be times? Or, if the lights of heaven should cease, and a potter's wheel run round, should there be no time by which we might measure those whirlings, and say, that either it moved with equal pauses, or if it turned sometimes slower, otherwhiles quicker, that some rounds were longer, other shorter? Or, while we were saying this, should we not also be speaking in time? Or, should there in our words be some syllables short, others long, but because those sounded in a shorter time, these in a longer? God, grant to men to see in a small thing notices common to things great and small. The stars and lights of heaven, are also *for signs, and for seasons, and for years, and for days*; they are; yet neither should I say, that the going round of that wooden wheel was a day, nor yet he, that it was therefore no time.

I desire to know the force and nature of time, by which we measure the motions of bodies, and say (for example) this motion is twice as long as that. For I ask, Seeing "day" denotes not the stay only of the sun upon the earth, (according to which day is one thing, night another;) but also its whole circuit from east to east again; according to which we say, "there passed so many days," the night being included when we say, "so many days," and the nights not reckoned apart;—seeing then a day is completed by the motion of the sun and by his circuit from east to east again, I ask, does the motion alone make the day, or the stay in which that motion is completed, or both? For if the first be the day; then should we have a day, although the sun should finish that course in so small a space of time, as one hour comes to. If the second, then should not that make a day, if between one sun-rise and another there were but so short a stay, as one hour comes to; but the sun must go four and twenty times about, to complete one day. If both, then neither could that be called a day, if the sun should run his whole round in the space of one hour; nor that, if, while the sun stood still, so much time should overpass, as the sun usually makes his whole course in, from morning to morning. I will not therefore now ask, what that is which is called day; but, what time is, whereby we measuring the circuit of the sun, should say that it was finished in half the time it was wont, if so be it was finished in so small a space as twelve hours; and comparing both times, should call this a single time, that a double time; even supposing the sun to run his round from east to east, sometimes in that single, sometimes in that double time. Let no man then tell me, that the motions of the heavenly bodies constitute times, because, when at the prayer of one, the sun had stood still, till he could achieve his victorious battle, the sun stood still, but time went on. For in its own allotted space of time was that battle waged and ended. I perceive time them to be a certain extension. But do I perceive it, or seem to perceive it? Thou, Light and Truth, wilt shew me.

Dost Thou bid me assent, if any define time to be "motion of a body?" Thou dost not bid me. For that no body is moved, but in time, I hear; this Thou sayest; but that the motion of a body is time, I hear not; Thou sayest it not. For when a body is moved, I by time measure, how long it moveth, from the time it began to move, until it left off? And if I did not see whence it began; and it continue to move so that I see not when it ends, I cannot measure, save perchance from the time I began, until I cease to see. And if I look long, I can only pronounce it to be a long time, but not how long; because when we say "how long," we do it by comparison; as, "this is as long as that," or "twice so long as that," or the like. But when we can mark the distances of the places, whence and whither goeth the body moved, or his parts, if it moved as in a lathe, then can we say precisely, in how much time the motion of that body or his part, from this place unto that, was finished. Seeing therefore the motion of a body is one thing, that by which we measure how long it is, another; who sees not, which of the two is rather to be called time? For and if a body be sometimes moved, sometimes stands still, then we measure, not his motion only, but his standing still too by time; and we say, "it stood still, as much as it moved;" or "it stood still twice or thrice so long as it moved;' or any other space which our measuring hath either ascertained, or guessed; more or less, as we use to say. Time then is not the motion of a body.

And I confess to Thee, O Lord, that I yet know not what time is, and again I confess unto Thee, O Lord, that I know that I speak this in time, and that having long spoken of time, that very "long" is not long, but by the pause of time. How then know I this, seeing I know not what time is? or is it perchance that I know not how to express what I know? Woe is me, that do not even know, what I know not. Behold, O my God, before Thee I lie not; but as I speak, so is my heart. *Thou shalt light my candle; Thou O Lord my God, wilt enlighten my darkness.*

Does not my soul most truly confess unto Thee, that I do measure times? Do I then measure, O my God, and know not what I measure? I measure the motion of a body in time; and the time itself do I not measure? Or could I indeed measure the motion of a body how long it were, and in how long space it could come from this place to that, without measuring the time in which it is moved? This same time then, how do I measure? do we by a shorter time measure a longer, as by the space of a cubit, the space of a rood? for so indeed we seem by the space of a short syllable, to measure the space of a long syllable, and to say that this is double the other. Thus measure we the spaces of stanzas, by the spaces of the verses, and the spaces of the verses, by the spaces of the feet, and the spaces of the feet, by the spaces of the syllables, and the spaces of long, by the spaces of short syllables; not measuring by pages, (for then we measure spaces, not times;) but when we utter the words and they pass by, and we say "it is a long stanza, because composed of so many verses; long verses, because consisting of so many feet; long feet, because prolonged by so many syllables; a long syllable because double to a short one." But neither do we this way obtain any certain measure of time; because it may be, that a shorter verse, pronounced more fully, may take up more time than a longer, pronounced hurriedly. And so for a verse, a foot, a syllable. Whence it seemed to me, that time is nothing else than protraction; but of what, I know not; and I marvel, if it be not of the mind itself? For what I beseech Thee, O my God, do I measure, when I say, either indefinitely "this is a longer time than that," or definitely "this is double that?" That I measure time, I know; and yet I measure not time to come, for it is not yet; nor present, because it is not protracted by any space; nor past, because it now is not. What then do I measure? Times passing, not past? for so I said.

Courage, my mind, and press on mightily. God is our helper, He *made us, and not we ourselves.* Press on where truth begins to dawn. Suppose, now, the voice of a body begins to sound, and does sound, and sounds on, and list, it ceases; it is silence now, and that voice is past, and is no more a voice. Before it sounded, it was to come, and could not be measured, because as yet it was not, and now it cannot, because it is no longer. Then therefore while it sounded, it might; because there then was what might be measured. But yet even then it was not at a stay; for it was passing on, and passing away. Could it be measured the rather, for that? For while passing, it was being extended into some space of time, so that it might be measured, since the present hath no space. If therefore then it might, then, lo, suppose another voice hath begun to sound, and still soundeth in one continued tenor without any interruption; let us measure it while it sounds; seeing when it hath left sounding, it will then be past, and nothing left to be measured; let us measure it verily, and tell how much it is. But it sounds still, nor can it be measured by from the instant it began in, unto the end it left in. For the very space between is the thing we measure, namely, from some beginning unto some end. Wherefore, a voice that is not yet ended, cannot be measured, so that it may be said how long, or short it is; nor can it be called equal to another, or double to a single, or the like. But when ended, it no longer is. How may it then be measured? And yet we measure times; but yet neither those which are not yet, nor those which no longer are, nor those which are not lengthened out by some pause, nor those which have no bounds. We measure neither times to come, nor past, nor present, nor passing; and yet we do measure times. . . .

And now will I stand, and become firm in Thee, in my mould, Thy truth; nor will I endure the questions of men, who by a penal disease thirst for more than they can contain, and say, "what did God before He *made heaven and earth ?*" "Or, how came it into His mind to make any thing, having never before made any thing?" Give them, O Lord, well to bethink themselves what they say, and to find, that "never" cannot be predicated, when "time" is not. This then that He is said "never to have made;" what else is it to say, than "in 'no time' to have made?" Let them see therefore, that time cannot be without created being, and cease to *speak* that *vanity*. May they also be *extended towards those things which are before*; and understand Thee before all times, the eternal Creator of all times, and that no times be coeternal with Thee, nor any creature, even if there be any creature before all times. . . .

14

JAMES OTTEN

---

introduction

The metaphysically puzzling thing about time, as we have noted, is that it seems to *pass*, which means that in some sense or other it is something that is *moving*. The common sense of mankind is agreed on this. Things that were once future come into being, are briefly present, and then begin an endless recession into the past, becoming ever more distant. Sometimes this thought is oppressive, as when people reflect, for example, that their youth is now behind them and growing ever more distantly past, or that their extinction by death is approaching and growing ever closer.

Yet this movement of time—or, what amounts to the same thing, this steady movement of things out of the future, into the present, and then on into the past—has seemed to metaphysicians so deeply mysterious that most of them have declared it to be an illusion. Plato called time a "moving image of eternity," making clear his view that eternity, in which there is no temporal passage, is what is real. The flowing time with which we are familiar is but an "image"—that is, an illusion. Immanuel Kant declared time to be no "real being," Spinoza found it to be only a human way of viewing eternity, and so it has been with most philosophers. Henri Bergson was an exception, declaring the utter reality of passing time: "Time bites into things and leaves on them the mark of its tooth."

Nor is it hard to see why philosophers have been so puzzled by time. The relations of *before*, *after*, and *simultaneous with* are clearly fixed, as Otten, in the selection that follows, makes clear. Once established, nothing about those relations undergoes any change; they remain the same forever. But the properties things have of being *future, present,* or *past* do seem to change —that which is future becomes less so, finally enters the present, then begins its everlasting recession into the past. And this, whatever might be the verdict of common sense, appears highly irrational to a philosopher. For one thing, as Otten notes, it is not easy to say *how fast* things are passing through time in this way. Equally puzzling, they must all be moving at exactly the same rate—otherwise the relations of *before, after,* and *simultaneous* would not remain fixed. And, no less puzzling, this kind of movement cannot be stopped or reversed, unlike any other kind of motion we know of.

Yet Otten does defend this common-sense view that things move through time, and he tries to reduce the main obstacles that metaphysics has always found in it.

James Otten, who teaches at Purdue University, is best known for his theories of human action. This previously unpublished selection is used with his kind permission.

The Passage of Time*

One of the seemingly brute facts of our existence is the inexorable passage of time. We commonly express this supposed fact in a variety of colorful ways. Time advances, we say. It flows by, marches on, moves along, pushes on, passes by. No matter what may happen, even if the heavens fall, time does not stop. Things that are once future come to be present and then vanish into the emptiness of the past. While they exist, things steadily grow older, but never does their age freeze and never do they become younger. Presentness perpetually journeys along the time axis in the direction of the future. Or, at least, so it all seems.

Among philosophers there exists a fascinating dispute about the passage of time, involving two conflicting views. The *passage view* maintains that the passage of time is something real; the *static view* claims that it only seems to take place, that it is illusory. I shall first examine the dispute between these two views, and then I shall defend the passage view against two objections commonly brought to bear on it by adherents to the static view.

THE MEANING OF 'THE PASSAGE OF TIME'

At the outset we need to determine what the meaning of 'the passage of time' is in this dispute. Conceivably it could mean any one of a number of different things. Three possible meanings immediately come to mind.

*An unpublished essay by James Otten, used with the author's permission.

First, by speaking of the passage of time one could mean that *time itself* is the subject of passage or motion—that it flows like a river, or that it moves along like a locomotive. However, there is a devastating objection to construing the passage of time in this way. The concept of motion is a relational concept. That is, to say that something moves is to imply that it moves in relation to something else. But what is this something else that time is supposed to move in relation to? Unless this question can be satisfactorily answered, and I am sure that it cannot be, then certainly we must conclude that time itself cannot move and that therefore this first meaning is completely unintelligible.

Second, by speaking of the passage of time one could mean, not necessarily that anything in particular is the subject of passage or motion, but rather than one's apprehension of the duration of things matches to some extent the actual duration of those things. For instance, it might be remarked in the midst of a football game that time is passing quickly or slowly, that it is flying by or creeping along. This means that the game, or a certain segment of it, seems to be of shorter or longer duration than it in fact is. In such contexts, one's judgments about the passage of time are comparative judgments concerning perceived duration and real duration. Indeed, we sometimes do have this second meaning in mind when talking of the passage of time.

And, third, by speaking of the passage of time one could mean that *things in time* are the subject of passage or motion through time—that they move through time in a fashion similar to that in which they move through space, except that things move through time only in *one* direction and always at the *same* rate. Perhaps this meaning would be expressed more clearly if we were to speak, not of the *passage of time*, but rather of the *passageway of time* through which things move, or, even better, of the *passage through time* of things.

At any rate, it is precisely this third meaning that 'the passage of time' has in the dispute between the two views of time. In other words, both views are in total agreement that the idea of the passage of time is equivalent to the idea that things move through time, the passage view claiming that they do, and the static view claiming they do not.

THE TWO VIEWS OF TIME

Let us now examine the two views of time in greater depth so that we can see more clearly the difference between them. Interestingly enough, these views are rooted in two fundamental but starkly different ways in which we conceive of things as temporal.

On the one hand, we conceive of things as having the "transitory temporal properties" of *being past, being present,* and *being future*. These temporal properties are transitory in the obvious sense that anything once possessing such a property necessarily lacks it at some other time. For instance, if the Third World War is indeed a real event in the future, then at some time yet to come it must lose its status as a future event by becoming present and then past.

On the other hand, we conceive of things as bearing to each other the "static temporal relations" of *being earlier than, being simultaneous with,* and *being later than.* Of course, these temporal relations are static inasmuch as anything once bearing such a relation to another thing necessarily bears that relation to it forever. Thus, since Caesar's birth was once earlier than Napoleon's death, his birth must once and forever be earlier than Napoleon's death.

Quite in line with our common-sense beliefs, the passage view of time maintains that not only do things bear the "static temporal relations" to each other, but they also possess the "transitory temporal properties." To put it more simply, things not only are earlier than, simultaneous with, and later than other things, according to the passage view, but they also are, at diverse times, in the past, present, and future.

Now the static view of time asserts that things do bear the "static temporal relations" to each other, but that, contrary to our common-sense beliefs, things do not possess the "transitory temporal properties." In other words, the static view admits that things are earlier than, simultaneous with, and later than other things, but it denies that things really are past, present, or future in any nonrelative sense.

Thus, the difference between the two views of time amounts simply to this: whereas the passage view holds that it is a *fact* that things possess the "transitory temporal properties" of *being past, being present,* and *being future,* the static view holds that it is a *myth.* It hardly needs mentioning here that the passage view's notion that the passage of time is something real is equivalent to the notion that things actually do possess the "transitory temporal properties." As the passage view would have it, things move relentlessly through time on the onrushing wave of the present, constantly encroaching on the future and leaving behind ever larger expanses of the past.

METAPHORS EMPLOYED BY THE TWO VIEWS

Time is an amazingly difficult thing to understand, and an even more difficult thing to explain in words. Because of this, we often resort to metaphors in our attempts to express the nature of time. Each of the two views that we are considering uses its own peculiar type of metaphor to explain time.

Consider an example of a metaphor that the passage view would employ to express the idea of the passage of time—or, what comes to the same thing, the idea that things move through time. Such an example would be the metaphor that *things move through time much as ships move through a waterway.* Naturally the static view would maintain that the motion of things through time in the sense expressed by this metaphor does not actually occur and is simply an illusion.

However, according to the static view, things can be said to "pass" through time in a static sense. This is not the same as the motion of things through time, but rather it is a kind of extendedness of things through time. It is aptly expressed by the metaphor that *things pass through time much as the planks of a fence pass through a field in which the fence is situated.*

By elaborating upon these metaphors, we can see how both views are able to explain our seeming awareness of the passage of time. For the passage view, a person is like a ship passing through a waterway, a person's awareness of the passage of time is like a spotlight on a ship that can focus on other ships located on either side of it but not on ships located in front of or behind it. And, for the static view, a person is like a plank (or a cross section of many planks) on a fence situated in a field, and a person's awareness of the passage of time is like a spotlight that seemingly can focus successively on different planks of the fence, thus giving rise to the illusion that the planks themselves are in motion.

THE FIRST OBJECTION: CONCEPTUAL CONFUSION

At this point we have a fairly complete picture of the two views of time, and so we are ready to consider the two objections raised by the static view against the passage view.

Probably the most challenging objection is that the passage view is at bottom the result of conceptual confusion over the concept of motion through time. Once this concept is gotten straight, the objection says, it becomes apparent that there can be no such phenomenon as the passage of time. In detail, the objection runs this way. In order to explicate the obscure concept of motion through time, we need to appeal to the relatively clear concept of motion through space. Now obviously *something moves through space only if it varies in spatial position over time*—that is, only if it is in different places at different times. To derive the temporal analogue of this, we need to substitute temporal for spatial terms and vice versa. Accordingly, we find that *something moves through time only if it varies in temporal position over space*—that is, only if it is in different places at different times. But then motion through time is one and the same thing as motion through space. And therefore, just as motion through space must be motion through space from one place to another, so also motion through time must be motion through time from one present moment to another only if present moments are places, which, of course, is totally absurd. The objection concludes that places, which, of course, is totally absurd. The objection concludes that there can be no motion through time from one present moment to another, or, in simpler terms, that the passage of time cannot be real.

Indeed, this is a powerful objection, for unless it can be met, the passage view must be forsaken as a conceptual hodgepodge. However, it is not very difficult to discover the point at which the objection goes wrong: its description of something moving through time is incorrect, and because of this the whole objection collapses.

A correct description would be that *something moves through time if and only if it varies in temporal position over time.* One can see that this is a correct description from the following considerations. Motion is essentially variation in some respect over time. Thus, to say that Jones moves from one income bracket to another is to imply that his income varies over time. Similarly, to say that something moves from one temporal position to another is to imply that its temporal position varies over time. In generating the description of something moving through time from the description of something moving through space, the static view erred by replacing variation in some respect over *time* with variation in some respect over *space*. Ironically enough, the static view rather than the passage view falls prey to conceptual confusion here.

Finally, we should observe that there is no more difficulty in the idea that things move through time from one present moment to another, than there is in the perfectly harmless idea that things move through space from one here to another.

THE SECOND OBJECTION: HOW FAST?

The second objection to consider is a very simple one, which can be expressed in the following way. If something moves through a certain frame of reference, then it must make sense to ask how fast or at what rate it is moving. For instance, if a satellite moves through space, it must make sense to ask how fast it is moving through space. However, says the objection, it does not make any sense at all to ask how fast things move through time. Therefore, it must be concluded that things do not move through time.

Now this objection seems to be plainly mistaken in its claim that it makes no sense to ask the question, How fast or at what rate do things move through time? For we do know at least two general facts about the rate at which things move through time. First, we know that things move through time at some rate or other, since if they were at a standstill in time then change would not take place, but quite obviously it *does* take place. Second, we know that all things move through time at the same rate. So, we can answer the above question by saying that things move through time at some rate or other, and that all things move through time at one and the same rate. Hence, the second objection, like the first, carries no weight against the passage view.

AN UNNOTICED IMPLICATION

Finally, I want to point out a very surprising implication of the passage view of time, which I believe has gone unnoticed until now. If the passage view of time is correct, and we have not found any reason to think otherwise, then we may not be nearly so alone in the vast expanse of time as we previously thought ourselves to be.

Recall the metaphor that was used earlier to explain the passage view. According to that metaphor, things are like ships passing through a waterway, and a person's awareness of the passage of time is like a spotlight on a ship that can focus on the other ships located on either side of it but not on ships located in front of or behind it. Of course, the area on the sides of a ship represents its present, the area in front represents its future, and the area behind represents its past. We would represent the universe as we know it by a fleet of ships lined up side by side across the width of the waterway at some point; like a line of soldiers, this fleet would march down the waterway.

Now the surprising implication I have in mind is that, besides the fleet that comprises the universe as we know it, there very well may be numerous other fleets floating down the waterway. Perhaps the different fleets are packed in like sardines. Perhaps they are moving at different speeds and will sometime collide. Perhaps some are standing still. At any rate, the novel possibilities that the passage view implies are enormous.

15

DAVID HUME

___

introduction

The idea of causation has always been basic to metaphysics and to philosophy generally. Philosophers, like everyone else, have assumed that the *explanation* of anything consists of discovering its cause. To some extent this is perfectly true. An infectious disease is explained when its causative bacterium or virus is identified; tides are explained by the gravitational forces that cause them; and so with other things. Metaphysicians have always sought the highest and most universal causes, declaring God to be the cause of the world itself. Physics, or the understanding of physical nature, was once thought to consist of the knowledge of the causes operative there; psychology, or the understanding of human nature, was thought to require the knowledge of the passions and feelings that cause human behavior; and natural theology has sought to establish, by reason, the nature and attributes of the ultimate cause of the world.

This concept has been so fundamental to philosophy that it has been a foundation of whole metaphysical systems, and until Hume's destructive analysis certain presuppositions were widely thought to be self-evident and incontrovertible. It was thought, for example, that no effect can be greater than its cause. This seemed to Descartes so immune to doubt that he rested his entire escape from skepticism upon it. Similarly, it was claimed that similar causes must always have similar effects, this being not merely a generalization from experience, but a deliverance of reason. Again, causes were thought to produce their effects by virtue of an inherent power to do so, and understanding a cause was assumed to involve the rational understanding of that power. Thus, one moving object was thought to impart its motion to another, upon impact, by virtue of its inherent power to set something in motion, and to understand this causal relationship one needed to understand that power, to grasp the connection between the two events, or to see, not merely that the one is followed by the other, but *why* this is so—to see that the one *must* be followed by the other.

The significance of David Hume's discussion of causation is that he claimed to divest this concept of all its metaphysical entanglements and to explain it entirely empirically, in terms of what is actually observed. Though philosophers since then have abandoned the archaic psychology in terms of which Hume pursued his analysis, many believe that he was successful at least in abolishing the claim that there is some sort of necessary connection between causes and their effects.

Hume, following a tradition, believed that all our ideas arise from experience. This is what he means by saying that every idea is traceable to an "impression." By an impression he meant either some sense experience, such as the feeling of warmth or a sensation of some sound, or else some inner experience, such as the feeling of sadness or anger or joy. These latter he referred to as impressions arising from "reflection." To have a clear understanding of an idea, then, or of some word that we use to express an idea, we must be able to trace it to the clear external or internal impression from which it is derived or copied.

Whence then, Hume asks, arises our idea of any necessary connection between a cause and its effect? Do we really have such an idea at all? Are we entitled to believe, as a deliverance of reason, that there is in a cause anything like a *power* to compel the occurrence of a given effect? When we see one billiard ball impart its motion to another, we think that the second ball *had* to move, given the impact of the first, that no other effect was possible, given the conditions that obtained, or in short that there was here, as in every causal relationship, a necessary connection between the cause that occurred and the effect that followed.

Hume claims, in effect, that this is a groundless prejudice. He finds no ordinary impression, or simple experience, to which this idea of a necessary connection can be traced. It arises simply from a feeling of expectation that past experience has given rise to. Hence, that is all we are entitled to infer, upon experiencing some familiar cause—namely, that its accustomed effect can be expected to follow. We cannot infer why it will follow, or that it must follow. The connection between them exists only in our minds.

When we observe some familiar cause and its effect—such as one moving ball imparting its motion to another—all we actually observe is these two motions, the one following upon the other. We see no connection whatever between them, nor is there anything in what we see that would rule out the possibility of some other effect—of both balls simply stopping, for example, or suddenly rolling sideways, or igniting into flame. That the first ball should, upon impact, stop rolling, and the second suddenly begin rolling, is something we have come to expect from our experience. But experience does not show us why this happens, or that it must happen as it does.

So our idea of a necessary connection cannot be traced to any external impression. Can it then, perhaps, be traced to an internal one? Can we, upon reflecting on our own acts of will and their effects, find any kind of necessary or rational connection between them? Not at all, Hume says. All we find is that, upon our willing some motion, such as the motion of one of our limbs, that motion usually follows. We can find no reason why it should, nor indeed can we make any rational connection at all between the inner workings of our minds and the outer motions of our bodies. The connection between the mind and the body is utterly mysterious. We learn from experience that we can move certain parts of our bodies at will. We never see how, nor do we ever understand why we have such command over some parts of our bodies and not others.

All we ever find in causation, therefore, is conjunction, the effect following upon the cause. We never find any connection, nor are we ever able, by reason alone, to infer either from the other. We find that this conjunction or sequence is more or less constant. The same causes are followed by the same effects. This we find in experience. That they must be followed by the same effects, we do not find, nor will we ever be able to see why a given cause is followed by the effect that does follow it. We only find that it is.

Do we have, then, no real idea of a necessary connection? In other words, is there no impression to which such an idea could be traced? Hume said that there is. The impression is not derived from anything connecting the causes and effects themselves; rather, it is an internal one, something within our own minds. It consists of that feeling of expectation that our experience of causes and effects has given rise to. Upon seeing some familiar cause—a rolling ball approaching another, for example—we *expect* to see a familiar effect—the motion of the second ball—simply because we have seen this so many times before. The repetition of this experience has created in us a habit of expectation. And it is this inner feeling that gives rise in us to the idea of a necessary connection between cause and effect. We say that the effect *must* follow, that no other effect would be *possible*—really meaning by this only that we have come to expect that effect and no other. That is what the supposed connection amounts to, and nothing more.

David Hume, a Scottish philosopher and historian who died in 1776, has probably had more influence on academic philosophers than any other modern classical thinker. His theory of causation, set forth in the selection below, constitutes one of the most original ideas in the history of philosophy.

Causation and Sequence*

There are no ideas, which occur in metaphysics more obscure and uncertain, than those of *power, force, energy* or *necessary connection*, of which it is every moment necessary for us to treat in all our disquisitions. We shall, therefore, endeavor, in this section, to fix, if possible, the precise meaning of these terms, and thereby remove some part of that obscurity, which is so much complained of in this species of philosophy.

It seems a proposition, which will not admit of much dispute, that all our ideas are nothing but copies of our impressions, or, in other words, that it is impossible for us to *think* of anything, which we have not antecedently *felt*, either by our external or internal senses. I have endeavored to explain and prove this proposition, and have expressed my hopes, that, by a proper application of it, men may reach a greater clearness and precision in philosophical reasonings, than what they have hitherto been able to attain. Complex ideas may, perhaps, be well known by definition, which is nothing but an enumeration of those parts or simple ideas, that compose them. But when we have pushed up definitions to the most simple ideas, and find still some ambiguity and obscurity; what resource are we then possessed of? By what invention can we throw light upon these ideas, and render them altogether precise and determinate to our intellectual view! Produce the impressions or original sentiments, from which the ideas are copied. These impressions are all strong and sensible. They admit not of ambiguity. They are not only placed in a full light themselves, but may throw light on their correspondent ideas, which lie in obscurity. And by this means, we may, perhaps, attain a new microscope or species of optics, by which, in the moral sciences, the most minute, and most simple ideas may be so enlarged as to fall readily under our apprehension, and be equally known with the grossest and most sensible ideas, that can be the object of our inquiry.

To be fully acquainted, therefore, with the idea of power or necessary connection, let us examine its impression; and in order to find the impression with greater certainty, let us search for it in all the sources, from which it may possibly be derived.

When we look about us towards external objects, and consider the operation of causes, we are never able, in a single instance, to discover any power or necessary connection; any quality, which binds the effect to the cause, and renders the one an infallible consequence of the other. We only find, that the one does actually, in fact, follow the other. The impulse of one billiard ball is attended with motion in the second. This is the whole that appears to the *outward* senses. The mind feels no sentiment or *inward* impression from

*From David Hume, "Of the Idea of Necessary Connection," *An Enquiry Concerning Human Understanding*, 3rd ed., Clarendon Press (Oxford, 1975).

this succession of objects: consequently there is not, in any single, particular instance of cause and effect, anything which can suggest the idea of power or necessary connection.

From the first appearance of an object, we never can conjecture what effect will result from it. But were the power or energy of any cause discoverable by the mind, we could foresee the effect, even without experience; and might, at first, pronounce with certainty concerning it, by mere dint of thought and reasoning.

In reality, there is no part of matter, that does ever, by its sensible qualities, discover any power or energy, or give us ground to imagine, that it could produce anything, or be followed by any other object, which we could denominate its effect. Solidity, extension, motion; these qualities are all complete in themselves, and never point out any other event which may result from them. The scenes of the universe are continually shifting, and one object follows another in an uninterrupted succession; but the power of force, which actuates the whole machine, is entirely concealed from us, and never discovers itself in any of the sensible qualities of body. We know, that, in fact, heat is a constant attendant of flame; but what is the connection between them, we have no room so much as to conjecture or imagine. It is impossible, therefore, that the idea of power can be derived from the contemplation of bodies, in single instances of their operation; because no bodies ever discover any power, which can be the original of this idea.

Since, therefore, external objects as they appear to the senses, give us no idea of power or necessary connection, by their operation in particular instances, let us see, whether this idea be derived from reflection on the operations of our own minds, and be copied from any internal impression. It may be said, that we are every moment conscious of internal power; while we feel, that, by the simple command of our will, we can move the organs of our body, or direct the faculties of our mind. An act of volition produces motion in our limbs, or raises a new idea in our imagination. This influence of the will we know by consciousness. Hence we acquire the idea of power or energy; and are certain, that we ourselves and all other intelligent beings are possessed of power. This idea, then, is an idea of reflection, since it arises from reflecting on the operations of our own mind, and on the command which is exercised by will, both over the organs of the body and faculties of the soul.

We shall proceed to examine this pretension; and first with regard to the influence of volition over the organs of the body. This influence, we may observe, is a fact, which, like all other natural events, can be known only by experience, and can never be foreseen from any apparent energy or power in the cause, which connects it with the effect, and renders the one an infallible consequence of the other. The motion of our body follows upon the command of our will. Of this we are every moment conscious. But the means, by which this is effected; the energy, by which the will performs so extraordinary an operation; of this we are so far from being immediately conscious, that it must for ever escape our most diligent inquiry.

For *first*, Is there any principle in all nature more mysterious than the union of soul with body; by which a supposed spiritual substance acquires such an influence over a material one, that the most refined thought is able to actuate the grossest matter? Were we empowered, by a secret wish, to remove mountains, or control the planets in their orbit; this extensive authority would not be more extraordinary, nor more beyond our comprehension. But if by consciousness we perceived any power or energy in the will, we must know this power; we must know its connection with the effect; we must know the secret union of soul and body, and the nature of both these substances; by which the one is able to operate, in so many instances, upon the other.

Secondly, We are not able to move all the organs of the body with a like authority; though we cannot assign any reason besides experience, for so remarkable a difference between one and the other. Why has the will an influence over the tongue and fingers, not over the heart and liver? This question would never embarrass us, were we conscious of a power in the former case, not in the latter. We should then perceive, independent of experience, why the authority of will over the organs of the body is circumscribed within such particular limits. Being in that case fully acquainted with the power or force, by which it operates, we should also know, why its influence reaches precisely to such boundaries, and no farther.

A man, suddenly struck with palsy in the leg or arm, or who had newly lost those members, frequently endeavors, at first to move them, and employ them in their usual offices. Here he is as much conscious of power to command such limbs, as a man in perfect health is conscious of power to actuate any member which remains in its natural state and condition. But consciousness never deceives. Consequently, neither in the one case nor in the other, are we ever conscious of any power. We learn the influence of our will from experience alone. And experience only teaches us, how one event constantly follows another; without instructing us in the secret connection, which binds them together, and renders them inseparable.

Thirdly, We learn from anatomy, that the immediate object of power in voluntary motion, is not the member itself which is moved, but certain muscles, and nerves, and animal spirits, and, perhaps, something still more minute and more unknown, through which the motion is successfully propagated, ere it reach the member itself whose motion is the immediate object of volition. Can there be a more certain proof that the power, by which this whole operation is performed, so far from being directly and fully known by an inward sentiment or consciousness, is, to the last degree, mysterious and unintelligible? Here the mind wills a certain event: immediately another event, unknown to ourselves, and totally different from the one intended, is produced: this event produces another, equally unknown: till at last, through a long succession, the desired event is produced. But if the original power were felt, it must be known: were it known, its effect also must be known; since all power is relative to its effect. And *vice versa*, if the effect be not known, the power cannot be known nor felt. How indeed can we be conscious of a power to move our limbs, when we have no such power, but only that to move certain animal spirits, which, though they produce at last the motion of our limbs, yet operate in such a manner as is wholly beyond our comprehension?

We may, therefore, conclude from the whole, I hope, without any temerity, though with assurance; that our idea of power is not copied from any sentiment or consciousness of power within ourselves, when we give rise to animal motion, or apply our limbs, to their proper use and office. That their motion follows the command of the will is a matter of common experience, like other natural events: but the power or energy by which this is effected, like that in other natural events, is unknown and inconceivable.

Shall we then assert, that we are conscious of a power or energy in our own minds, when, by an act or command of our will, we raise up a new idea, fix the mind to the contemplation of it, turn it on all sides, and at last dismiss it for some other idea, when we think that we have surveyed it with sufficient accuracy? I believe the same arguments will prove, that even this command of the will gives us no real idea of force or energy.

First, It must be allowed, that, when we know a power, we know that very circumstance in the cause, by which it is enabled to produce the effect: for these are supposed to be synonymous. We must, therefore, know both the cause and effect, and the relation between them. But do we pretend to be acquainted with the nature of the human soul and the nature of an idea, or the aptitude of the one to produce the other? This is a real creation; a production of something out of nothing: which implies a power so great, that it may seem, at first sight, beyond the reach of any being, less than infinite. At least it must be owned, that such a power is not felt, nor known, nor even conceivable by the mind. We only feel the event, namely, the existence of an idea, consequent to a command of the will: but the manner, in which this operation is performed, the power by which it is produced, is entirely beyond our comprehension.

Secondly, The command of the mind over itself is limited, as well as its command over the body; and these limits are not known by reason, or any acquaintance with the nature of cause and effect, but only by experience and observation, as in all other natural events and in the operation of external objects. Our authority over our sentiments and passions is much weaker than that over our ideas; and even the latter authority is circumscribed within very narrow boundaries. Will anyone pretend to assign the ultimate reason of these boundaries, or show why the power is deficient in one case, not in another?

Thirdly, This self-command is very different at different times. A man in health possesses more of it than one languishing with sickness. We are more master of our thoughts in the morning than in the evening; fasting, than after a full meal. Can we give any reason for these variations, except experience? Where then is the power, of which we pretend to be conscious? Is there not here, either in a spiritual or material substance, or both, some secret mechanism or structure of parts, upon which the effect depends, and which, being entirely unknown to us, renders the power or energy of the will equally unknown and incomprehensible?

Volition is surely an act of the mind, with which we are sufficiently acquainted. Reflect upon it. Consider it on all sides. Do you find anything in it like this creative power, by which it raises from nothing a new idea, and with a kind of *fiat*, imitates the omnipotence of its Maker, if I may be allowed so to speak, who called forth into existence all the various scenes of nature? So far from being conscious of this energy in the will, it requires as certain experience as that of which we are possessed, to convince us that such extraordinary effects do ever result from a simple act of volition. . . .

But to hasten to a conclusion of this argument, which is already drawn out too great a length: we have sought in vain for an idea of power or necessary to connection in all the sources from which we could suppose it to be derived. It appears that, in single instances of the operation of bodies, we never can, by our utmost scrutiny, discover anything but one event following another, without being able to comprehend any force or power by which the cause operates, or any connection between it and its supposed effect. The same difficulty occurs in contemplating the operations of mind on body—where we observe the motion of the latter to follow upon the volition of the former, but are not able to observe or conceive the tie which binds together the motion and volition, or the energy by which the mind produces this effect. The authority of the will over its own faculties and ideas is not a whit more comprehensible: so that, upon the whole, there appears not, throughout all nature, any one instance of connection which is conceivable by us. All events seem entirely loose and separate. One event follows another; but we never can observe any tie between them. They seem *conjoined*, but never *connected*. And as we can have no idea of anything which never appeared to our outward sense or inward sentiment, the necessary conclusion *seems* to be that we have no idea of connection or power at all, and that these words are absolutely without any meaning, when employed either in philosophical reasonings or common life.

But there still remains one method of avoiding this conclusion, and one source which we have not yet examined. When any natural object or event is presented, it is impossible for us, by any sagacity or penetration, to discover, or even conjecture, without experience, what event will result from it, or to carry our foresight beyond that object which is immediately present to the memory and senses. Even after one instance or experiment where we have observed a particular event to follow upon another, we are not entitled to form a general rule, or foretell what will happen in like cases; it being justly esteemed an unpardonable temerity to judge of the whole course of nature from one single experiment, however accurate or certain. But when one particular species of event has always, in all instances, been conjoined with another, we make no longer any scruple of foretelling one upon the appearance of the other, and of employing that reasoning which can alone assure us of any matter of fact or existence. We then call the one object, *cause*; the other, *effect*. We suppose that there is some connection between them; some power in the one, by which it infallibly produces the other, and operates with the greatest certainty and strongest necessity.

It appears, then, that this idea of a necessary connection among events arises from a number of similar instances which occur of the constant conjunction of these events; nor can that idea ever be suggested by any one of these instances, surveyed in all possible lights and positions. But there is nothing in a number of instances, different from every single instance, which is supposed to be exactly similar; except only, that after a repetition of similar instances, the mind is carried by habit, upon the appearance of one event, to expect its usual attendant, and to believe that it will exist. This connection, therefore, which we *feel* in the mind, this customary transition of the imagination from one object to its usual attendant, is the sentiment or impression from which we form the idea of power or necessary connection. Nothing farther is in the case. Contemplate the subject on all sides; you will never find any other origin of that idea. This is the sole difference between one instance, from which we can never receive the idea of connection, and a number of similar instances, by which it is suggested. The first time a man saw the communication of motion by impulse, as by the shock of two billiard balls, he could not pronounce that the one event was *connected*; but only that it was *conjoined* with the other. After he has observed several instances of this nature, he then pronounces them to be *connected*. What alteration has happened to give rise to this new idea of *connection*? Nothing but that he now *feels* these events to be *connected* in his imagination, and can readily foretell the existence of one from the appearance of the other. When we say, therefore, that one object is connected with another, we mean only that they have acquired a connection in our thought, and give rise to this inference, by which they become proofs of each other's existence: a conclusion which is somewhat extraordinary, but which seems founded on sufficient evidence. Nor will its evidence be weakened by any general diffidence of the understanding, or sceptical suspicion concerning every conclusion which is new and extraordinary. No conclusions can be more agreeable to scepticism than such as make discoveries concerning the weakness and narrow limits of human reason and capacity.

And what stronger instance can be produced of the surprising ignorance and weakness of the understanding than the present? For surely, if there be any relation among objects which it imports to us to know perfectly, it is that of cause and effect. On this are founded all our reasonings concerning matter of fact or existence. By means of it alone we attain any assurance concerning objects which are removed from the present testimony of our memory and senses. The only immediate utility of all sciences, is to teach us, how to control and regulate future events by their causes. Our thoughts and inquiries are, therefore, every moment, employed about this relation: yet so imperfect are the ideas which we form concerning it, that it is impossible to give any just definition of cause, except what is drawn from something extraneous and foreign to it. Similar objects are always conjoined with similar. Of this we have experience. Suitably to this experience, therefore, we may define a cause to be *an object, followed by another, and where all the objects similar to the first are followed by objects similar to the second.* Or in other words *where, if the first object had not been, the second never had existed.* The appearance of a cause always conveys the mind, by a customary transition, to the idea of the effect. Of this also we have experience. We may, therefore, suitably to this experience, form another definition of cause, and call it, *an object followed by another, and whose appearance always conveys the thought to that other.* But though both these definitions be drawn from circumstances foreign to the cause, we cannot remedy this inconvenience, or attain any more perfect definition, which may point out that circumstances in the cause, which gives it a connection with its effect. We have no idea of this connection, nor even any distinct notion what it is we desire to know, when we endeavor at a conception of it. We say, for instance, that the vibration of this string is the cause of this particular sound. But what do we mean by that affirmation? We either mean *that this vibration is followed by this sound, and that all similar vibrations have been followed by similar sounds*: Or, *that this vibration is followed by this sound, and that upon the appearance of one the mind anticipates the senses, and forms immediately an idea of the other.* We may consider the relation of cause and effect in either of these two lights; but beyond these, we have no idea of it.

To recapitulate, therefore, the reasonings of this section: every idea is copied from some preceding impression or sentiment; and where we cannot find any impression, we may be certain that there is no idea. In all single instances of the operation of bodies or minds, there is nothing that produces any impression, nor consequently can suggest any idea of power or necessary connection. But when many uniform instances appear, and the same object is always followed by the same event; we then begin to entertain the notion of cause and connection. We then feel a new sentiment or impression, to wit, a customary connection in the thought or imagination between one object and its usual attendant; and this sentiment is the original of that idea which we seek for. For as this idea arises from a number of similar instances, and not from any single instance, it must arise from that circumstance, in which the number of instances differ from every individual instance. But this customary connection or transition of the imagination is the only circumstance in which they differ. In every other particular they are alike. The first instance which we saw of motion communicated by the shock of two billiard balls (to return to this obvious illustration) is exactly similar to any instance that may, at present, occur to us; except only, that we could not, at first, *infer* one event from the other; which we are enabled to do at present, after so long a course of uniform experience. I know not whether the reader will readily apprehend this reasoning. I am afraid that, should I multiply words about it, or throw it into a greater variety of lights, it would only become more obscure and intricate. In all abstract reasonings there is one point of view which, if we can happily hit, we shall go farther towards illustrating the subject than by all the eloquence in the world. This point of view we should endeavor to reach, and reserve the flowers of rhetoric for subjects which are more adapted to them.

16

BRAND BLANSHARD

introduction

Brand Blanshard's philosophy, particularly with respect to causation, represents the extreme opposite of Hume's. Blanshard is one of the few metaphysical philosophers who manages to express his ideas clearly, and therefore rather little is needed here by way of interpretation or clarification. It will be enough to put his theory of causation within the context of his larger views, and to comment briefly on his more fundamental contentions.

Blanshard views the entire world as interconnected in a rational way, so that it is susceptible to being understood by human reason. The world is not merely a huge congeries of odds and ends having little to do with each other. A thorough understanding of any of it would, on the contrary, yield an understanding of the whole. Thus understanding is not achieved just by looking at things. What is seen must then be understood, and understanding consists of grasping the rational, and hence to some extent necessary, connections between things. It was, of course, precisely this kind of philosophical outlook that Hume's skeptical arguments were meant to undermine.

Hume, believing that we can have no meaningful idea that does not rest upon some kind of perception, declared that we have no real perception of any necessary connections in nature, hence we really have no meaningful idea of such connections other than what we project from our own subjective habits of expectation. But Blanshard, standing on Hume's own ground of direct perception, declares that this is simply untrue. We do see necessary connections between certain ordinary things we experience. Upon seeing two pebbles from one's left hand placed next to two pebbles from one's right hand, for example, we see not only that four pebbles result, but that this results *necessarily*, that it could come out no other way. And this necessity is immediately and easily seen. Or upon seeing a square inscribed within a circle, we not only see that the former encloses a smaller area than the latter, we also see immediately that this is necessarily so.

But even granting such fairly obvious observations, can we then go on to say, as Hume denied, that we see any similar necessity in the relationship of a cause to its effect? Do we merely see one thing following upon another, with no more connection between them than mere sequence? Or do we also see that one *must* follow upon the other? And if we are tempted to say this, should we then say, with Hume, that this "must" expresses no more than our inner expectation of a certain effect from a certain cause?

Blanshard argues rather convincingly that the lack of apparent necessity between causes and effects is usually the result of an incomplete description of both. We do not, to be sure, see why a specific case of malaria fever *must* result from the bite of a particular mosquito—why it could not just as well result from, say, a dog bite, or from anything under the sun. But this is because we are here referring to links within a causal chain that are quite far removed from each other. When we fill in the description, to include all the links, then we see that the immediate cause of the malady, namely, the destruction of hemoglobin within the blood cells, does have a necessary connection with it, such that we can see not only that starvation of tissue results, but how it necessarily results. Effects appear conceptually inseparable from their causes, once those causes and those effects are described in detail. We may not, at first, see why gasoline must ignite in the presence of flame, instead, say, of solidifying; but once one understands in some detail the chemical nature of gasoline, and the nature of heat, then the connection between these events ceases to appear accidental. Gasoline, sufficiently understood, comes to be seen as something whose nature is to react the way that it does. Such understanding is not a mere habit of expectation but the perception of a necessary connection. And so it is, Blanshard believes, with respect to the whole of nature. We often do not see why things must be as they are. But as we come to understand more and more *what* something is, then we come to understand more and more, not only what its causal relations with other things turn out to be, but why they are what we find them to be.

Brand Blanshard was born in 1892, educated at the University of Michigan, Columbia, Oxford, and Harvard, and was until his retirement Sterling professor of philosophy at Yale. In the arguments that follow, excerpted from his book *Reason and Analysis*, he attempts to reinstate much of what Hume's critical analysis was aimed at destroying.

Causation as Rational Connection*

Causation is only one strand in the network of relations that holds things together, and any one of these relations might in theory be singled out by the philosopher for special attention. Most of them have in fact been passed over as of minor importance. But a few of them have held a continued fascination for both the scientific and the speculative mind. Among this select few causation is perhaps the most conspicuous member. Why is this? There are several reasons.

(1) It is a relation, as Hume pointed out, to which we have to appeal if we are to take one step beyond the given into the world of physical things, or to past or future. If we perceive a voice as a wife's or a friend's, or assume that the postman has left the mail in the hall, or expect the floor to hold us up when we walk, we are depending on causal relations. If there were no such relations, we should have no reason for believing that there were any physical things or that anything would behave in one way rather than another. Causation is the lifeline connecting us with the world.

(2) It is also our instrument of *control*. Our intellectual interest, as Dewey has emphasized, tends to follow our practical needs, and science to enlist in the service of technology. A grasp of the causes of things will give us command over them if anything can. As long as the causes of malaria and yellow fever were unknown, we were helpless about them; once their causes were brought to light, we could see what must be done to eradicate them. If such other plagues of mankind as cancer, juvenile delinquency and senile decay are to be eliminated, the first step is to master their causes.

(3) But science does not aim merely at control; its primary aim is at *understanding*. It considers that the understanding of a thing or event has been achieved when the laws that govern it have been formulated. Not all these laws, indeed, are causal laws. The laws of motion, the laws that all mammals are vertebrates, the law that all ruminating animals have cloven hooves, the law that light travels at a certain speed, are not statements of causal connection. Nevertheless, causal laws are the staple of science. They are laws that would have first mention as examples of scientific explanation, for they carry with them the strongest sense of understanding. When we ask

the question Why? about any event—a disease, a tidal wave, a war, a motor 'accident'—what we are asking for is an explanation in terms of its causes. In natural science that is what explanation normally means.

(4) If the mastery of causal laws gives control and understanding, it is because such laws are more than devices of our own. They belong to nature; they are part of the network, the set of objective ties, that bind events together. The scientist's traditional assumption has been that nothing happens by accident, that whether he knows the cause of an event or not, it is there to be found and is the condition of the event's occurrence. Indeed every event seems to be implicated with every other. Not only does each event have a precursor in a line that stretches backward without beginning and forward without end, but these lines of causation intercross. My use of a pen at this moment would seem to have no causal connection with someone's eating his lunch at the same moment in Los Angeles. And this is no doubt true if one means a connection in a straight temporal line. But there are indirect causal lines. After all, it is not fancy but highly probable fact that the occurrence of either event depends on another celebrated event that happened at Marathon some twenty-five centuries earlier, so that each of the present events is connected through a common cause with the other. The universe itself may be regarded as one gigantic congeries of events linked directly or indirectly by a network of causal laws. And since the strands that form this network belong to the nature of things no less than the items linked, philosophers have often felt that to understand them fully would be to grasp the necessary order of the universe.

The philosophy of science that has been most popular in recent years denies that there is any such order. A causal law is a statement that an event of the kind A is regularly followed by an event of the kind B. That is the end of the matter; the question *why* B should follow is an idle question; it asks for what cannot be given because it is not there. Here Russell and Wittgenstein returned to Hume. According to Hume, 'we may define a cause to be an object followed by another, and where all the objects similar to the first are followed by objects similar to the second'.[1] We know that a billiard ball, when struck by another, does in fact roll away; a child knows, after sticking its finger in a candle flame, that the flame does in fact burn; that is all we know in either case and, in principle, all we shall ever know.

This doctrine, when first announced, was a shock to both common sense and philosophy, and rumblings of discontent continue in both quarters. There was no objection to holding that causality did involve regular sequence; the objection from both parties was that the regular-sequence view left out something that was plainly there and was of prime importance. The missing element, however, was not the same for the two parties. What common sense thought had been left out was the element of constraint or

---

[1] *Inquiry Concerning Human Understanding, Sec. VII, Pt. 2.*

compulsion. When one billiard ball struck another, it surely gave it a push; it compelled it to move by exerting force on it. For ordinary thought, this is surely the essential element in the case, and to ignore it seemed perverse. On the other hand, what philosophers particularly objected to was the exclusion of necessity. They had been in the habit of thinking that one could *reason* from effect to cause, that the two were so related that, given the first, one could with sufficient acumen *deduce* the second. Aquinas thought that, given the existence of the world, he could deduce its Creator; Spinoza that, given the existence of a pebble, he could deduce an absolute substance; Locke that, given his percept of a sphere, he could deduce a physical thing that caused it and was like it. If such reasoning was illicit, much that had passed as sound metaphysics would have to be discarded. Plain men and philosophers were thus united in feeling that a causality from which force and necessity were omitted was a mere shell of itself.

The genius of Hume is apparent in the persuasive clearness with which he met these objections. Never perhaps, except by Berkeley, has a major metaphysical upset been effected with arguments so simple. In causation, rightly seen, he held, there is no trace of either compulsion or necessity, and without these all that is left is regular sequence. To the contention that the cause exercises force or compulsion he replied that this supposed force is really our own experience wrongly projected into things. It is true that when we push a table we feel sensations of strain and resistance, but the billiard ball that strikes another has no such sensations. It is true that when, after repeatedly seeing a ball roll away upon being struck, we next see a ball rolling toward another, there is a felt tendency to expect the second to roll away. To that extent there exists in our minds a gentle feeling of constraint. It is natural and easy to project this constraint, belonging only to our habit of thought, into the action of the outward cause. But the projection is plainly illicit. Does it follow that when a hammer strikes a nail or a bolt of lightning splits an oak, we speak uncritically in ascribing to the cause any exercise of force? Yes, Hume would reply, the inference is not to be escaped. The only force we know is a kind of sensation. There is no such sensation in the hammer that strikes the nail or the bolt that splits the oak. To place it there is a regression to animism.

As for the element of necessity in causation, Hume dismisses it in a similar though slightly more complicated way. He bases his argument on the assumption that ideas are copies of sensations, and that if we claim to have a certain idea, we must be prepared to point to the sensation or sensations from which it is derived. Now rationalists had said that when the flame produced the burn, or one ball made another roll, there was a logical *must* in the situation; the effect *had* to happen; we could see that once the cause occurred, the result *could* not have been otherwise.

Hume's reply was threefold. (1) If it is true that we have this idea of necessity, we must be able to point to the sensation that gave rise to it. Now a logical relation of this kind is not the sort of thing that could be seen or heard or smelt or otherwise sensed at all. Hence, never having sensed it, we have no copy of it in the way of an idea. We only delude ourselves if we think we have. (2) Hume undertook to confirm this view by means of a rapid survey. There were three types of situation in which causality appeared, and he sought to show that necessity was to be found in none of them. (a) Cause and effect might both be physical, as when the rolling of one ball made another roll. We have seen already how he handled this. What we are experiencing is the fact of sequence, not the necessity of it; the necessity ascribed only reflects the firmness of our habit of expectation. (b) Cause and effect may both be mental; the thought of Theodore Roosevelt 'suggests by association' the thought of Franklin Roosevelt. But in such association of ideas, which is no doubt a fact, is there any logical necessity? If we think of the first Roosevelt, *must* we go on to think of the second? Obviously not, and of course we often do not in fact. (c) A physical event may cause a mental one, or a mental a physical one. (i) A flame, to take our former example, may cause a burning sensation. Now we have no doubt that flames have been followed by burning sensations, or that they will continue to be. But do we see that they *must* produce them, in the same transparent way in which we can see that the diameter of a circle must cut it in equal halves? Clearly not. The question why?, asked about this latter statement, would be pointless, since we have already reached the necessity which the question why? is asking. But between the action of the flame on the finger and the feeling of a burning sensation there is a long series of intermediate steps about any one of which, let alone the series as a whole, we could perfectly well ask why. And if we did, we should not get a glimmering of an answer. Why a change in the skin on our fingertips should be followed by the mental event called pain lies in total darkness. (ii) Nor do we seem to be better off as to the action of mind on body. We will to lift our hand and the hand comes up, and it may be thought captious to make a mystery of it. But after all, familiarity is not intelligibility. Hume pointed out that if the volition was to make our arm move, it must somehow affect the motion of the atoms in our heads, and that there was no profounder mystery in the world than how it did this; we are as ignorant of the process as we should be if our wish were to move mountains or enable beggars to ride.

(3) Hume offered a third argument which he thought clinched the case completely. This was a *reductio ad absurdum* designed to show that the cause-effect relation could not possibly contain the ground-consequent or implying relation. Take any case of logical implication, for example that in which being the diameter of a given circle implies that it cuts the circle in half. If you know that the 'halves' of the circle before you are not equal, you know that the line cannot be a diameter; in logical jargon, $(p \supset q. \sim q) \supset \sim p$; to deny the consequent and still affirm the antecedent is

held to be self-contradiction. Now is there any self-contradiction in saying that the effect in a causal sequence might not have occurred, while the cause occurred nevertheless? None whatever. There is no contradiction in supposing that I make the same volition that has always caused my arm to rise, and that nothing happens. If this were self-contradictory, it would be strictly inconceivable, whereas it is perfectly easy to conceive; indeed it is what actually occurs when the man with paralysis wills to lift his arm. Can the effect equally be conceived without the cause? Undoubtedly, Hume would reply. It is entirely conceivable that the second billiard ball should roll away by itself, or should suddenly secede from the universe, or start talking Hebrew. To say that this is improbable is to miss the point. What is alleged is that it is logically impossible, and this it clearly is not, since such an impossibility could not be conceived, and this quite obviously can.

For Hume and his many followers, such considerations were decisive. It seemed clear to them that causation had no necessity about it. The linkage that it supplies between events is not intelligible in the sense that entailment is intelligible; that two events should accompany each other is just as little necessary as the chance that two dice should both fall with a six up. The man who argued that because one die showed a six the next must do so too would be regarded as absurd; and he would really be arguing with equal absurdity if he held that because one event happens any other event *must* happen. Nor does the fact that, so far as we know, events of this kind have always gone together make any difference in principle. The fact that snow has always been white does not make it more intelligible *why* it is white, or less thinkable that it should be black or purple. Regularities we can admit. But there is no ground whatever for converting these regularities into necessities. All that we can sensibly mean by saying that A causes B is that whenever there occurs an event of the kind A—defined as precisely as possible—it is followed by an event of the kind B—defined with similar care. And this is what is meant by the 'uniform-sequence' view.

What are we to say of this defence? It evidently depends on three propositions: first, that all our ideas come from sense; second, that we never apprehend necessity as having a part in causation; third, that cause and effect may be dissociated without contradiction. I may as well say at once that no one of these arguments, as stated, seems to me convincing.

(1) No doubt Hume is right that a relation of necessity cannot be touched, seen, or tasted, indeed is not a sense content of any kind. But the conclusion that we never find it in our experience of nature does not follow unless in conjunction with the further premise that our experience of nature is wholly sense experience. And to say that is to beg the question. For the contention of the non-Humians is that they do in fact apprehend (if not by sense, then by some other appropriate faculty such as reason or intelligence) necessary connections between certain sensibly presented qualities. It is no sufficient

answer to this to say that experience is confined to sense qualities. Whether it is so confined is precisely the point at issue.

The question, then, is whether we do find in experience nonsensible necessities. And it seems plain enough that we do. Here are six or eight of them chosen at random: that this scarlet patch is more like this crimson patch than like that azure patch; that this surface cannot at once be blue and red; that this pink shade is a colour; that the space between the ends of this ruler can be divided without limit; that any two leaves on that tree and any other two make four; that these two lines do not enclose a space; that if this triangle has equal sides it has equal angles; that this sweet taste is different from that sour one. This last example is extremely simple, and if admitted, it will carry necessity right through our perceptual world. And does it not have to be admitted? What we mean by 'sweet' is not the same as not being sour, but if any taste is sweet it excludes sourness, not in fact merely, but necessarily. The world of perceptual experience is honeycombed with necessary involvements and exclusions. Hume's suggestion that since ideas come from experience, they must all come from sense experience turns on a prejudgment of what experience is like.

(2) It will be convenient to look next at the third argument. This is that if causality involves necessity, then a denial of the consequent would, as in hypothetical reasoning, commit us to denying the antecedent, whereas in this case it does not. We can perfectly well imagine the second billiard ball's not rolling while supposing the first to behave normally, or the failure of our arm to rise, though we make the customary volition. If the cause entailed the effect, we should see that, given the antecedent, the consequent *had* to happen; to say this and also to admit that sometimes it does not happen should be merely to contradict oneself. Yet no such contradiction is involved.

Now note, to begin with, that the argument is stated, following Hume, in terms of imagination. We can *imagine* the first ball's rolling without the second doing so; we can *imagine* resolving to lift an arm and the arm's not rising. But the question whether, given a set of conditions, something might have happened other than what did happen is not to be settled by asking whether we can imagine it to have happened. It is likely enough that we can, but that proves nothing beyond the liveliness of our imagination. I can imagine myself stealing off to a work-room in the cellar and emerging with a perpetual motion machine; I can imagine myself spending an evening over figures and diagrams and showing the world next morning that at last the circle has been squared. But the ability to imagine such events does not show that they are in fact possible. This depends on whether they are consistent with certain conditions, consistent in the second instance with the postulates of geometry and in the first instance with the laws of mechanics. It may be said that the laws of mechanics at least are themselves empirical only, so there would be no inconsistency in supposing them suspended. But whether they are or not is hardly a point to be settled by appeal to the imagination. If a scientist maintained that there was something in the nature of matter that rendered Newton's three laws of motion necessary, we could not refute him by imagining a ball to cease rolling when there is no obstruction or to turn suddenly into a cow and leap over the moon. [2]

Whether causality involves necessity can be tested only by a case in which the cause and the effect are conceived clearly and distinctly and one then asks oneself whether the first conception entails the second. A causal law, whether stating a uniform sequence or an entailment, is always a statement that something of the *kind* A causes something of the *kind* B, and a kind is something conceived rather than imagined, as is also the linkage of kinds. Now just as the disproof that such linkage is necessary is not to be found in imagination, so also it is not to be found in actual cases. At first we seem to have such a case in the paralysed man who wills to lift his arm without result. If the cause entails the effect, it is argued, we should be able to see that the arm *must* rise, but since it does not, we have here a clear case in which the cause does not necessitate the effect. But the example proves nothing. For if the arm does not rise, then even in the uniform-sequence view, what we have is not a case of cause and effect at all; the failure of the 'effect' to follow shows that the sequence is not uniform, and therefore not causal. Indeed the uniform-sequence theory cannot hope to disprove the entailment theory by instances in which cause and effect are disjoined, for if they are thus disjoined, they are *ipso facto* not cause and effect.

If the entailment theory is to be disproved, then, it must be not through an imagined or actual disjoining of cause and effect, but through a conceived disjoining. The critic must produce a case in which two events are admitted to be causally related and in which we have a clear and complete apprehension of the connected terms; and we must then be able to see that no necessity connects them. In the abstract, this test may seem easy to apply. Unfortunately it is very hard to apply, for the reason that the full and clear grasp of either cause or effect is itself so difficult to achieve. The critic produces a sample in which cause and effect, though never disjoined in fact, seem divorceable in theory, only to find, when challenged, that the true cause or effect or both have not yet been arrived at. It is not improbable, indeed, that one ground for doubt whether A is really the cause is the inability to see any reason why it should produce B. At any rate, as long as there remains an interval not bridged by any visible necessity, the reflective mind continues to look further. Perhaps the commonest of these intervals are those presented, on the one hand, by space and time, and on the other, by the increasing complexity of the cause as we study it.

---

[2] Speaking strictly, we must admit that the logically impossible is unimaginable as well as inconceivable. If Flatland or a square equal in area to a given circle is not logically possible, one cannot imagine it in full detail. I am using 'imagination' here in its looser popular sense.

Consider how we reject an antecedent as the cause until it achieves approximate identity with the effect. A man gets malaria, and we say that he has been bitten by an anopheles mosquito. Of course there is nothing in such a bite, so far as we can see, to make malaria necessary. But then are we quite clear that the bite *is* the cause? It clearly happens at times without an ensuing malaria. The disease must be caused by something nearer to it in time and space. This would seem to be the pouring into the bloodstream, by means of the bite, of a mass of parasites called *plasmodia*. But we cannot stop here either. The mere presence of the parasites in the bloodstream is not the cause; they may be present while their host shows no sign of the disease. They must not only be present; they must attack the red blood corpuscles in the stream. But even this is not the proximate cause, for there is still a temporal interval between it and the appearance of the recognized forms of the disease. Following the attacks of the parasites, the blood corpuscles are systematically drained of their haemoglobin. Is this, then, the cause? It is natural enough to say so, but we might still intelligibly ask, Could not this happen and the disease still not happen? So we again move nearer to the effect. Since haemoglobin is the means by which oxygen is conveyed to the tissues, its disappearance means that these tissues are starved and cannot function. Here at last we have reached a condition which cannot occur without the occurrence of the disease. But then this condition *is* the disease; this starvation of bodily tissues is the essential constitutive factor in it. As long as the series of changes presents us merely with state A followed unintelligibly by a different state B, we continue to hunt for a cause that will somehow bridge the gap in both necessity and time.

Consider again how, with reflection, we broaden the scope of the cause. We begin by taking it as the efficient or precipitating cause, that is, the one change occurring immediately before the effect and in proximity with it. What caused the gun to go off was pulling the trigger; what caused the window to break was the impact of the stone; what caused malaria was the bite of the mosquito, or some other event known to physicians that preceded the disease more closely. But if the cause of an event includes that without which the event would not have happened, it includes much besides the efficient cause. 'The real cause of the phenomenon,' as Mill recognized, 'is the assemblage of all its conditions.'[3] A man's contracting malaria has many conditions that no one would think worth mentioning, but are as essential to what happened as anything that an expert would point out. If the patient had no air to breathe, if gravitation did not hold him to the earth, if the sun did not provide him with a certain amount of warmth, if any one of dozens of co-operating organs in his body were not functioning in its normal way, if his prevailing cast of mind were more sanguine or melancholic, the course of his

[3]System of Logic, Bk. III. Ch. 5, Sec. 3.

disease would not be precisely what it is. Each one of these is what is called a necessary condition of the disease's occurring as it did. When all of them are put together, they form the sufficient condition. And it is the sufficient condition that is here meant by the cause.

It will now perhaps be apparent why it is so difficult to show that causality does not involve necessity, even if it does not in fact. The critic would have to ascertain and clearly conceive the sufficient cause on the one hand and the total proximate effect on the other, and he would have to show that though these two were never in fact dissociated from each other, there were no reasons why they should not be, since there was no necessity lurking within this uniformity or behind it. This is an impossible undertaking. It would require one to prove a negative by exhausting in thought the nature of the cause and the effect, and we have just seen two reasons why this is impracticable. We never reach the proximate cause of anything, since between any alleged cause and effect an intermediate state exists, and since the cause as the sum of the conditions is too complex to be exhausted. Hume's argument, then, to show that causation excludes necessity carries little conviction. That argument was that whereas in a case of genuine necessity the denial of the consequent committed us by clear necessity to denying the antecedent, in a case of cause and effect we could always deny the effect and see that there was *no* necessity constraining us to deny the cause. But any such negative insight would require a knowledge of the terms and their sequence that we do not in fact possess. . . .

We must surely admit Hume's contention that through the larger part of the known world—he would say all of it—the nature of the causal process is at present impenetrable to us. We do not know why a volition moves a muscle, or why a burn hurts, or why a nail sinks at the blow of a hammer. Is it reasonable to believe that there is necessity in such behaviour, in spite of our failure to detect it? I think it is, and shall try to state the chief grounds for thinking so.

(1) The first is that, hard as it may be to accept the necessity thesis, it is still harder to accept the alternative. Scientists sometimes say that uniformity is all they need or want. Perhaps it is; their interest is in the discovery of laws, not in the explanation of why laws should be what they are. Nevertheless uniformity cannot by itself be the whole story, for if it were, there would not be even that. Let us suppose for a moment that between two events, A and B, there is no sort of constraint or inner connection, no reason why B should follow rather than anything else. If this were true, B's regular attendance upon A would be a miracle. With no ground for its appearance in the nature of anything preceding it, B's occurrence along with A would be a matter of chance, and if we made any calculations about it, they would have to be based on the theory of chance. This theory is clear enough in simple cases. Suppose we throw a die and get a 3. We then ask what the chances are

that we shall get a 3 on the next throw. They are 1 in 6. What are the chances that we shall get two successive 3's? They are 1 in 36. The probability that we should get any of the numbers in the die n times in succession is $1/6n$, and it is obvious that this fraction dwindles with enormous speed as one goes on. In an actual game with dice where it was important to get 3's, how long should we be willing to assume that nothing but chance was involved if an opponent continued to get them? Suppose he got 3's three times in succession. The odds against that are 215 to 1, and we should regard him as remarkably lucky. Suppose he got five 3's running; the odds against that are 7775 to 1, and we should certainly grow suspicious. A few more such successes, and we should be confident that either he or the dice or both were in need of rigorous inspection.

Now suppose that one billiard ball hits another which rolls away, and suppose there is no link whatever between these events but chance conjunction. If that were true, the likelihood that the second ball would behave in that way again when struck by the first will have to be calculated, if at all, by the theory of chances. It is true that since the ball could behave not in one of six ways only but in any one of an unlimited number of ways, the chances are not definitely calculable; but we can see that the odds against a single repetition would be enormous, and the odds against this repetition continuing would be enormous beyond conception. Yet it is just this constant repetition that we actually find. It continues not merely for a few cases, or a few hundred ones, but so far as we can see, through an inexhaustible series of cases. To suggest that this constant accompaniment is a matter of chance is to abuse the meaning of the word. If it were a matter of chance in the strict sense, the lawfulness we find in nature would simply not be there. Something more is clearly at work.

(2) If asked what this is, we can only say that it is some kind of necessity. Here we shall probably meet the question, 'How can you insist that necessity is present and also admit that you cannot see it? When you say that the diameter bisects a circle or that what has shape has size, you can say that necessity is present because you do see it; you are laying hold of what is self-evident. When you say that the causal connection is necessary, one assumes that you can point to something that is similarly self-evident. But you have just admitted that causal connections throughout the physical and psycho-physical realm are entirely opaque to us.'

We have granted, it is true, that we cannot generally see why the effect follows the cause. But that is not the same as to say that we wholly lack a priori insight into causation. I am inclined to follow Professor Broad in holding that we do have such insight. He thinks we know a priori several propositions that apply to the causation of changes generally. [4] (a) 'Every

---

[4]*Examination of McTaggart's Philosophy*, I, 232–235. In *The Philosophy of C. D. Broad* (ed. by P. A. Schilpp), 741–744, he offers a further analysis of some of these propositions.

change has a cause.' It is perhaps not self-evident that the mere continuance of a process requires a special explanation—the continued resting of a ball, for example; but if anyone were to suggest to us that at some point the ball began to move, or increased the speed of its movement without any cause at all, we should say he must certainly be mistaken. (b) The second proposition goes on to say something about the natures of A and B, though what it says remains highly abstract. It says that 'the cause of any *change* contains a change as a factor. This seems to me as evident,' Broad adds, 'as any proposition that I have ever met with.' A change cannot come from nothing at all; *ex nihilo nihil fit*. Nor could it come from a state that remained unchanged through time, for then there would be nothing to account for its appearance at one time rather than another. We are convinced that there must be something to account for this, and that it can only be another change. Thirdly (c) 'if a change issues from a moment *t*, then all changes which are factors in its cause are changes which enter into *t*'. 'I think,' says Broad, 'that this proposition is the accurate expression of the common dictum that a cause must precede its effect and be continuous with it in time.'[5] (d) To these propositions I would add another, namely that the cause and the effect are linked through their characters, that it is in virtue of A's being a change of the character *a* that it produces B with the character *b*. This does not exclude the possibility of alternative causes of B. It does imply that if there are such causes, it is something in the nature of each of the alternate causes in virtue of which the effect is produced.

I am inclined to think that these are all a priori insights into causality. If they are, it is untrue to say that the causal relation is wholly opaque and impenetrable to us. Even if we do not know why a particular change produced another, we do have necessary knowledge about the causation of changes generally.

(3) Can we say anything more about the nature of this necessary knowledge? Here again we may start from Broad. 'It may be noticed,' he writes, 'that in English we have the three sentences, "Nothing has ϕ and lacks ψ", "Nothing can have ϕ and lack ψ", and "Nothing could have had ϕ and lacked ψ". The first expresses a Universal of Fact, the second a Universal of Law, and the third an Absolute Necessity.'[6] The universal of fact, 'nothing has ϕ and lacks ψ', would be exemplified, I suppose, by the observation made by Darwin that tom-cats that are white and blue-eyed are also deaf. The universal of law, 'nothing can have ϕ and lack ψ', Broad illustrates by 'anything that had inertial mass would have gravitational mass'. Absolute necessity he illus-

---

[5]*Examination*, I, 233. Broad adds a fourth proposition about causality that seems to him self-evident: 'A given change in a given process issuing from a given moment cannot have more than one total cause.' But upon further analysis of this proposition in *The Philosophy of Broad*, 744, he writes that it seems not impossible that a change should have several co-existing total causes. I doubt therefore whether he would wish to hold to his original proposition.

[6]*Examination of McTaggart's Philosophy*, I, 243.

trates by the proposition, 'anything that had shape would have extension'. To which of these types does a causal statement belong?

Suppose I decide to lift my arm, and the arm moves; here we should say that the decision caused the movement. Regarding this sort of sequence Broad says, 'I *know* that *this* change would not have issued from that moment unless *that* decision had entered into that moment.' If it is objected that my body might have been electrically stimulated to such behaviour, the statement may be amended by the addition 'if the other conditions were as I believed them to be'. Two points about this case should be noted, for when put together they make it clear why causality is such a puzzle to philosophers. On the one hand, the way mind acts on body is as mysterious as anything in our experience. On the other hand, if one can say, as Broad does, and perhaps most people would, 'I *know* that *this* change would not have issued from that moment unless *that* decision had entered into that moment', then one is claiming a very different kind of knowledge from that of a 'universal of fact'. To say of a tom-cat simply on the ground of its not being deaf, 'I *know* that it is not white and blue-eyed', would seem presumptuous, since between these characters we see no linkage except that they have in certain cases been found together. To say that I know that my arm would not have moved as it did if I had not decided to move it is certainly to claim more than such events have regularly accompanied each other; it is to claim that the decision was a *necessary* condition of the movement. What sort of necessity belongs to such a condition?

Broad suggests only two types of necessity in terms of which it could be understood, the 'universal of law' and 'absolute necessity'. The universal of law he illustrates, as we have seen, by the connection between inertial mass and gravitational mass. What distinguishes this necessity from absolute necessity is that it is contingent in the following sense: though, given the structure of the actual world, a thing could not have the one kind of mass without having the other, still there *might have been* a world in which the one appeared without the other, whereas if the characters were connected by absolute necessity, there *could not have been* a world in which a thing had the one character (e. g. shape) without the other (e. g. extension).

Now it seems to me that the notion of contingent necessity is a half-way house in which we cannot rest. To be sure, it is a notion continually used in scientific and other explanation; to explain a fact, we bring it under a law; to explain the law, we show that it follows necessarily from a more general law, and the more general the better. But the necessity here lies merely in the linkage between the propositions, not in the propositions themselves; if the more general law is true, the less general follows, but there is no implication that the general law is itself a necessary truth, nor therefore that the derived truth is. Such explanation is of course valid, but it leaves the question of chief interest unanswered. Suppose we have traced our derivative laws back to ultimate laws; we explain the fall of a particular raindrop in the end by appeal to the law of gravitation. These ultimate laws will state principles on which the universe is constructed. To say that they are themselves contingently necessary would be meaningless, since there is nothing further on which they could be contingent. Of the three types of universal statement with which Broad provides us, then, only two are available; these ultimate principles must be either universals of fact, presumed to be mere conjunctions, or absolute necessities.

Confronted with this choice, we hold them to be absolute necessities. We cannot show them to be so by simple appeal to self-evidence. But there is other evidence available. Let us look again at the fourth of our a priori causal propositions. This was that if A produces B, it was in virtue of a linkage between the characters *a* and *b*. Now what could be meant by saying that A produces B *in virtue of* its character unless the character of A *determined* what was to emerge?

> If two plants, whose nature is really the same, can determine the growth of totally different seeds, how can we call either the seed *of* that plant at all? Grant that a seed may sometimes be produced by a plant of its own kind, and sometimes by a plant of another kind, without any difference of circumstances, and merely because causes do not act uniformly, and you have really granted that anything may produce anything; flint and steel may produce seed instead of a spark, and oil raise the waves or quench a conflagration. But to say that anything may produce anything is to empty the word "produce" of all its meaning. For the causal relation is a necessary relation, such that if you have one thing you *must* have another. To add that it does not matter what that other is, destroys the force of the *must*. [7]

The point here is a simple one. To say that A produces B in virtue of its special nature *is* to assert necessity. If it is in virtue of a certain character in A and not of something else that B comes into being, then if B was not there, A was not there, and could not have been there. If it was in virtue of being belladonna that something dilated the pupil yesterday, then you know that if, under circumstances otherwise the same, something does not dilate the pupil today, it *cannot* be belladonna; to say that it might be would be to deny that belladonna *as such* acts in a certain way, which is what our causal statement meant. We should be saying that though it was of the nature of belladonna to dilate the pupil, nevertheless, since it sometimes fails to do so, it is *not* of its nature to do so. That is mere incoherence.

Joseph goes so far as to hold that to deny necessity in causation is to deny the law of identity itself. 'To assert a causal connection between *a* and *x* implies that *a* acts as it does because it is what it is; because in fact, it is *a*. So long therefore as it is *a*, it must act thus; and to assert that it may act otherwise on a subsequent occasion is to assert that what is *a* is something else than the *a* which it is declared to be.' [8] Now this is obviously true if the causal properties of a thing are introduced into its nature by definition. We

[7]H. W. B. Joseph, *Introduction to Logic*, 2nd ed., 407.
[8]*Ibid.*, 408.

often conceive things in terms of such properties. 'Glass is brittle, fusible, transparent, hard; gold is malleable, soluble in *aqua regia*, of a certain specific gravity, etc. Matter is impenetrable, mobile, etc. A man is wise, benevolent, quick-tempered, etc.'[9] These may all be taken as causal properties. If gold did not dissolve on being placed in *aqua regia* we should not call it gold because its so behaving is taken as a defining property of gold. But as Professor Stebbing pointed out, we do not commonly include in the nature of a thing all its causal properties.[10] A billiard ball has the causal property of being able to initiate motion in another billiard ball if it strikes it with a certain velocity, but this causal property, Miss Stebbing would say, forms no part of the nature of the ball as we ordinarily think of it. In this she seems to me right. She then goes on to argue that, for all we can see, it is a completely external relation, that is, that the ball could still be precisely what it is if it did not have this property. Here I think she is mistaken. To include a causal property in the definition of a term is not the only way of arguing for its internality. Even if a thing *is* not its behaviour, still if we say that it behaves in this way in virtue of having this nature, that it is *such as* to behave in this way, then we are saying, I suggest, that it *could not* lack the causal property while possessing this nature. The roundness of the ball is a constitutive, not a behavioural property, but if it is in virtue of its roundness that the ball rolls, then a ball that was unable to roll would not be a ball.

I do not think that any of the three arguments we have offered, or all of them together, *prove* that the link between a particular cause and a particular effect involves necessity. It is just conceivable that the regularities in the world, though infinitely improbable on the theory of chances, are what Montague calls 'an outrageous run of luck'. It is conceivable that while we have some self-evident knowledge of causality generally, there remain enclaves of contingency in the occurrence of particular events. It seems barely possible that we are suffering from a deep and distorting illusion in thinking that A's acting as it does follows from its being what it is. We should be adducing more impressive evidence—granted—if we could show in a particular case of hammer and nail that the cause entails the effect, as we can show that being a triangle entails having angles equal to 180 degrees. This we cannot do. But 'C may perfectly well entail E without our being able to see that it does so, and we may have general grounds for assuming the presence of a logical necessity which we cannot grasp ourselves, or at least see that this assumption is really presupposed in all our scientific reasoning'.[11] It is the part of reasonableness to accept a conclusion, even when indemonstrable, if it makes sense of things and no alternative does.

[9]G. F. Stout, *Studies in Philosophy and Psychology*, 305.
[10]*A Modern Introduction to Logic*, 285 ff.
[11]A. C. Ewing, *Idealism*, 167. For another defence of the view that 'natural laws are principles of necessitation', see W. Kneale, *Probability and Induction*, 70 ff.

V

What Can I Hope for?

GOD AND THE CONQUEST OF DEATH

17

SAMUEL CLARKE

introduction

While most of mankind are religious, no one imagines that they arrived at their religious convictions through metaphysical speculation. Religious beliefs arise from human needs, not from human reason. Still, human beings do pride themselves on being rational, so it is not surprising that philosophers, who declare reason to be their light and guide in all things, should raise the question whether theism might be provable as a purely metaphysical hypothesis.

Many philosophers have declared that it is. They have claimed that, quite independently of faith or revelation, drawing its data from experience, unaided human reason can prove the existence of God and, up to a point, describe the divine nature as well.

One of the clearest such proofs is Samuel Clarke's. This author begins with what he takes to be the simplest and most obvious facts of experience, known to everyone, and then step by step deduces from them the foundations of Judeo-Christian theology—that is to say, the existence and chief attributes of God, considered as the creator of heaven and earth.

Clarke composed this discourse as part of a larger set of lectures to the public, which were delivered in St. Paul's in 1704–1705. This may account

for the clarity and beauty of his exposition. Little is needed here by way of
clarifying his thought, but, since it is not a mode of thinking that is popular in
the present age, it will be desirable to say something in order to preclude
needless misunderstanding.

Clarke sets out to demonstrate twelve propositions, of which the first
three, to the effect that there is one eternal god, are purely metaphysical in
character. Seven of the remaining propositions undertake to prove the most
important attributes of this God, such as that He is infinite, omnipotent,
wise, and so on, and the remaining two deal with matters ancillary to the
main line of thought.

Clarke's first proposition, that something has always existed, is really a
very modest claim. He does not say that this something is God nor, indeed,
that some one thing has always existed: only, rather, that there has never
been a time when something or other did not exist. This claim follows, of
course, from the presupposition that no existent thing can arise from sheer
nothingness, together with the incontestable observation that something
does *now* exist. But the second proposition, and certainly the most important, goes much farther. Clarke here shows that some *one* thing must always
have existed, and that this being must be unchangeable and must depend on
nothing else for its existence. This claim follows from the observation that, if
there were *not* such an eternal and changeless being, then reality would be
comprised entirely of a series of beings dependent on each other for their
existence. Of course we know that all the things in the world *are* thus
dependent on each other for their existence—nothing in the world creates
itself, nor does anything arise from nothing. But the question Clarke is
considering is whether that totality of dependent beings—all that do, will, or
have ever existed—can by itself be the sum of reality. If it could, then we
would have to suppose, contrary to reason, *either* that something that
exists—namely, that totality of finite and dependent things—depends on
nothing at all for its existence, *or* that it is the cause of its own existence. And
this is no more possible for the totality of finite and dependent things than it
is for any one of them—the merest flower or raindrop, for instance.

Here we must pause to consider two misguided but common responses to
this line of thought. The first consists of asking whether the totality of finite
things, each dependent on others within that totality, might not *itself* be the
eternal being whose existence Clarke seems to have proved. This response is
simply beside the point; for it is not merely the *eternity* of that being that is
at issue, but its independent existence.

To see this important point, consider the following. Suppose, for the
purpose of discussion, that the sun were an eternal thing; that is, suppose it
had always existed, and had at no point in time first come into existence.
Then it would follow that sunlight had always existed. But the eternity of that

sunlight would not in the least suggest its independent existence. Sunlight depends for its existence on the sun—there can be no sunlight without a sun that is shining. And this dependence is in no way reduced by supposing the sun, hence the sunlight, always to have existed.

And the other misguided response to Clarke's reasoning is to ask whether the totality of finite and dependent things (the world, as we normally think of it) might not be both eternal *and* independent—that is, why *it* might not be the very being whose existence Clarke has established. But it cannot be, for that eternal and independent being has to exist by its own nature. Otherwise, it would be a dependent being, dependent on something *other* than itself for its existence. And the world clearly does not exist by its own nature—there is no reason at all, within the world itself, why anything at all should exist, or why there should be any world. If everything *in* the world is finite and dependent, as it clearly is, then the totality of these things (the world), though it might indeed be infinite and eternal, cannot be independent of anything but itself for its existence. A more common but less accurate way to make this point would be to say that, just as nothing in the world creates *itself*, neither does the world. This we derive from our knowledge of what the world consists of, and not from the requirements of logic, for there is no *logical* reason why the world might not depend on nothing but itself, just as God, according to theology, depends on nothing but Himself.

The third proposition—that the eternal being is "self-existent" or necessary—really follows right from the second. For even an eternal being, as we have seen, cannot be without any cause at all for its existence. Nor can this eternal and independent being require some cause other than itself for its existence—for if it did, then it would be a *dependent* being, and hence, just another item within the totality of dependent beings (the world). That eternal being must, accordingly, be self-caused.

But, as Clarke notes, this must not be taken to mean that it has *produced* itself, or that at some point in time it brought itself into existence. That idea is absurd. The being of which we are speaking is eternal and hence never *came* into existence—it has always existed. But this does not remove the need for a cause of its existence—for nothing (not even God) can depend on *nothing at all* for its existence. This eternal and independent being must, therefore, depend on nothing but itself for its existence. And this is but another way of saying that it exists by its own nature—an idea that is obscure only if applied to the familiar things in the world, which plainly do not exist by their own nature but are dependent on other things.

Again the troublesome question arises, however: If, as seems to be proved, there is some eternal being that exists by its own nature, why cannot that being be simply the world itself, considered as a whole, as Spinoza suggested? Even granting that nothing *in* in the world—not even the most durable and seemingly changeless thing, such as a star—exists by its own nature, why may not the totality of such things, or the totality of *matter*, exist by its own nature, independently of anything else?

This is the crucial question upon which all of Clarke's metaphysical theology turns, and his response to it is most ingenious and metaphysically elegant. If, he says, matter existed by its very nature, then there could be no place where it did not exist, and the world would be one completely solid mass, without any degrees of rarefication or density, and without any vacuum. For if there is any place where no matter exists, this shows that it is possible for matter not to exist there, and hence, possible for it not to exist elsewhere, where perhaps it *does* exist, and hence, possible for it to exist nowhere at all. If it can fail to exist at one place, it can fail to exist at another or at all places. Hence, it does not exist by its own nature.

Those are Clarke's fundamental metaphysical conclusions. The remainder of his work is devoted to establishing some of the attributes of this eternal and changeless being, which, of course, turns out to be God, the creator of heaven and earth. God is shown to be infinite and omnipresent by a line of thought similar to that just considered; namely, if God could fail to exist at one place, then He could fail to exist at another, and hence, could fail to exist altogether, contrary to what has been proved. He is shown to be one by the ingenious argument that, if there were two gods, each independent of the other (and neither could, of course, be *dependent* on the other), then it would follow that either one of them *could* exist alone, and hence, that the other could fail to exist, and hence, that neither would exist by its very nature—contrary to what has been proved. The intelligence of God is shown, Clarke thinks, not only by the order and beauty of the world, but by the intelligence of His creatures, together with the presupposition that no such perfection could arise from something less perfect. And His power of free choice is thought to follow from his intelligence, it being contradictory to think of intelligent action as being nothing more than a passive response to causes. God's infinite power, wisdom, and goodness are thought by Clarke to follow from similar considerations.

Little metaphysical acumen is needed to see that Clarke's arguments for some of God's attributes, particularly those meant to establish His personality, lack rigor. But the metaphysical foundations of his theology, namely, his arguments for the first three propositions, are not easily put aside.

Samuel Clarke (1675–1729) was an associate of Sir Isaac Newton and one of the early defenders of the Newtonian physics. His *Discourse Concerning the Being and Attributes of God*, from which the following selections are taken, is not only the clearest exposition of the cosmological argument to be found in ancient or modern classical philosophy, but a model of metaphysical argumentation as well. Clarke's conclusions, as his method too, are no longer sympathetically received either by the religious or the philosophical irreligious, but this is mostly because people today distrust pure reasoning as an avenue to religious belief. There is nothing really wrong with the reasoning itself, and it takes a sophisticated and agile mind to show why Clarke's inferences are not binding on any rational person, if, indeed, they are not.

The Being and Attributes
of God*

All those who either are, or pretend to be *Athiests*; who either disbelieve the Being of God, or would be thought to do so; or, (which is all one,) who deny the Principal Attributes of the Divine Nature, and suppose God to be an Unintelligent Being, which acts merely by Necessity; that is, which, in any tolerable Propriety of Speech, acts not at all, but is only acted upon: All Men that are *Atheists*, I say, in this Sense, must be so upon one or other of these three Accounts.

Either, *First*, Because being extremely ignorant and stupid, they have *never duly considered* any thing at all; nor made any just use of their natural Reason, to discover even the plainest and most obvious Truths; but have spent their Time in a manner of Life very little Superiour to that of Beasts.

Or, *Secondly*, Because being totally debauched and corrupted in their *Practice*, they have, by a vicious and degenerate Life, corrupted the Principles of their Nature, and defaced the Reason of their own Minds; and, instead of fairly and impartially enquiring into the Rules and Obligations of Nature, and the Reason and Fitness of Things, have accustomed themselves only to mock and scoff at Religion; and, being under the Power of Evil Habits, and the Slavery of Unreasonable and Indulged Lusts, are resolved not to hearken to any Reasoning which would oblige them to forsake their beloved Vices.

Or, *Thirdly*, Because in the way of *Speculative Reasoning*, and upon the Principles of Philosophy, they pretend that the Arguments used Against the Being or Attributes of God, seem to them, after the strictest and fullest inquiry, to be more strong and conclusive, than those by which we endeavour to prove these great Truths.

These seem the only Causes that can be imagined, of any Man's disbelieving the Being or Attributes of God; and no Man can be supposed to be an Atheist, but upon one or other of these three Accounts. Now to the *two former* of these three sorts of Men; namely, to such as are wholly ignorant and stupid, or to such as through habitual Debauchery have brought them-

---

*From Samuel Clarke, A *Discourse Concerning the Being and Attributes of God, the Obligations of Natural Religion, and the Truth and Certainty of the Christian Revelation*, 10th ed., corrected (London: John and Paul Knapton, 1749).

selves to a Custom of mocking and scoffing at all Religion, and will not hearken to any fair Reasoning; it is *not* my *present* Business to apply my self. The One of these, wants to be instructed in the first Principles of *Reason*, as well as of *Religion*. The Other disbelieves only for a present false *Interest*, and because he is desirous that the Thing should not be true. The One has *not yet arrived* to the use of his natural Faculties: The Other has *renounced* them; and declares he will not be argued with, as a rational Creature. 'Tis therefore the *third sort* of Atheists only (namely those who in the way of Speculative *Reasoning*, and upon the Principles of Philosophy, pretend that the Arguments brought Against the Being or Attributes of God, do, upon the strictest and fullest Examination, appear to them to be more strong and conclusive, than those by which these great Truths are attempted to be proved;) These, I say, are the only Atheistical Persons, to whom my present Discourse can be supposed to be directed, or indeed who are capable of being reasoned with at all. . . .

I. First then, it is Absolutely and Undeniably certain, that *Something has existed from all Eternity*. This is so evident and Undeniable a Proposition, that no Atheist in any Age has ever presumed to assert the contrary; and therefore there is little need of being particular in the proof of it. For since Something now Is, 'tis evident that Something always Was: Otherwise the Things that Now Are, must have been produced out of Nothing, absolutely and without Cause: Which is a plain Contradiction in Terms. For, to say a Thing is *produced*, and yet that there is no *Cause* at all of that Production, is to say that Something is *Effected*, when it is *Effected by Nothing;* that is, at the same time when it is *not Effected at all*. Whatever Exists, has a Cause, a Reason, a Ground of its Existence; (a Foundation, on which its Existence relies; a Ground or Reason why it doth *exist*, rather than *not exist*;) either in the Necessity of its own Nature, and then it must have been *of it self Eternal*: Or in the Will of some Other Being; and then That Other Being must, at least in the order of Nature and Causality, have Existed before it.

That *Something* therefore *has really Existed from Eternity*, is one of the certainest and most evident Truths in the World; acknowledged by all Men, and disputed by none. Yet as to the *Manner* how it can be; there is nothing in Nature more difficult for the Mind of Man to conceive, than this very first Plain and Self-evident Truth. For, *How any thing can have existed eternally*; that is, *How an Eternal Duration can be now actually Past*; is a thing utterly as impossible for our narrow Understandings to comprehend, as any thing that is not an express Contradiction can be imagined to be: And yet to deny the Truth of the Proposition, that an *Eternal Duration is now actually past*; would be to assert *something still far more Unintelligible*, even a *real and express Contradiction*. . . .

II. *There has Existed from Eternity, Some One Unchangeable and Independent Being*. For since Something must needs have been from Eternity; as has been already proved, and is granted on all hands: Either there has always

Existed some one Unchangeable and *Independent* Being, from which all other Beings that are or ever were in the Universe, have received their Original; or else there has been an infinite Succession of changeable and *dependent* Beings produced one from another in an endless Progression, *without* any Original Cause at all. Now this latter Supposition is so very absurd, that tho' all Atheism must in its Account of most things (as shall be shewn hereafter) terminate in it, yet I think very few Atheists ever were so weak as openly and directly to defend it. For it is plainly impossible, and *contradictory* to itself. I shall not argue against it from the *supposed* Impossiblity of Infinite Succession, *barely* and *absolutely considered in itself*; for a Reason which shall be mentioned hereafter. But, if we consider such an infinite Progression, as *One* entire endless *Series of Dependent* Beings; 'tis plain this *whole Series of Beings* can have no Cause *from without*, of its Existence; because in it are supposed to be included *all Things* that are or ever were in the Universe: And 'tis plain it can have no Reason *within itself*, of its Existence; because no one Being in this Infinite Succession is supposed to be Self-existent or *Necessary*, (which is the only Ground or Reason of Existence of any thing, that can be imagined *within the thing itself*, as will presently more fully appear,) but every one *Dependent* on the foregoing: And where *no Part* is necessary, 'tis manifest *the Whole* cannot be necessary: Absolute Necessity of Existence, not being an *extrinsick, relative,* and *accidental* Denomination; but an *inward and essential* Property of the Nature of the Thing which so Exists. An infinite Succession therefore of merely *Dependent* Beings, without any Original Independent Cause; is a *Series* of Beings, that has neither Necessity, nor Cause, nor any Reason or Ground *at all* of its Existence, either *within itself* or *from without*: That is, 'tis an express Contradiction and Impossibility; 'tis a supposing *Something* to be *caused*, (because it is granted in every one of its Stages of Succession, *not* to be *necessarily and of itself*;) and yet that, in the whole, 'tis caused *absolutely by Nothing.* Which every Man knows is a Contradiction to imagine done *in Time*, and, because Duration in this Case makes no Difference, 'tis equally a Contradiction to suppose it done *from Eternity*. And consequently there must, *on the contrary*, of necessity have existed from Eternity, *some One* Immutable and *Independent* Being.

To suppose an *infinite Succession* of changeable and *dependent* Beings produced one from another in an endless Progression, *without* any Original Cause at all; is only a driving back from one step to another, and (as it were) removing out of Sight, the Question concerning the Ground or Reason of the Existence of Things. 'Tis in reality, and in point of Argument, the very same Supposition; as it would be to suppose *One continued Being*, of *beginningless* and endless Duration, neither self-existent and Necessary in itself, nor having its Existence founded in Any Self-existent Cause. Which is directly absurd and contradictory.

Otherwise, thus. Either there has always existed some One Unchangeable and *Independent* Being, from which all other Beings have received their

Original; or else there has been an infinite Succession of changeable and *dependent* Beings, produced one from another in an endless Progression, without any Original Cause at all. According to this latter Supposition; there is Nothing, in the Universe, Self-Existent or Necessarily-existing. And if so; then it was originally *equally possible*, that from Eternity there should never have existed any thing at all; as that there should from Eternity have existed a Succession of changeable and dependent Beings. Which being supposed, then, *What* is it that has from Eternity determined such a Succession of Beings to exist, rather than that from Eternity there should never have existed any thing at all? *Necessity* it was not; because it was equally possible, in this Supposition, that they should not have existed at all. *Chance* is nothing but a mere Word, without any Signification. And *Other Being* 'tis *supposed* there was none, to determine the Existence of these. Their Existence therefore was determined by *Nothing*; neither by any Necessity in the nature of the Things themselves, because 'tis supposed that none of them are Self-existent; nor by any other Being, because no other is supposed to Exist. That is to say; Of two *equally possible* things, (*viz.* whether *any thing* or *nothing* should from Eternity have existed,) the one is determined, rather than the other, *absolutely by Nothing*: Which is an express Contradiction. And consequently, as before, there must on the contrary, of Necessity have existed from Eternity, *some One* Immutable and *Independent* Being. Which, *what* it is, remains in the next place to be inquired.

III. *That unchangeable and independent Being, which has Existed from Eternity, without any external Cause of its Existence; must be Self-Existent, that is, Necessarily-existing.* For whatever Exists, must either have come into Being out of Nothing, absolutely without Cause; or it must have been produced by some External Cause; or it must be Self-Existent. Now to arise out of Nothing, absolutely without any Cause; has been already shown to be a plain Contradiction. To have been produced by some External Cause, cannot possibly be true of every thing; but something must have existed Eternally and Independently; As has likewise been shown already. It remains therefore, that That Being which has existed Independently from Eternity, must of Necessity be Self-existent. Now to be *Self-existent*, is not, to be *Produced by itself*; for that is an express Contradiction. But it is, (which is the only Idea we can frame of Self-existence; and without which, the word seems to have no Signification at all:) It is, I say, to *exist by an Absolute Necessity originally in the Nature of the Thing itself.* And this Necessity, must be *Antecedent*; not indeed in Time, to the Existence of the Being itself; because That is Eternal; But it must be *Antecedent* in the Natural Order of our Ideas, to our *Supposition* of its Being. That is; This Necessity must not barely be *consequent* upon our Supposition of the Existence of such a Being; (For then it would not be a Necessity *Absolutely* such in itself, nor be the Ground or Foundation of the Existence of any thing, being on the contrary only a Consequent of it;) But it must *antecedently* force itself upon us, whether we will or no, even when we are endeavouring to suppose that no such Being Exists. For Example: When we are endeavouring to suppose, that there is *no Being* in the Universe that exists Necessarily; we always find in our Minds, (besides the foregoing Demonstration of Something being Self-existent, from the *Impossibility of every Thing's being dependent;) We always find in our Minds, I say, some Ideas, as of Infinity and Eternity*; which to remove, that is, to suppose that there is no Being, no Substance in the Universe, to which these Attributes or Modes of Existence are necessarily inherent, is a Contradiction in the very Terms. For Modes and Attributes exist only by the Existence of the Substance to which they belong. Now he that can suppose Eternity and Immensity (and consequently the Substance by whose Existence these Modes or Attributes exist,) removed out of the Universe; may, if he please, as easily remove the Relation of Equality between twice two and four.

That to suppose *Immensity* removed out of the Universe, or not necessarily *Eternal*, is an *express contradiction;* is *intuitively* evident to every one who attends to his own Ideas, and considers the Essential Nature of Things. To suppose *any part* of Space *removed,* is to suppose it removed *from* and *out of* itself: And to suppose the *Whole* to be *taken away,* is supposing it to be *taken away from itself,* that is, to be *taken away* while it *still remains*: Which is a *Contradiction in Terms.* There is no Obscurity in This Argument, but what arises to those who think *Immense Space* to be absolutely *Nothing.* Which Notion, is *itself* likewise an *express contradiction.* For *Nothing,* is That which has *No Properties or Modes whatsoever.* That is to say; 'tis That *of which nothing can truly be affirmed,* and *of which Every thing can truly be denied.* Which is not the Case of *Immensity or Space.*

From this *Third Proposition* it follows,

1st, That the *only true Idea of a Self-existent or Necessarily Existing Being, is the Idea of a Being, the Supposition of whose Not-existing is an express Contradiction.* For since it is absolutely impossible but there must be Somewhat Self-existent; that is, which exists by the Necessity of its own Nature; 'Tis plain that *That necessity* cannot be a Necessity consequent upon any foregoing Supposition, (because Nothing can be Antecedent to that which is Self-Existent, no not its own *Will,* so as to be the Cause or Ground of its own Existence,) but it must be a Necessity *absolutely such in its own Nature.* Now a Necessity, not *relatively* or *consequentially,* but *absolutely such* in its own Nature; is nothing else, but its being a plain Impossibility or implying a Contradiction to suppose the contrary. For Instance: The Relation of Equality between twice two and four, is an absolute Necessity; only because 'tis an immediate Contradiction in Terms to suppose them unequal. This is the only Idea we can frame, of an absolute Necessity; and to use the word in any other Sense, seems to be using it without any Signification at all.

If any One now asks, *what sort of Idea* the Idea of that Being is, the Supposition of whose Not-Existing is thus an express Contradiction: I answer, 'tis the first and Simplest Idea we can possibly frame; an Idea *necessarily and essentially* included or presupposed, as a *fine quâ non*, in every other Idea whatsoever; an Idea, which (unless we forbear thinking at all)we cannot possibly extirpate or remove out of our Minds; of *a most simple Being, absolutely Eternal and Infinite, Original and Independent*. For, that he who supposes there is no *Original Independent* Being in the Universe, suppose a Contradiction; hath been shown already. And that he who supposes there may possibly be no *Eternal* and *Infinite* Being in the Universe, supposes likewise a Contradiction, is evident from hence; (besides that these two Attributes do necessarily *follow* from Self-originate Independent Existence, as shall be shown hereafter;) that when he has done his utmost, in indeavouring to imagine that no such Being Exists; he cannot avoid imagining an Eternal and Infinite *Nothing*; that is, he will imagine Eternity and Immensity removed out of the Universe, and yet that at the same time they still continue there. As has been *above* distinctly explained. . . .

2dly, From hence it follows; that *there is no Man whatsoever, who makes any use of his Reason, but may easily become more certain of the Being of a Supreme Independent Cause, than he can be of any thing else besides his own Existence.* For how much Thought soever it may require to demonstrate the *Other* Attributes of such a Being, as it may do to demonstrate the greatest Mathematical Certainties; (of which more hereafter:) Yet, as to its *Existence;* that there *Is* somewhat Eternal, Infinite, and Self-existing, which must be the Cause and Origin of all other Things; this is one of the First and most natural Conclusions, that any Man, who thinks at all, can frame in his Mind: And no Man can any more doubt of this, than he can doubt whether twice two be equal to four. 'Tis possible indeed a Man may in some sense be *ignorant* of this first and plain Truth, by being utterly stupid, and not thinking at all: (For though it is absolutely impossible for him to imagine the Contrary, yet he may possibly neglect to conceive this: Though no Man can possibly Think that twice two is not four, yet he may possibly be stupid, and never have thought at all whether it be so or not.) But this I say: There is no Man, who thinks or reasons at all, but may easily become more certain, that there is Something Eternal, Infinite, and Self-existing; than he can be certain of any thing else.

3dly, Hence we may observe, that *Our first Certainty of the Existence of God, does not arise from this, that* in the Idea *our Minds frame of him, (or rather* in the Definition *that we make of the word,* God, *as signifying a Being of all possible Perfections,) we include Self-Existence: But from hence, that 'tis demonstrable both* negatively, *that neither can all Things possibly have arisen out of Nothing, nor can they have depended one on another in an endless Succession; and also* positively, *that there* is *Something in the Universe*, actually existing without us, *the Supposition of whose Not-Existing, plainly implies a Contradiction.* . . .

4thly, From hence it follows, that *The Material World cannot possibly be the First and Original Being, Uncreated, Independent, and of itself Eternal.* For since it hath been already demonstrated, that Whatever Being hath Existed from Eternity, Independent, and without any External Cause of its Existence, must be Self-Existent; and that Whatever is Self-Existent, must Exist Necessarily by an absolute Necessity in the Nature of the Thing itself: It follows evidently, that unless the Material World Exists Necessarily by an Absolute Necessity in its own Nature, so as that it must be an Express Contradiction to suppose it not to Exist; it cannot be Independent, and of itself Eternal. Now that the Material World does not Exist thus necessarily, is very Evident. For absolute Necessity of Existing, and a Possibility of not Existing, being contradictory Ideas; 'tis manifest the Material World cannot Exist Necessarily, if without a Contradiction we can Conceive it either *Not to Be*, or to be in any respect *otherwise* than it Now is. Than which, nothing is more easy. For whether we consider the *Form* of the World, with the *Disposition* and *Motion* of its Parts; or whether we consider the *Matter* of it, as such, without respect to its present Form; Every Thing in it, both the *Whole* and every one of its *Parts*, their *Situation* and *Motion*, the *Form* and also the *Matter*, are the most Arbitrary and Dependent Things, and the farthest removed from Necessity, that can possibly be imagined. A Necessity indeed of *Fitness*, that is, a Necessity that Things should be as they are, in order to the *Well-being* of the whole, there may be in all these Things: But an absolute Necessity of *Nature* in any of them, (which is what the Atheist must maintain,) there is not the least appearance of. If any Man will say in This sense, (as every Atheist must do,) either the *Form* of the World, or at least the *Matter* and *Motion* of it, is necessary; Nothing can possibly be invented more Absurd.

If he says, that the particular *Form* is Necessary; that is, that the World, and *all Things* that are therein, exist by Necessity of Nature; he must affirm it to be a Contradiction to suppose that any Part of the World can be in any respect *otherwise* than it now is. It must be a Contradiction in Terms, to suppose *more* or *fewer* Stars, *more* or *fewer* Planets, or to suppose their *Size*, *Figure* or *Motion*, Different from what it now is; or to suppose *more* or *fewer* Plants and Animals upon Earth, or the present ones of different *Shape* and *Bigness* from what they now are. In all which things there is the greatest Arbitrariness, in respect of Power and Possibility, that can be imagined; however necessary any of them may be, in respect of Wisdom, and Preservation of the Beauty and Order of the whole.

If the Atheist will say, that the *Motion in General* of all Matter is necessary; it follows that it must be a Contradiction in Terms, to suppose any

Matter to be at *Rest*. Which is so absurd and ridiculous, that I think hardly any Atheists, either Ancient or Modern, have presumed directly to suppose it. . . .

IV. *What the Substance or Essence of that Being, which is Self-Existent, or Necessarily-Existing, is; we have no Idea, neither is it at all possible for us to comprehend it.* That there *is* such a Being actually Existing without us, we are sure (as I have already shown) by strict and undeniable Demonstration. Also *what* it is *not*; that is, that the Material World is *not* it, as Modern Atheists would have it; has been already Demonstrated. But *what* it *is*, I mean as to its *Substance* and Essence; this we are infinitely unable to comprehend. Yet this does not in the least diminish the Certainty of the Demonstration of its Existence. For 'tis one thing, to know certainly that a Being Exists; and another, to know *what* the Essence of that Being is. And the one may be capable of the strictest Demonstration, when the other is absolutely beyond the Reach of all our Faculties to understand. A Blind or Deaf Man has infinitely more Reason to deny the Being, or the Possibility of the Being, of Light or Sounds; than any Atheist can have to deny, or doubt of, the Existence of God. For the One can at the utmost have no other Proof, but credible *Testimony*, of the Existence of certain Things, whereof 'tis absolutely impossible that he himself should frame any manner of Idea, not only of their Essence, but even of their Effects or Properties: But the other may, with the least Use of his Reason, be assured of the Existence of a Supreme Being, by undeniable *Demonstration;* and may also certainly know abundance of its Attributes, (as shall be made appear in the following Propositions,) though its *Substance* or Essence be intirely incomprehensible. Wherefore nothing can be more Unreasonable and Weak, than for an Atheist upon this account to deny the Being of God, merely because his weak and finite Understanding cannot frame to itself any adæquate Notion of the Substance or Essence of that First and Supreme Cause. We are utterly ignorant of the *Substance* or Essence of *all other* things; even of those things which we converse most familiarly with, and think we understand best. There is not so mean and contemptible a Plant or Animal, that does not confound the most inlarged Understanding upon Earth: Nay, even the simplest and plainest of all inanimate Beings, have their Essence or *Substance* hidden from Us in the deepest and most impenetrable Obscurity. How weak then and foolish is it, to raise Objections against the Being of God, from the Incomprehensibleness of his Essence! and to represent it as a strange and incredible thing, that there should Exist any incorporeal Substance, the Essence of which we are not able to Comprehend! As if it were not far more strange, that there should exist numberless Objects of our Senses, things subject to our daily Inquiry, Search, and Examination; and yet we not be able, no not in any Measure, to find out the *real Essence* of any one even of the least of *these* Things.

Nevertheless, 'tis very necessary to observe here by the way, that it does
not at all from hence follow, that there *can possibly* be in the *unknown
Substance* or *Essence* of God, any thing *contradictory* to our clear Ideas. For
as a Blind-man, though he has no *Idea* of *Light* and *Colours*, yet knows
certainly and infallibly that there *cannot possibly* be any kind of *Light* which
is *not Light*, or any sort of *Colour* which is *not a Colour:* So, though we have
no Idea of the *Substance* of God, nor indeed of the *Substance* of any Other
Being; yet we are as infallibly certain that there cannot possibly be, either in
the One or the Other, any *contradictory* Modes or Properties; as if we had
the *clearest* and *most distinct* Idea of them. . . .

V. *Though the Substance or Essence of the Self-Existent Being, is in itself
absolutely Incomprehensible to us; yet many of the Essential Attributes of his
Nature, are strictly Demonstrable, as well as his Existence.* Thus, in the first
place, the *Self-Existent Being must of Necessity be Eternal.* The Ideas of
Eternity and Self-Existence are so closely connected, that because Something must of necessity be Eternal *Independently and without any outward
Cause of its Being,* therefore it must necessarily be Self-existent; and because 'tis impossible but Something must be Self-existent, therefore 'tis
necessary that it must likewise be Eternal. To be Self-existent, is (as has
been already shown) to Exist by an Absolute Necessity in the Nature of the
Thing it self. Now this Necessity being Absolute, and not depending upon
any thing External, must be always unalterably the same; Nothing being
alterable, but what is capable of being affected by somewhat without it self.
That Being therefore, which has no other Cause of its Existence, but the
absolute Necessity of its own Nature; must of necessity have existed from
everlasting, without Beginning; and must of necessity exist to everlasting
without End.

As to the *Manner* of this Eternal Existence; 'tis manifest, it herein infinitely transcends the Manner of the Existence of all Created Beings, even of
such as shall exist for ever; that whereas 'tis not possible for Their finite
Minds to comprehend all that is past, or to understand perfectly all things
that are at present, much less to know all that is future, or to have entirely in
their Power any thing that is to come; but their Thoughts, and Knowledge,
and Power, must of Necessity have degrees and periods, and be successive
and transient as the Things themselves: The Eternal, Supreme Cause, on the
contrary, (supposing him to be an *Intelligent Being,* which will hereafter be
proved in the Sequel of this Discourse,) must of necessity have such a
perfect, independent and unchangeable Comprehension of all Things,
that there can be no One Point or Instant of his Eternal Duration, wherein
all Things that are past, present, or to come, will not be *as* entirely known
and represented to him in one single Thought or View and all Things present
and future, be equally entirely in his Power and Direction; *as if* there was
really no Succession at all, but all things were actually present at once. Thus

far we can speak Intelligibly concerning the Eternal Duration of the Self-existent Being; And no *Atheist* can say this is an Impossible, Absurd, or Insufficient Account. It is, in the most proper and Intelligible Sense of the Words, to all the purposes of Excellency and Perfection, *Interminabilis vitæ tota simul & perfecta Possessio:* the *Entire and Perfect Possession of an endless Life.*

VI. *The Self-Existent Being, must of necessity be Infinite and Omnipresent.* The Idea of Infinity or Immensity, as well as of Eternity, is so closely connected with that of Self-Existence, that because 'tis impossible but Something must be infinite *independently and of it self,* (for else it would be impossible there should be any Infinite at all, unless an Effect could be perfecter than its Cause;) therefore it must of necessity be Self-Existent: And because Something must of necessity be Self-Existent, therefore 'tis necessary that it must likewise be Infinite. To be Self-Existent (as has been already shown,) is to Exist by an Absolute Necessity in the Nature of the Thing itself. Now this Necessity being Absolute in itself, and not depending on any Outward Cause; 'tis evident it must be *every where,* as well as *always,* unalterably the same. For a Necessity which is not every where the same, is plainly a Consequential Necessity only, depending upon some External Cause, and not an Absolute one in its own Nature: For a Necessity absolutely such in itself, has no Relation to Time or Place, or any thing else. Whatever therefore Exists by an Absolute Necessity in its own Nature, must needs be Infinite as well as Eternal. To suppose a Finite Being, to be Self-Existent; is to say that 'tis a Contradiction for That Being not to Exist, the Absence of which may yet be conceived without a Contradiction. Which is the greatest Absurdity in the World. For if a Being can without a Contradiction be absent from one Place, it may without a Contradiction be absent likewise from another Place, and from all Places: And whatever Necessity it may have of Existing, must arise from some External Cause, and not absolutely from itself: And consequently, the Being cannot be Self-Existent.

From hence it follows,

1*st,* That the Infinity of the Self-Existent Being, must be an Infinity of *Fullness* as well as of *Immensity;* That is, it must not only be without *Limits,* but also without *Diversity, Defect,* or *Interruption:* For Instance: Could *Matter* be supposed *Boundless,* it would not therefore follow that it was in this compleat Sense *Infinite;* because, though it had no Limits, yet it might have within itself many assignable Vacuities. But whatever is Self-Existent, must of necessity Exist absolutely in every Place alike, and be equally present every where; and consequently must have a true and absolute Infinity, both of *Immensity* and *Fullness.*

2*dly,* From hence it follows, that the Self-Existent Being, must be *a most Simple, Unchangeable, Incorruptible* Being; *without Parts, Figure, Motion, Divisibility,* or any other such Properties as we find in Matter. For all these things do plainly and necessarily imply Finiteness in their very Notion, and are utterly inconsistent with complete Infinity. *Divisibility* is a separation of Parts, real or mental: Meaning by *mental Separation*, not barely a *partial Apprehending*; (for *Space*, for instance, which is *absolutely* indivisible and inseparable either really or mentally, may yet be *partially apprehended*;) but a removing, disjoining, or separating of Parts one from another, even so much as *in the Imagination*. And any such Separation or Removing of Parts one from another, is *really* or *mentally* a setting of Bounds: Either of which, destroys Infinity. *Motion*, for the same reason, implies Finiteness: And *to have Parts*, properly speaking, signifies either Difference and Diversity of Existence; which is inconsistent with Necessity: or else it signifies Divisibility, *real* or *mental* as before, which is inconsistent with compleat Infinity. *Corruption*, *Change*, or *any Alteration whatsoever*, implies Motion, Separation of Parts, and Finiteness. And any Manner of *Composition*, in opposition to the most perfect *Simplicity*, signifies Difference and Diversity in the manner of Existence; which is inconsistent with Necessity.

'Tis evident therefore, that the Self-Existent Being must be *Infinite* in the *strictest* and most *compleat* Sense. But as to the *particular Manner* of his being Infinite or every where present, in opposition to the manner of Created Things being present in such or such finite Places; This is as impossible for our finite Understanding to comprehend or explain, as it is for us to form an adæquate Idea of Infinity. Yet that the Thing is true, that he *is* actually *Omnipresent*, we are as certain, as we are that there must Something be Infinite; which no Man, who has thought upon these Things at all, ever denied. The *Schoolmen* indeed have presumed to assert, that the Immensity of God is a *Point*, as his Eternity (they think) is an *Instant*. But, this being altogether Unintelligible; That which we can more safely affirm, and which no Atheist can say is absurd, and which nevertheless is sufficient to all wise and good Purposes, is this: That whereas all Finite and Created Beings, can be present but in One definite place at Once, and Corporeal Beings even in That One Place very imperfectly and unequally, to any Purpose of Power or Activity, only by the Successive Motion of different Members and Organs; The Supreme Cause on the contrary, being an Infinite and most Simple Essence, and comprehending all things perfectly in himself, is *at all times equally* present, both in his Simple Essence, and by the Immediate and Perfect Exercise of all his Attributes, to *every Point* of the Boundless Immensity, *as if* it were really all but one Single Point.

VII. *The Self-Existent Being, must of necessity be but One.* This evidently follows from his being *Necessarily-Existent*. For *Necessity* Absolute in it self, is *Simple* and *Uniform* and *Universal*, without any possible *Difference*, *Difformity*, or *Variety* whatsoever: And all *Variety* or *Difference* of *Existence*, must needs *arise from* some *External* Cause, and be *dependent upon* it, and *proportionable* to the *efficiency* of That *Cause*, whatsoever it be. *Absolute Necessity*, in which there can be *no Variation* in *any kind* or *degree*, cannot be the *Ground* of existence of a *Number* of Beings, however *similar* and *agreeing* : Because, without any *Other difference*, even *Number* is *itself* a manifest *Difformity* or *Inequality* (if I may so speak) of *Efficiency* or *Causality*.

Again : To suppose *Two* (or more) *distinct Beings* existing *of themselves*, necessarily, and *independent* from each other; implies this plain *Contradiction;* that, *each* of them being *independent* from the other, they may *either of them* be supposed to exist *alone*, so that it will be no contradiction to imagine the other not to exist; and consequently *neither of them* will be Necessarily-Existing. Whatsoever therefore Exists necessarily, is the One Simple Essence of the Self-Existent Being; And whatsoever differs from that, is not Necessarily-Existing: Because in absolute Necessity there can be no *Difference*, or *Diversity*, of Existence. Other Beings there may be innumerable, besides the One Infinite Self-Existent: But no Other Being can be Self-Existent, because so it would be individually the same, at the same time that it is supposed to be different. . . .

VIII. *The Self-existent and Original Cause of all things, must be an intelligent Being.* In this Proposition lies the main Question between us and the Atheists. For, that something must be Self-existent; and that That which is Self-existent, must necessarily be Eternal and Infinite and the Original Cause of all things; will not bear much Dispute. But all Atheists, whether they hold the World to be of *itself* Eternal both as to the Matter and Form, or whether they hold the Matter only to be Necessary and the Form Contingent, or whatever Hypothesis they frame; have always asserted and must maintain, either directly or indirectly, that the Self-existent Being is not an *Intelligent* Being, but either pure unactive *Matter*, or (which in other Words is the very same thing) a mere *necessary Agent*. For a mere *necessary Agent* must of necessity either be plainly and directly in the grossest sense *Unintelligent;* which was the ancient Atheists' Notion of the Self-existent Being: Or else its Intelligence (which is the Assertion of *Spinoza* and some Moderns,) must be wholly separate from any Power of Will and Choice; which, in respect of any Excellency and Perfection, or indeed to any common Sense, is the very same thing as no Intelligence at all.

Now that the Self-existent Being is not such a Blind and *Unintelligent* Necessity, but in the most proper Sense an *understanding* and *really active* Being; does not indeed so *obviously* and directly appear *to Us* by Considerations *a priori* ; because (through the Imperfection of our Faculties) we know not *wherein* Intelligence consists, nor can see the Immediate and Necessary connexion of it with Self-existence, as we can that of Eternity, Infinity, Unity, Etc. But *a posteriori*, almost every thing in the World, demonstrates to us this great Truth; and affords undeniable Arguments, to prove that the World, and all Things therein, are the Effects of an *Intelligent* and *Knowing* Cause.

And l*st*, Since in general there are manifestly in Things, *various kinds* of *Powers*, and very *different Excellencies* and Degrees of Perfection; it must needs be, that, in the Order of Causes and Effects, the Cause must always be more Excellent than the Effect: And consequently the Self-existent Being, whatever that be supposed to be, must of necessity (being the Original of all things) contain in itself the Sum and highest Degree of all the Perfections of all things, Not because That which is Self-existent, must *therefore* have all possible Perfections: (For This, though most certainly true in itself, yet cannot be so easily demonstrated *a priori:*) But because 'tis impossible that any Effect should have any Perfection, which was not in the Cause. For if it had, then That Perfection would be caused by nothing; which is a plain Contradiction. Now an *Unintelligent* Being, 'tis evident, cannot be endued with all the Perfections of all things in the World; because *Intelligence* is one of those Perfections. All things therefore cannot arise from an Unintelligent Original: And consequently the Self-existent Being, must of necessity be *Intelligent.*

There is no possibility for an Atheist to avoid the Force of this Argument any other way, than by asserting one of these *two* things: Either that there is *no Intelligent Being at all* in the Universe; or that *Intelligence* is *no distinct Perfection*, but merely a Composition of Figure and Motion, as Colour and Sounds are vulgarly supposed to be. Of the *Former* of these Assertions, every Man's own *Consciousness* is an abundant Confutation. For they who contend that Beasts are mere Machines, have yet never presumed to conjecture that *Men* are so too. And that the *Latter* Assertion (in which the main strength of Atheism lies,) is most absurd and impossible; shall be shown presently. Though if That Assertion *could* be supposed to be *True*, yet even *still* 'twould unavoidably follow, that the Self-existent Being must needs be *Intelligent*; as shall be proved in my *4th Argument* upon this present Head. In the mean time; that the Assertion itself, *viz.* that *Intelligence* is not any *distinct Perfection*, properly speaking, but merely a Composition of Unintelligent Figure and Motion; that This Assertion, I say, is most absurd and impossible, will appear from what shall be said in the ensuing Argument.

2dly, Since in *Men in particular* there is undeniably that Power, which we call Thought, *Intelligence,* Consciousness, Perception or Knowledge; there must of Necessity *either* have been from Eternity *without any Original Cause at all,* an infinite Succession of Men, whereof *no one* has had a *Necessary,* but *every one* a *Dependent and Communicated* Being; *or else* these Beings, indued with Perception and Consciousness, must at some time or other have arisen purely out of that which had no such Quality as Sense, Perception or Consciousness; *or else* they must have been produced by some *Intelligent* Superiour Being. There never was nor can be any Atheist whatsoever, that can deny but One of these *Three* Suppositions *must* be the Truth. If therefore the *two former* can be proved to be false and impossible, the *latter* must be own'd to be demonstrably true. Now that the *First* is impossible, is evident from what has been already said in proof of the *Second* General Head of this Discourse. And that the *Second* is likewise impossible, may be thus demonstrated. *If* Perception or *Intelligence*, be a *distinct Quality* or Perfection, and not a mere Effect or Composition of Unintelligent Figure and Motion; then Beings endued with Perception or Consciousness, can never have arisen purely out of that which had no such Quality as Perception or Consciousness; because nothing can ever give to another any Perfection, which it hath not either actually in itself, or at least in a higher degree. *But* Perception or Intelligence is a *distinct Quality* or Perfection, and not a mere Effect or Composition of Unintelligent Figure and Motion. . . .

IX. *The Self-existent and Original Cause of all Things, is not a necessary Agent, but a Being indued with Liberty and Choice.* The contrary to this Proposition, is the Foundation and the Sum of what *Spinoza* and his Followers have asserted concerning the Nature of God. What Reasons or Arguments they have offered for their Opinion, I shall have occasion to consider briefly in my Proof of the Proposition itself. The Truth of which, appears

1*st*, In that it is a Necessary Consequence of the foregoing Proposition. For *Intelligence* without *Liberty* (as I there hinted) is really (in respect of any Power, Excellence, or Perfection,) *no Intelligence* at all. It is indeed a *Consciousness*, but it is merely *a Passive One*; a Consciousness, not of Acting, but purely of being Acted upon. Without *Liberty*, nothing can in any tolerable Propriety of Speech, be said to be an Agent, or Cause of anything. For to Act necessarily, is really and properly not to Act at all, but only to be Acted upon. What therefore *Spinoza* and his Followers assert concerning the Production of all Things from the Necessity of the Divine Nature, is mere Jargon and Words without any meaning at all. For if by the Necessity of the Divine Nature they understand not the Perfection and Rectitude of his Will, whereby God is unalterably determined to do always what is best in the whole; (as confessedly they do not; because this is consistent with the most perfect Liberty and Choice;) but, on the contrary, mean an Absolute and strictly Natural Necessity: It follows evidently, that when they say, God by the Necessity of his Nature, is the Cause and Author of all Things; they understand him to be a Cause or Agent in no other sense, than as if a Man should say, that a Stone, by the Necessity of its Nature, is the Cause of its own falling and striking the Ground: Which is really not to be an Agent or Cause at all; But their Opinion amounts to this, that all things are equally Self-Existent, and consequently that the Material World is God: Which I have before proved to be a Contradiction. In like manner, when they speak of the Intelligence and Knowledge of God; they mean to attribute these Powers to him in no other sense, than the ancient *Hylozoicks* attributed them to *all Matter;* that is, that a Stone, when it falls, has a Sensation and Consciousness; but that That Consciousness is no Cause at all, or Power, of Acting. Which kind of Intelligence, in any tolerable Propriety of Speech, is no Intelligence at all. And consequently the Arguments, that proved the

Supreme Cause to be *properly* an Intelligent and Active Being; do also undeniably prove that he is likewise indued with *Liberty* and Choice, which alone is the Power of Acting.

2*dly*, If the Supreme Cause, is not a Being indued with *Liberty* and Choice, but a mere Necessary Agent, whose Actions are all as absolutely and naturally Necessary as his Existence: Then it will follow, that nothing which is not, could *possibly* have been; and that nothing which is, could *possibly* not have been; and that no Mode or Circumstance of the Existence of any thing, could *possibly* have been in any respect otherwise, than it now actually is. All which being evidently most false and absurd: it follows on the contrary, that the Supreme Cause is not a mere necessary Agent, but a Being indued with Liberty and Choice. . . .

X. *The Self-Existent Being, the Supreme Cause of all Things, must of Necessity have infinite Power.* This Proposition is evident, and undeniable. For since nothing (as has been already proved) can possibly be Self-Existent, besides himself; and consequently all Things in the Universe were made by Him, and are entirely dependent upon Him; and all the *Powers* of all Things are derived from Him, and must therefore be perfectly Subject and Subordinate to Him: 'Tis manifest that nothing can make any Difficulty or Resistance to the Execution of his Will; but he must of Necessity have absolute Power to do every thing he pleases, with the perfectest Ease, and in the perfectest Manner, at once and in a Moment, whenever he Wills it. . . . The only Question is, *what* the true meaning of what we call *Infinite Power*, is; and to *what things* it must be understood to extend, or not to extend.

Now in determining this Question, there are some Propositions, about which there is no dispute. Which therefore I shall but just mention. As,

1*st*, That infinite Power reaches to all *Possible* things, but cannot be said to extend to the working any thing which implies a *Contradiction*: As, that a Thing should *be* and *not be* at the same time; that the same thing should *be made* and *not be made*, or *have been* and *not have been*; that *twice two* should *not make four*, or that *That which is necessarily False*, should *be True*. The Reason whereof is plain: Because the Power of making a Thing to be, at the same time that it is not; is only a Power of doing that which is Nothing, that is, no Power at all.

2*dly*, Infinite Power cannot be said to extend to those things, which imply *Natural* Imperfection in the Being to whom such Power is ascribed: As, that it should destroy its own Being, weaken itself, or the like. These Things imply *Natural* Imperfection, and are by all Men confessed to be such, as cannot possibly belong to the Necessary Self-existent Being. There are also other things which imply Imperfection in another kind, *viz. Moral* Imperfection: Concerning which, Atheism takes away the Subject of the Question, by denying wholly the Difference of Moral Good and Evil; and therefore I shall omit the Consideration of them, 'till I come to deduce the *Moral* Attributes of God. . . .

XI. *The Supreme Cause and Author of all Things, will of Necessity be infinitely Wise*. This Proposition is evidently Consequent upon those that have already been proved: And those being established, This, as admitting no further Dispute, needs not to be largely insisted upon. For nothing is more evident, than that an *Infinite, Omnipresent, Intelligent Being*, must know perfectly *all Things that are;* And that He who alone is *Self-Existent and Eternal, the sole Cause and Author of all Things; from whom alone all the Powers of all Things are derived*, and *on whom they continually depend;* must also know perfectly all the Consequences of those Powers, that is, *all Possibilities of Things to come*, and what in every respect is Best and Wisest to be done: And that, having infinite *Power*, he can never be controuled or prevented from doing what he so knows to be Fittest. From all which, it manifestly follows, that every Effect of the Supreme Cause, must be the Product of Infinite Wisdom. More particularly: The Supreme Being, because he is *Infinite*, must be every where present: And because he is an Infinite *Mind* or *Intelligence*, therefore wherever he Is, his Knowledge Is, which is inseparable from his Being, and must therefore be infinite likewise: And wherever his Infinite Knowledge is, it must necessarily have a *full and perfect* Prospect of all Things, and nothing can be conceal'd from its Inspection: He includes and surrounds every thing with his boundless Presence; and penetrates every part of their Substance with his All-seeing Eye: So that the inmost Nature and Essence of all things, are Perfectly Naked and Open to his View; and even the deepest Thoughts of Intelligent Beings themselves, manifest in his fight. Further; All Things being not only present to him, but also entirely *Depending* upon him, and having *received* both their Being itself, and all their Powers and Faculties *from Him;* 'tis manifest that, as he knows all Things that *are*, so he must likewise know all Possibilities of things, that is, all Effects that *Can be*: For, being himself Alone Self-Existent, and having Alone *given* to all Things all the Powers and Faculties they are endued with; 'tis evident He must of Necessity know perfectly what All and Each of those Powers and Faculties, which are *derived wholly from himself*, can possibly Produce: And Seeing at one boundless View, all the possible Compositions and Divisions, Variations and Changes, Circumstances and Dependencies of Things; all their possible Relations one to another, and their Dispositions or Fitnesses to certain and respective Ends, he must, without Possibility of Errour, know exactly what is Best and Properest in every one of the Infinite Possible Cases or Methods of Disposing things; and understand perfectly how to order and direct the respective Means, to bring about what he so knows to be, in its Kind, or in the Whole, the Best and Fittest in the End. This is what we mean by *Infinite Wisdom*. And having before shown, (which indeed is also evident of itself,) that the Supreme Cause is moreover *All-Powerful*; so that He can no more be prevented by Force or Opposition, than he can be hindered by Errour or Mistake from *Effecting* always what is absolutely Fittest and Wisest to be done: It follows undeniably, that he is *actually and effectually*, in the highest and most complete sense, *Infinitely Wise;* and that the World, and all Things therein, must be and are Effects of Infinite Wisdom. This is Demonstration *à priori.* The Proof *à posteriori*, of the Infinite Wisdom of God, from the Consideration of the Exquisite Perfection and Consummate Excellency of his Works; is no less strong and undeniable. But I shall not inlarge upon This Argument; because it has often already been accurately and strongly urged, to the everlasting Shame and Confusion of Atheists, by the ablest and learnedest Writers both of Antient and Modern Times. I shall here observe only this One Thing; That the older the World grows, and the deeper Men inquire into Things and the more Accurate Observations they make, and the more and greater Discoveries they find out; the stronger this Argument continually grows: Which is a certain Evidence of its being founded in Truth. . . .

XII. Lastly; *The Supreme Cause and Author of all Things, must of necessity be a Being of Infinite Goodness, Justice and Truth, and all other Moral Perfections; such as Become the Supreme Governour and Judge of the World.* That there are *different Relations* of Things one towards another, is as certain as that there are *Different Things* in the World. That from these *Different Relations* of *Different Things*, there necessarily arises an *Agreement* or *Disagreement* of some things to others, or a *Fitness* or *Unfitness* of the Application of Different Things or Different Relations, one to another; is likewise as certain, as that there is any Difference in the Nature of Things, or that Different Things do Exist. Further; that there is a *Fitness* or *Suitableness* of certain *Circumstances* to certain *Persons*, and an *Unsuitableness* of Others, founded in the *Nature of Things* and in the *Qualifications of Persons*, antecedent to *Will*, and to All *Arbitrary or Positive Appointment whatsoever;* must unavoidably be acknowledged by every one, who will not affirm that 'tis *equally Fit and Suitable*, in the *Nature and Reason of Things*, that an Innocent Being should be *extremely and eternally Miserable*, as that it should be Free from such Misery. There *is* therefore such a thing as *Fitness* and *Unfitness*, eternally, necessarily, and unchangeably in the Nature and Reason of Things. Now What these *Relations of Things*, absolutely and necessarily, *Are* in Themselves; That also they *Appear to be*, to the Understanding of all Intelligent Beings; except Those only, who understand Things to Be what they are not, that is, whose Understandings are either very imperfect or very much depraved. And by this *Understanding or Knowledge* of the Natural and Necessary Relations of Things, the *Actions likewise* of all Intelligent Beings are constantly Directed, (which *by the way* is the true Ground and Foundation of all Morality:) unless their *Will* be corrupted by particular *Interest or Affection*, or swayed by some unreasonable and prevailing Lust. The Supreme Cause therefore, and Author of all Things, since (as has already been proved) he must of necessity have Infinite *Knowledge*, and the Perfection of *Wisdom*; so that 'tis absolutely impossible he should *Err*, or be in any respect *Ignorant* of the True Relations and Fitness or Unfitness of things, or be by any means *Deceived* or imposed upon herein: And since he is likewise *Self-Existent*, absolutely *Independent* and *All-Powerful;* so that, having no *want* of any thing, 'tis impossible his *Will* should be influenced by any wrong *Affection;* and having no *Dependence,* 'tis impossible his *Power* should be limited by any Superiour Strength; 'Tis evident He must of necessity, (meaning, not a *Necessity of Fate,* but such a *Moral Necessity* as I before said was consistent with the most perfect Liberty,)*Do* always what he *Knows* to be *Fittest to be done;* That is, He must act always according to the strictest Rules of Infinite *Goodness, Justice,* and *Truth,* and all other *Moral Perfections.* In Particular: The Supreme Cause must in the first place be infinitely *Good;* that is, he must have an unalterable Disposition to *Do* and to *Communicate* Good or Happiness: Because, being himself necessarily *Happy* in the Eternal Injoyment of his own infinite Perfections, he cannot possibly have any other Motives to make any Creatures at all, but only that he may communicate to Them his Own Perfections; according to their different *Capacities,* arising from that *Variety of Natures,* which it was fit for *Infinite Wisdom* to produce; and according to their *different Improvements,* arising from that *Liberty* which is essentially Necessary to the Constitution of *Intelligent* and *Active Beings.* That he must be infinitely *Good,* appears likewise further from hence; that, being necessarily *All-Sufficient,* he must consequently be infinitely removed from all *Malice* and *Envy,* and from all other possible Causes or Temptations of doing Evil; which, 'tis evident, can only be Effects of *Want* and *Weakness,* of *Imperfection* or *Depravation.* Again; The Supreme Cause and Author of all things, must in like manner be infinitely *Just:* Because, the *Rule of Equity* being nothing else but the *Very Nature* of Things, and their *necessary Relations* one to Another; And the *Execution of Justice,* being nothing else but a suiting the *Circumstances of Things* to the *Qualifications of Persons,* according to the Original *Fitness* and *Agreeableness,* which I have before shown to be *Necessarily in Nature,* antecedent to *Will* and to *all positive Appointment;* 'Tis manifest, that He who knows *Perfectly* this Rule of Equity, and necessarily *judges of Things as they are;* who has *compleat Power* to Execute Justice according to that Knowledge, and *No possible Temptation* to deviate in the least therefrom; who can neither be *imposed upon* by any *Deceit,* nor *swayed* by any *Byass,* nor *awed by any Power;* must, of necessity, do always that which is *Right;* without Iniquity, and without Partiality; without Prejudice, and without Respect of Persons. Lastly, That the Supreme Cause and Author of all things, must be *True and Faithful,* in all his *Declarations* and all his Promises; is most evident. For the only Possible Reason of Falsifying, is either *Rashness* or *Forgetfulness, Inconstancy* or *Impotency, Fear of Evil,* or *Hope of Gain;* From all which, an Infinitely *Wise, All-Sufficient* and *Good*

Being, must of Necessity be infinitely removed; And consequently, as 'tis impossible for him *to be deceived himself,* so neither is it possible for him in any wise *to deceive* Others. In a Word: All Evil and all Imperfections whatsoever, arise plainly either from *Shortness of Understanding, Defect of Power,* or *Faultiness of Will*; And this last, evidently from some *Impotency, Corruption,* or *Depravation;* being nothing else, but a direct Choosing to Act contrary to the known Reason and Nature of Things. From all which, it being manifest that the Supreme Cause and Author of all Things, cannot but be infinitely removed; it follows undeniably, that he must of Necessity be *a Being of Infinite Goodness, Justice, and Truth, and all other Moral Perfections.*

And now from what has been said upon this Argument, I hope 'tis in the whole sufficiently clear, that the Being and Attributes of God, are, to attentive and considering Minds, abundantly capable of just Proof and Demonstration; and that the Adversaries of God and Religion, have no *Reason* on their side, (to which they would pretend to be strict Adherers,) but merely vain Confidence, and great Blindness and Prejudice; when they desire it should be thought, that, in the Fabrick of the World, God has left himself wholly without Witness; and that all the Arguments of Nature, are on the side of Atheism and Irreligion. Some Men, I know, there are, who having never turned their Thoughts to Matters of this Nature, think that these Things are all absolutely above our Comprehension; and that we talk about we know not what, when we dispute about these Questions. But since the most considerable Atheists that ever appeared in the World, and the Pleaders for Universal Fatality, have All thought fit to argue in this Way, in their Attempts to remove the First Foundations of Religion; 'tis Reasonable and Necessary, that they should be opposed in their own Way; it being most certain, that no Argumentation, of what kind soever, can possibly be made use of on the side of Errour, but may also be used with much greater Advantage on the behalf of Truth.

From what has been said upon this Argument, we may see how it comes to pass, that though nothing is so certain and undeniable as the Necessary Existence of God, and the consequent Deduction of all his Attributes; yet Men, who have never attended to the Evidence of Reason, and to the Notices that God hath given us of Himself, may easily be in great measure ignorant of Both. That the three Angles of a Triangle are Equal to two right ones, is so certain and evident, that whoever affirms the contrary, affirms what may very easily be reduced to an express Contradiction: Yet whoever turns not his Mind to consider it at all, may easily be ignorant of This and numberless other the like Mathematical and most infallible Truths.

Yet the Notices that God has been pleased to give us of himself, are so many and so obvious; in the Constitution, Order, Beauty, and Harmony of

the several Parts of the World; in the Frame and Structure of our own
Bodies, and the wonderful Powers and Faculties of our Souls; in the unavoidable Apprehensions of our own Minds, and the common Consent of all
other Men; in every thing within us, and everything without us: that no Man
of the meanest Capacity and greatest Disadvantages whatsoever, with the
slightest and most superficial Observation of the Works of God, and the
lowest and most obvious attendance to the Reason of Things, can be ignorant
of *Him*; but he must be utterly without Excuse. Possibly he may not indeed
be able to understand, or be affected by, nice and Metaphysical Demonstra-
tions of the Being and Attributes of God: But then, for the same Reason, he
is obliged also not to suffer himself to be shaken and unsettled, by the subtle
Sophistries of Sceptical and Atheistical Men; which he cannot perhaps answer, because he cannot understand. But he is bound to adhere to those
Things which he knows, and those Reasonings he is capable to judge of;
which are abundantly sufficient to determine and to guide the Practice of
sober and considering Men.

18

WALLACE I. MATSON

---

introduction

Samuel Clarke delivered his metaphysical speculations on God to his eighteenth-century contemporaries in a church. Wallace Matson, a contemporary philosopher, has set forth his reflections on the same theme in talks, papers, and books, and his audience is composed mostly of highly sophisticated university teachers and students of philosophy. Yet the two philosophers, at crucial points, say much the same thing, Matson explicitly deriving some of his inspiration from Clarke. These ideas are not, then, of mere historical interest.

Matson's version of the cosmological argument rests on the principle of sufficient reason—the presupposition that there is an explanation for everything that exists. In the case of everything in the world, that explanation can be found in other things in the world—a person's existence is explained in terms of his parents, a tree is explained in terms of the seed from which it sprang, the circumstances of its origin and germination, and so on. It is generally conceded that everything in the world is explainable, and that the explanation of any such thing must be in terms of other things in the world.

Another way of expressing this view is to say that everything in the world is *contingent*, or as Clarke expressed it, *dependent*—dependent on something else in the world. The converse of dependent is *independent*. Thus, a thing would be independent or noncontingent if it were *not* dependent on anything else for its existence. But this is the definition of *necessary*. A necessary or independent being, therefore, would be one that in no way depended, either for its existence or its properties, on anything else. And we can now ask: Does any such being exist?

Clearly, Matson notes, there is no such being *in* nature, for everything in nature is dependent *on something else* for its existence. Nothing within nature exists simply by its own nature. Nor is the totality of all those dependent things (the world as a whole) a necessary being—for infinitely many alternative worlds are just as *possible* as this one. Thus, a world in which a given housefly had never existed, but that otherwise was very much like the world in which we and that particular housefly find ourselves, is at least *possible*, even though no such world exists. This actual world, then, like everything in it, is contingent, and there must accordingly be some explanation, or some sufficient reason, why it should exist. The reason cannot be found within the world, for obvious reasons, nor can the world be explained entirely in terms of itself. If it could, then it would itself exist by its own nature, or be a necessary being—which, as we have seen, it is not.

What, then, would *count* as an explanation of the totality of contingent things? In other words, what could serve as a reason for the existence of a world? Matson suggests that this reason can consist of nothing less than the absolutely rational choice of an unlimited being that exists by its own nature—that is, a necessarily existent being, lacking nothing in power, knowledge, or goodness. In other words, the world depends for its existence upon God, as the concept of God has been traditionally understood. At this point Matson's thought departs most radically from that of Clarke and other classical defenders of this argument; for Matson, in proving God's existence, simultaneously proves (in case the proof is genuine) God's chief attributes as well. What is crucial to Matson's thinking at this point is the supposition that, since the world is rational, i.e., completely intelligible to reason, then the reason for its own existence must be absolutely rational, together with what he thinks this entails.

Matson's treatment of the classical design argument is less sympathetic. And this argument is indeed, as even those most sympathetic to it concede, certainly less rigorous and metaphysical in character than the one just considered.

What is crucial to the design argument, in its traditional formulation, is the concept of *analogy*. That is, it is thought that things in nature, or at least living things and certain of their parts, such as the eye, exhibit a certain relationship of means to ends. The parts of the eye, for example, and their arrangement, seem to constitute a means to a certain end or purpose, namely, vision. And so it is throughout living nature. And even the world itself, or the totality of heaven and earth, remarkably resembles a huge clock or machine, wherein order and harmony prevail, instead of the kind of chaos or haphazardness that might have been.

Now it has been claimed by the defenders of the design argument, or at least one common version of it, that these evidences of adaptation of means to ends in nature point to the existence of a grand designer, and the specific defense of that suggestion has, in at least some cases, rested on a claimed *analogy* between the supposed means-ends relationships found in nature and the same kind of relationships found in human artifacts. But at this point the argument has gone in several different directions. Some of its defenders have supposed, not merely that the structures of living things strongly *suggest* a purposeful origin, but, more strongly, that it is precisely the character of being a means to some end that enables us to distinguish things that are designed from things that are not. If, therefore, this characteristic is found in natural things not fabricated by men, then we must presuppose some other designer of them.

Matson challenges the supposition that this characteristic of being a means to an end is what enables us to identify artifacts as such. If it were, then we would indeed be driven to infer some designer of natural things that have that characteristic. But Matson claims, convincingly, that we do not in fact use that as our criterion in identifying artifacts, but instead we look for marks of tools and manufacture, and so the argument is simply invalid.

Perhaps the so-called "argument from design" should not be treated as a metaphysical *argument* at all, for on the basis of the most elementary logical considerations it can be seen to be invalid. Why, then, does it exercise such force over people's thought? Why are both ignorant and learned people often so deeply impressed by it? Perhaps the answer is that, while the specific characteristics of nature, and especially living things, certainly supply no metaphysical proof of God's existence, they do strongly *suggest* it; and that even when this suggestion seems, as it often does to some minds, quite irresistible, it still cannot be reduced to an argument that will withstand the most elementary tests of reason. Perhaps this is why the so-called arguments from design will never really be refuted: while the character of the world certainly seems, to some minds, to suggest a grand designer of it, there is simply no argument here to refute.

Wallace Matson (1921–) teaches at the University of California at Berkeley. He has with great acumen reformulated and analyzed all of the traditional metaphysical arguments for God's existence, some of which he considers strong, others weak. Here we shall consider the main points in his formulations of two of these arguments, the cosmological argument and the classical argument from design.

God as Cause and Designer
of the World*

THE COSMOLOGICAL ARGUMENT

A brief preliminary summary of the argument is this: If the world is intelligible, then God exists. But the world is intelligible. Therefore God exists.

"Intelligibility" is defined in terms of the principle of sufficient reason: "There is a Sufficient Reason why everything that is, is so and not other-wise."[1] That is to say, a mere fact, of itself in isolation, is not intelligible, understandable; it becomes intelligible when it is explained—when it is put into a context enabling us to see not just *that* it is, but *why* it is "so and not otherwise."

There are, I am told, at least 93 different kinds of explanation; and though I think that that is an exaggeration, there is admittedly danger in talking, as I am about to do, in terms of only two kinds: mechanical and purposive. These two may be considered, however, as genera embracing many particular species. If they do not jointly exhaust the field, they very nearly do so; and at any rate, it does not seem that anyone has proposed a different kind of explanation that could qualify as universal or cosmic.

A mechanical explanation is one in terms of causes, regularities, laws of nature. It is the type of explanation usually—though as I shall point out in a moment, perhaps not always—encountered in the natural sciences. Explanations of how an airplane works, or why it failed and crashed, are mechanical. Life, or the evolution of a galaxy, is explained mechanically if states at one time are related to states at another via laws, which in the more sophisticated sciences take the form of differential equations; in the less developed disciplines these laws may be no more than statements to the effect that one kind of occurrence has been observed always to be followed by another (cause-effect).

The kind of account we naturally give of why a rational creature is engaged in a certain activity is purposive or teleological. Such explanations commonly include references to motives, choices, deliberations, reasons, not to mention emotions and passions. . . .

To return to the principle of sufficient reason: it is just the claim that there are no brute facts, that everything has an explanation—though we may not be able to find out what it is. The principle thus includes the causal princi-

---

[1] Leibniz, *Monadology*, sec. 32, and elsewhere.

ple, that everything has a cause; but it is broader. It says that everything has a cause, or serves a purpose, or both.

But then, why should we accept the principle—if we should? This is a curious question: is there a sufficient reason for accepting the principle of sufficient reason? We shall not face it squarely in this book. It might be maintained that the principle is an assumption that we are obliged to make if our attempts to understand the world are not to be pointless. That is to say, our efforts to explain particular things presuppose that there is some explanation. We do not know what the cause of cancer is, but the biochemist does not for a moment entertain the possibility that cancer has no cause at all. The psychoanalyst does not know what the pattern of his patient's behavior is in all its details; but however "irrational" and apparently meaningless the actions, psychoanalysis is committed to the assumption that there is a meaning to be found in them. Furthermore, the principle does not let us down; our successes in finding reasons why things are "so and not otherwise" are so many confirmations of it, and our failures we ascribe to the difficulty, not the impossibility, of understanding. These may not be adequate reasons for accepting the principle; but we shall simply assume it in what follows.

"So *and not otherwise.*" This boulder is here in this gorge; but it "might just as well" have been somewhere else? So it might, considered just in itself. But it used to be on the edge of the precipice above, and someone pushed it; that is why it is here, why it has to be here. But then, why could it not have flown through the air when pushed? Well, heavy bodies, near the surface of the earth, fall when unsupported. This, then, is just a brute fact? No, it follows from the property of matter that bodies attract one another. But why . . . ?

Someone pushed it? He "might just as well" not have pushed it. But inasmuch as unfriendly Indians were pursuing him up the gorge. . . .

Explanation, the finding of sufficient reasons, we see to be a process of ruling out alternative possibilities. Without an explanation we do not know why the boulder should not be in just any old place. The explanation tells us why it is here rather than there—why just this possibility, out of the indefinite or infinite number of conceivable ones, was realized. We know further why it was pushed by just this man at just this time; and so on.

We say that a thing or event is *contingent* if the reason why it is what it is, is not otherwise, is not ascertainable without looking beyond the thing or event itself. To be contingent is just to be dependent on something else, to be the effect of something else. The opposite of "contingent" in this sense is "necessary." Something is necessary if it is what it is no matter what else is the case—if it is something entirely independent, in its existence and all its properties, of the existence and properties of everything else.

We have now defined the term "necessary being." The question is whether there is any reason to believe that a necessary Being exists. (We might as well use capitals, as it will not have escaped the reader that such a Being = God.) The argument proceeds:

It is obvious that there is no necessary Being in nature. This is just another way of saying that everything in nature has a cause. There is no particular thing that would not have been otherwise if something else had been otherwise. Now one may be tempted to say that although this is true of particular things—objects and events—at any rate the laws of nature are exceptions. There might have been more or fewer boulders in this gorge, but the law of gravitation must be what it is. We should note, however, that science explains laws as well as particulars. In Kepler's day, it was one brute fact that heavy bodies near the earth fall when unsupported, another brute fact that smoke goes up, and a third that the planets move around the sun. Newton exhibited the sufficient reason for these in terms of a more comprehensive generalization: given that all matter has the property of gravitating, it follows that all these things must behave as they do and not otherwise. But as to why bodies gravitate, Newton himself knew not, "and [he said] I frame no hypotheses."[2] Before Newton there were the three brute laws we have mentioned, plus a lot of others; after Newton, just one. What are to us, today, the brute laws of gravitation, electromagnetism, nuclear forces, etc., await their explanation in, presumably, a general field theory. Once physicists enunciate such a theory, the number of separate brute facts will be again reduced. But even so, at least one will remain: we shall not know why the general field equation is what it is, and not otherwise. We will be able to imagine other possibilities, and we shall not know why just this one is realized. It will be contingent, but we shall not know on what it is contingent. Or so it appears.

Thus not only is there no necessary thing in nature, but there is no necessary characteristic of nature either. Given that some things in nature are what they are, we understand how it is necessary (relative to them) that other parts of nature are as they are. Given that nature has certain characteristics, we understand why necessarily (relative to them) nature must have certain other characteristics also. But nowhere in nature is there a thing, or a characteristic, of which we can say: This is as it is, and could not be otherwise than it is, no matter what else were to change.

Not only is this last statement true of things in, and characteristics of, nature: nature as a whole is not a necessary Being. The world—the totality of everything that was and is and will be—is only one among an infinitude of possible worlds. By a "possible world" is meant any assemblage of coherently describable things and occurrences. Thus for example one possible world is that in which everything is exactly the same as in this one, with the single exception that there is a misprint in this line of this book. (More grammati-

[2]In note "Concerning the Law of Gravitation," added at close of Book III of *Principia*, 2d ed., 1713.

cally: it is possible that there should be such a world.) It is possible that your parents might never have met, and in consequence that you would not have existed: we have described another possible world. Still another is inhabited by unicorns, mermaids, and centaurs. This is not to say that such creatures are biologically possible; only that no contradiction is involved in supposing that they could exist were the laws of biology different from what they are. Novelists and painters, including surrealists, describe possible worlds. The only limitation on imagining them—and it is not really a limitation—is that a possible world cannot be such that description of it would involve logical contradiction. Thus there is no possible world containing round squares.

This world that we live in, then, is not the only possible world; but it is the only real or actual world. Now when one state of affairs, out of a plurality of possibilities, is realized, there must be a sufficient reason why just that one exists. Yet it is clear that the sufficient reason for this world's existence cannot be contained within it, in nature.

Must we then abandon the principle of sufficient reason? Each part of nature has its sufficient reason in some other part of nature: in its cause at least, perhaps also in its purpose if it has one. And that sufficient reason has its sufficient reason in some other part; and so on . . . ad infinitum? It appears that if we stay within nature, we must either come in the end to at least one brute fact (maybe the "big bang" of the astrophysicists) or one "brute law" (maybe a unified field theory); or else we are confronted with an infinite regress of sufficient reasons, such that no reason is absolutely sufficient, only relatively so. In any case, as we have just seen, nature cannot contain within itself the sufficient reason for its own being, considered as a whole: in particular, why should there not have been just nothing at all? If we confine ourselves within nature in our search for a reason for nature, assuredly we shall find none; the totality of things will have to be taken as one stupendous brute fact; and as a brute fact it will be unintelligible, irrational.

Perhaps it is so. Perhaps the principle breaks down. Perhaps existence, at base, is a surd, and there is no use trying to adequate it to the intellect. Perhaps we must make shift to comprehend only the parts, never the whole.

However, let us not give up so easily. Let us at least ask ourselves what a sufficient reason for the whole might be like, if there were one.

We see immediately that it could not be a cause in the mechanical sense. The attempt to explain everything, whether piecemeal or all at once, in terms of a cause obviously leads us into an infinite regress—just what we are trying to escape. There remains for investigation, then, the possibility of finding a sufficient reason that is a choice.

Are we not faced here at the outset with the same difficulty of infinite regress? For we have already admitted that choices have causes. So that if the sufficient reason for the world were a choice, we could still ask for the cause of the choice; and so on.

But, after all, the choices that we are familiar with are made by limited, contingent beings. We must not be led too hastily to generalize on the sole basis of them. Rather, let us consider, within the sphere of human activities, what are the criteria by which we judge the adequacy of any explanation made in terms of a choice. That is, if we are told that X is as it is because P chose it to be that way, we may demand a further explanation of the choice—the choice itself may puzzle us. But perhaps not always: maybe sometimes this kind of answer is satisfying in itself.

Now it seems that we go on the following principle: we assume that a person makes the best choice he can. If his choice does not strike us as being the best possible, we wonder why it was not, and we search for reasons for the failure; but insofar as it is the best, we demand no further explanation. For the choice seems to us perfectly rational. Let me illustrate.

Someone builds a house of cheap materials, in a run-down neighborhood, not even taking advantage of the best available site on his lot; the rooms are poorly arranged and ventilated; the style is grotesque. We ask: Why did he do this? We answer: He couldn't afford anything better; he is not clever at design, and he was brought up by an ignorant and vulgar aunt. In view of his limitations, that was the best he could do. If a wealthy, ingenious, and well-educated person built such a house, we should perhaps have to conclude that he was not quite sane; we should think it fruitless to search for reasons for such behavior , and should engage rather in a clinical investigation of the causes of his psychosis.

If, however, a man of wealth and taste builds a convenient and beautiful mansion, we are not puzzled at all. That is just what one would expect; that is the rational thing to do. No doubt, there are causes of his being wealthy and tasteful; but those causes, whatever they are, are of only secondary relevance at most in explaining the house. It is sufficient that the house is the result of a rational choice.

Now let us suppose, for the sake of argument, that the world is the outcome of a choice. Is there any kind of choice that would in itself put an end to all puzzlement—that would not tempt us to ask further questions about the causes of the choice?

If we follow our homely example, it seems that this condition could be satisfied only if the choice were an absolutely rational one. And to be absolutely rational, to be self-sufficient as an explanation, the choice would have to be made by a Being subject to no limitations. If the chooser lacked power to produce whatever he wished to produce, we should want to know what prevented him. If he lacked the knowledge of all the alternatives, we should need to explain this lack. If, having complete knowledge and power, he nevertheless did not make the best choice, that would be most puzzling of all; we should call his behavior irrational and demand a cause. But if the chooser were subject to no limitations of power, if he chose in full knowledge of all the alternatives (all the logically possible ones), and chose the best—then this choice would be absolutely rational and would in itself constitute the sufficient reason for the world's being so and not otherwise. Since we have eliminated causes, and choices not fulfilling these conditions, only such a choice by an omnipotent, omniscient, and benevolent Being could be the sufficient reason for the universe.

Therefore if nature is rational, God exists. But there is good reason to believe that nature is rational: to wit, all of science and the rest of experience. Therefore there is good reason to believe that God exists.

This completes the exposition of the subtle cosmological argument, which in ingenuity and elegance perhaps marks the high point of rational theology. A few points concerning it remain to be noted:

First, it is not appropriate to ask, "Who made God?" and "What are the causes of the infinite Being?" in this context. God, as sufficient reason for nature—chooser of its laws as well as of its furniture—must be outside nature; but it is only within nature, i.e., within a framework of causal presuppositions, that it makes sense to ask for causes.

Second, God is the necessary Being in the sense of our definition of this term: a Being not dependent on the existence of anything else for His existence; not such that He could be otherwise in any respect, whatever else were the case. This is not to say that God's existence is logically necessary, in the sense that His nonexistence is inconceivable. One can conceive of there being no universe at all and no God. One can (perhaps) also conceive of the universe being irrational, hence either the result of the choice of some small-g god or of no choice. The argument claims only that God, as the source of all being, including all causation, cannot conceivably be Himself limited by any causes—in other words, there cannot be any cause (or indeed any reason) why He should not exist. Only in this sense does His essence entail His existence.

Third, a word "choice" in this context must of course not be supposed to carry with it any connotation of an act in time. The choice of "the best" by God is not to be thought of as the result of long and painful deliberation; this would be inconsistent with omnipotence. Hence the argument is neutral with respect to the issue whether nature has a beginning or not. (Or is this quite true? Theologians since St. Augustine have been aware of the difficulty involved in the notion of a temporal world brought into existence by a timeless Being: if the sufficient reason for the world is eternal, must not the world be eternal? If not, there must have been a time when the sufficient reason existed, but what it was the sufficient reason *for* did not. This is still another problem that we shall pass by as not relevant to our main concern.)

Fourth, as Leibniz noted,[3] it follows as a corollary that this is the best of all possible worlds. The reader is begged to withhold his Voltairean laughter, pending discussion in due course.

[3]*The Principles of Nature and of Grace, Based on Reason* (1714), sec. 10.

Summary of the Argument

1. There is a sufficient reason why everything that is, is so and not otherwise. That is, wherever there is a plurality of logically possible alternatives, there is a sufficient reason why the alternative realized is the one realized.
2. Sufficient reasons are either causes or choices or both.
3. Of any cause, as distinguished from choice, one can always legitimately ask what its cause is.
4. Hence causes cannot be ultimately sufficient reasons.
5. Now the actual universe is not the only possible universe.
6. Hence (by 1, 2, and 4) its sufficient reason must be a choice.
7. But choices are sufficient reasons only insofar as they are rational choices.
8. A choice is rational insofar as it is choice of the best; and insofar as limitations of power or knowledge are imposed on the chooser, the choice is rational only relative to these limitations and requires further explanation.
9. Therefore an absolutely rational choice, requiring no further explanation, is a choice of the best, made by a Being subject to no limitations.
10. Therefore (by 5, 6, 9, and the definition of God) God exists.

THE ARGUMENT FROM DESIGN

Unlike the ontological and cosmological arguments, which are mostly the preserves of theologians and philosophers, the third member of the traditional triad is of great popular appeal. In skeleton outline it is this:

1. Nature everywhere exhibits orderly structures and processes.
2. Orderly structures and processes are always the work of intelligent personality.
3. Therefore nature is the work of an intelligent personality, i.e., of a god.

The Psalmist sang: "The heavens declare the glory of God; and the firmament sheweth his handywork." This, the central thought of the design argument, is virtually as old as humanity. . . . The universe is full of complex organizations exhibiting "curious adapting of means to ends." Our question is, how are these to be accounted for?

There are three (and, as far as I can see, only three) abstractly tenable hypothesis: Aristotelian, mechanistic, and teleological.

1. The order in the world might have existed eternally. Particular instances of order in the present would be the outcomes of pre-existing equivalent orders, and so on back ad infinitum. If we held this view, and also allowed that the cosmological argument is fallacious, there would be no need

to account further for order at all. However, facts available to us are incompatible with this hypothesis, which we therefore can omit from consideration.

2. Complex organisms—we can restrict our survey to living beings without loss of generality—might be the outcome of a progressive development from simpler organisms; and the simplest organisms might themselves have developed gradually from even simpler combinations of material constitutents, so that in the whole procession from the atom to the theologian there is nowhere any gap. Scientists, not philosophers, must decide whether this is in outline the picture of what has in fact happened; but at any rate I shall assume that it is correct.

The philosophical question does not concern the facts. It is this: Is evolution able to account for itself in its own terms? The mechanistic answer is affirmative. Given some initial distribution of matter in the universe (and we need not raise the question where *that* came from), the inherent properties—essentially, the energy distribution patterns—of the elementary particles are sufficient to account for their building up into all the complexes presently encountered, including living and conscious ones. Thus organisms would be "chance" products of the shifting distribution of energy in the universe—"chance" in the sense of not being directed by intelligent foresight, though not chance in the sense of being lawless. Leucippus, the first great Greek mechanist, expressed this in the only words of his that have survived: "Nothing happens at random, but everything for a reason and from necessity."[4]

It is essential to the mechanistic view that although a complex can arise only from pre-existing parts, the parts can and sometimes do pre-exist dissociated from each other, and can and sometimes do unite spontaneously—that is, a complex effect does not always require an equally complex cause. There is occasionally something new under the sun, though what is new is made from what is old.

3. The teleological hypothesis, while admitting the facts of evolution, insists that these facts are not self-explanatory. The effect cannot exceed the cause; in particular, organisms must be, ultimately, the effects of causes at least as complex and ordered as they themselves; and those organisms possessing consciousness could not exist unless their pre-existing cause were itself conscious and purposive. This is not to deny that the particular material configurations may have been produced out of simpler constituents, but it is to deny that the union could be merely spontaneous and inherent in the parts. "Dead matter" could no more form itself into an amoeba or a theologian than lumber, nails, and wire could, without the activity of a carpenter, form themselves into a chicken coop.

But the teleologist, in admitting the facts of evolution, really abandons his case. He has admitted that as far as immediate causes are concerned it is

[4]Fragment 2.

possible—since it is actual—that highly organized structures can evolve "naturally" out of relatively unorganized materials. If he insists that the remote, unobserved, and unobservable causes of order must be intelligent, what possible justification for this view can he put forward? Is this not just the final retreat, to the limits of the universe, of the animism that once triumphantly occupied the whole of it? If you ask, soberly and seriously, for an explanation of the order in the universe (says the mechanist to the teleologist), you are asking for an account of the causes of that order. Well, here is the outline of that explanation; here are some of the details that go to fill it out; and if you want more, scientists are uncovering them faster than you can assimilate them. What more can you ask for? To go on saying: but the ultimate cause of order must be orderly, the ultimate cause of adaptation must be purposive, the ultimate cause of consciousness must be conscious— to go on saying this is simply to betray the fact, suspected all along, that nothing will satisfy you but an animistic explanation; and this is a fact about your psychology, not a certain or probable inference about the nature of things.

Some Afterthoughts

Yet after the fallacies of the probability and entropy arguments have been exposed, and after the propensity to accept the design axiom has been ascribed to natural animism, the argument from design is but scotched. Its extraordinarily tough core continues to pulsate with life. That core is the impressive analogy between the universe and the products of intelligent foresight.

> You will find [the world] to be nothing but one great machine, subdivided into an infinite number of lesser machines. . . . All these various machines, and even their most minute parts, are adjusted to each other with an accuracy which ravishes into admiration all men who have ever contemplated them. The curious adapting of means to ends, throughout all nature, resembles exactly, though it much exceeds, the productions of human contrivance. . . . Since therefore the effects resemble each other, we are led to infer, by all the rules of analogy, that the causes also resemble.[5]

Hume himself, after he had done all he could to expose the weakness of the analogy, grudgingly admitted that it has sufficient force to justify the conclusion that "the cause or causes of order in the universe probably bear some remote analogy to human intelligence." May we not still say that this is a matter of opinion, and that it is reasonable for us to hold the analogy to be really strong and sufficient to validate the reasonableness of theism?

Perhaps we may, if the argument really establishes an analogy. But does it?

Stripped of rhetoric, the argument as presented by Hume (and accepted as a fair statement of it, by advocates and critics alike) is this:

[5]Hume, *Dialogues*, Pt. II (see text, p. 99).

PREMISE I. Natural objects share with artifacts the common characteristics of adjustment of parts and curious adapting of means to ends.
PREMISE II. Artifacts have these characteristics because they are products of design.
CONCLUSION. Therefore natural objects are probably products of a great
designer.

In form this is an argument by analogy. The proponents of the argument
maintain that the analogy is a strong one; the detractors judge it weak; all
agree that the argument is an analogy.

. . . If the argument is an analogy, then it is an extremely weak one—much
weaker even than Hume judged, so weak that we must be amazed that anyone
could have thought it to have any force whatsoever. For it is in fact at least as
weak as the following argument:

PREMISE I. Natural objects share with artifacts the common characteristic of being colored.
PREMISE II. Artifacts are colored by being painted or dyed.
CONCLUSION. Therefore natural objects are probably colored by a great
painter-dyer.

I take it as self-evident that this is an extremely weak argument, to which
no one would assent. Yet it cannot be weaker than the design analogy,
because it is of the same form and its premises are obviously true. (It may be
objected that the second premise is not true, since some artifacts retain their
"natural" colors. I mean, though, that when we know how they got their
colors, we know that they got them by being painted or dyed. And besides,
some artifacts retain as components, "natural" adaptation of means to ends:
e.g., squirrel cages.) How so weak an argument could seem strong needs
accounting for; and I doubt whether cynical references to the unbounded
credulity of *homo religiosus* will suffice.

I shall try to explain these anomalies by suggesting that the paint argument is less convincing than the design argument precisely because its premises are more obviously true. From this I shall conclude that the analogical
form disguises the real form of the design argument.

If it were quite obvious—as obvious as that everything (not transparent) is
colored—that everything has the property of curious adapting of means to
ends, would there then be any temptation to argue that the cause of adaptation in natural objects must be like that in artifacts? I do not think so; but
perhaps the thought-experiment is difficult and inconclusive. Let us go at it
indirectly.

Suppose someone wanted seriously to urge the paint argument. One thing
we can be sure of is that he would waste no effort on proving the first
premise. It is obvious that everything, artificial and natural objects alike, is

colored. No one would say: "Look here. Automobiles and billboards and books and wigs and so forth are colored, as you can plainly see. But look again and you will discern, on close inspection, that not only these but also peaches and strawberries and snow and the sky and natural hair and so forth are colored. Now, having established that beyond reasonable doubt, we can go on."

But this sort of thing is just what advocates of the design argument do at the greatest possible length. They take it for granted only that the curious adapting of means to ends is obvious where artifacts are concerned; they judge that the thesis they must devote their eloquence to convincing people of is the existence of adaptation in nature. In the heyday of the argument from design, books such as the eight volumes of the *Bridgewater Treatises*[6] were almost wholly devoted to establishing this fact. Their authors assumed, correctly, that they were presenting the public with information not otherwise available, and with inferences such as would not occur to just anyone.

Let us rewrite the argument in a way that will bring out this insistence on the nonobviousness of adaptation:

1. You can distinguish artifacts from natural objects; and you know two things about artifacts: first, that they exhibit curious adapting of means to ends; second, that they do so because they are consciously designed to do so. This you have learned from the experience of seeing them made.
2. If, then, you were to discover some object the origin of which was unknown to you, but which obviously resembled something else known to be an artifact, you would immediately, and correctly, infer that it too was an artifact and was the product of conscious design.
3. Now it is granted that natural objects, such as eyeballs and lizards, do not obviously resemble artifacts. But on closer inspection, they are seen to possess the essential characteristic of artifacts, that characteristic which when obviously present warrants an inference to design, namely, curious adapting of means to ends.
4. Therefore by parity of reasoning you should come to realize that natural objects too are products of conscious design.

[6]Eight books published 1833–1840 under the auspices of the Royal Society. The authors shared a legacy of L8,000 from the eighth earl of Bridgewater. In order of publication, they are: Thomas Chalmers, *The Adaptation of External Nature to the Moral and Intellectual Constitution of Man;* William Prout, *Chemistry, Meteorology, and the Function of Digestion,* Considered with Reference to Natural Theology; William Kirby, *The History, Habits, and Instincts of Animals with Reference to Natural Theology;* William Buckland, *Geology and Mineralogy Considered with Reference to Natural Theology;* Sir Charles Bell, *The Hand: Its Mechanism and Vital Endowments, as Evincing Design;* John Kidd, *On the Adaptation of External Nature to the Physical Condition of Man;* William Whewell, *Astronomy and General Physics Considered with Reference to Natural Theology;* and Peter Mark Roget, *Animal and Vegetable Physiology Considered with Reference to Natural Theology.*

This, I think, is a fair summary of the argument from design as it is actually argued (for example, by Paley[7]). Adverbs are often dispensable parts of speech, but not here. The gist of the argument comes in the third paragraph, and its force lies in the contrast between inspecting things superficially and inspecting them carefully.

There is nothing inherently illegitimate about argumentation of this form. It often happens that we divide a large class of things into two subclasses, those that have the property P and those that lack it—or so it seems; and then later we discover that really all the members of the class have P after all. Thus well into the nineteenth century biologists commonly divided living things into those that were generated from seed and those that were spontaneously generated. Then Pasteur showed conclusively that there is no such thing as spontaneous generation—all living things are generated from seed.

Reasoning of this kind is valid only when a division is made between two species on the basis of some clear and relevant criterion, such that things of one kind are found, on the evidence available, to satisfy it, and others are not; and subsequently it is discovered that the things thought not to satisfy the criterion really do. In the example, the criterion was a clear one: reproduction from germ cells provided by parent organisms. No one had discovered any bodies, produced by flies, mosquitoes, molds, etc., such that from them, and from them only, other organisms of the same kind would develop. All that was known was that in certain conditions (decaying vegetation, etc.) these flora and fauna seemed inevitably to develop. The criterion was clear, and the division in accordance with it was justified on the evidence available. It took ingenious investigation to demonstrate that in these cases too, seeds were present.

Does the reformulated argument from design conform to these requirements? Perhaps it satisfies the second. It is not obvious that very many natural objects, and features of nature, show fine adjustment of parts and curious adapting of means to ends; but closer scrutiny may establish this. And the criterion itself, though not so clear and easy to apply as that of presence or absence of seeds, may be conceded to be sufficiently definite.

The criterion assumed is the wrong one, however. Proponents of the design argument take it for granted that the properties according to which we judge whether or not some object is an artifact, are accurate adjustment of parts and curious adapting of means to ends. But that is not the way we judge, even provisionally, whether something is an artifact or not. This is clear from our being able to tell whether something is an artifact without knowing what it is for or whether its parts are accurately adjusted.

Suppose someone is given a heap of miscellaneous objects: watches, leaves, eyeballs, pistols, lizards, stone axes, sealing wax, abstract paintings, etc.; then suppose he is required to separate them into two piles, the one

[7]William Paley, *Natural Theology, or Evidences of the Existence and Attributes of the Deity* (1802).

containing only artifacts, the other only "natural" objects. Anyone can easily do this. The reason why one can accomplish the task so easily, though, is perhaps just that one knows in advance which are man-made and which are not. So let us make the task more difficult. Let us put in the heap a number of "gismos"—objects especially constructed for the test by common methods of manufacture, i.e., metallic, plastic, painted, machined, welded, but such that the subject of the test has never seen such things before, and they do not in fact display any "accurate adjustment of parts" or "curious adapting of means to ends." Put into the heap also a number of natural objects which the subject has never seen. Will he have any more difficulty? He will not. The gismos go into one pile, the platypuses and tektites into the other, quite automatically.

Of course one might conceivably make mistakes in this sorting procedure. And it is perhaps hazardous to predict that human visitors to another planet would be entirely and immediately successful in determining, from an inventory of random objects found on its surface, whether it was or had been the abode of intelligent beings. But space explorers would not be at a loss as to how to proceed in the investigation. They would look for evidences of machining, materials that do not exist in nature, regular markings, and the like. Presence of some of these would be taken as evidence, though perhaps not conclusive, of artifice.

This is how archaeologists decide hard cases. Is this object just a rock, or is it a hand ax? The scientist's inspection is not directed toward determining whether the object can serve a purpose; he looks instead for those peculiar marks left by flaking tools and not produced by weathering. Again: there is no question at all that Stonehenge is a human contrivance, though there is much controversy about its purpose.

We are now in a position to understand why the friends of Design go to so much trouble to show design in nature, and why the critics, blandly conceding all their opponents put forth, attack the argument at another point. Both accept the Humean formulation. For the advocate, the main job is to establish the first premise; once this is done, he thinks, the assimilation of natural objects to the category of machines follows immediately. The critic, on the other hand, goes to great lengths to resist this coalescence. His usual strategy is to show that the analogy—though proper in that natural objects and machines do both exhibit curious adapting of means to end—is "weak," on the ground that the total disanalogy is great. But in taking this line the critic falls into the snare set by the advocate. Thus even such astute and skeptical inquiries as Hume and J. S. Mill[8] conceded some force to the design argument. They need not have done so; for properly considered, the argument is not really an argument by analogy, strong or weak. It is just another argument with a false premise, and therefore of no force at all.

[8]John Stuart Mill, *Theism* (1874), "The Argument from Marks of Design in Nature."

19

ARTHUR SCHOPENHAUER

introduction

Schopenhauer's discussion of death is one of the most profound and beautiful to be found in the literature of philosophy. Where Plato, in his dialogue on the same subject, the *Phaedo*, elaborated more or less ingenious dialectical arguments in the effort to "prove" that his soul was indestructible, arguments which leave the reader puzzled and skeptical, Schopenhauer tried, through metaphor, poetic expression, analogy, and illustration to open our eyes to a clearer vision of what life really is and what, accordingly, death is.

We tend to think that whether we shall live on after death is simply the question of whether our individual souls or minds will continue on, somewhat as before, after our bodies have been left behind to decay. This is exactly how Plato presented it, and, while it is not the conception of immortality found originally in Christianity or in Judaism, it has become the view of popular religion. Whenever people begin to ponder the problem of death, and the possibility of their surviving it, it is within this framework that their thinking is carried on. It has become almost impossible for most people to formulate the question of life after death in any other way. To most people the question, "Will I entirely cease to exist when I die?" *means* simply: "Will my mind or soul die with my body?" It is seldom realized that this conception of ourselves is almost entirely an inheritance from ancient Greek philosophy, that it is quite foreign to the classical traditions of most of the world as well as to our own classical religious heritage.

The question, "What will happen to me when I die?" is obviously expressed wrongly, even meaninglessly. The only possible answer to the question, as thus ineptly formulated, is: "Then I shall be dead."

What Schopenhauer asks, instead, is the question that really underlies that one, namely, "Will I die? Will there be a time when I shall exist no longer?" And that question, quite clearly, depends on the prior one: "What *am* I? What is my true nature? And what is the relationship of my true nature to my visible and animated body that is destined for the grave?"

And his answer is, negatively, that I am not an individual ego, mind, or soul more or less temporarily lodged within a body, as Plato taught. This conception that people have of themselves, which they even consider to be the only view that would render immortal life possible, is in fact an absurdity. The question of the relationship between the individual ego or self and his body has no answer, because that ego or self does not even exist. Therefore, no question of its relationship to the body even arises. It is a myth, something created by philosophers out of pagan superstitions, then embodied in religion and passed from one generation to another as more or less a presupposition.

The proper analogy for understanding what one is, and his relationship to his body, is not, as in Plato's philosophy, that of a bird in a cage, eager to fly out for a nobler life when freed from confinement. It is, rather, that of a pendulum in relation to the gravitational force that moves it, or of the life force within a leaf in relation to the life of the tree, or of the individual droplets of a waterfall in relation to the energy of the moving river.

Thus, in this philosophy, there is only one reality, of which everything else is but a transitory manifestation, and that reality Schopenhauer calls *will*. In all living things it expresses itself as a will to life. It is common to every living thing, not as something that is possessed by all living things, but as that which each such thing truly is. It is blind and without reason, having as its purpose only to exist. This will to live explains our terror of death, a terror which we can raise to consciousness, and actually think about, but which finds expression in all living things, even though they have no idea of death, as the instinct of self-preservation. It is not thought or consciousness, for these are not the will itself, but its expressions. Nor is it to be identified with vital motions, such as the breath or pulse, for these too are only expressions of the underlying will.

And that will, common to all things, is eternal and indestructible. It never arose, but has always been, and will always be. Death and decay are processes within individual organisms; but no person, and no living thing, is identical with any organism. A physical organism is but an organization of material particles, constantly changing, never the same at two successive moments. But a person, or indeed anything that lives, is that which brings these particles into such organization. We should no more identify our bodies with ourselves, than the moving spinning wheel with the spinner, or the arising and perishing bubbles with the vast river on whose surface they momentarily appear.

Shall I, then, continue to live, after my body is no more? The element in Plato's philosophy that is true and profound, and not the mere tautology that it at first appears to be, is that life itself is not subject to death. Only our bodies can die. But his error was to think that each of us possesses an individual life, and hence, an individual soul, which thinks. It is not our thoughts that are immortal, nor our souls or individual selves, for these are but illusions to begin with. What is immortal in each of us is precisely what we truly are, our innermost natures in which distinctions between self and not-self disappear. That which perishes is that which arose and which has, from our births, had only a phenomenal and impermanent existence to begin with. And each person, seeing this, and understanding the partial reality of his body, his mind, his memories, his ego, and what he superifcially thinks of us as *himself*, is led by a profounder insight to see that he has always been and will always be, that he never really began to exist and can never cease. That which perishes, the individual and separate self, never existed at all except as illusion.

This essay of Schopenhauer's, like the first one included in this book, is taken from the second volume of *The World as Will and Representation*, and was originally composed as a supplement to what had been said, much earlier in the philosopher's life, in the first volume. His references to the earlier work, along with certain digressions, have been omitted.

The Indestructibility of Our True Nature*

Death is the real inspiring genius or Musagetes of philosophy, and for this reason Socrates defined philosophy as θανάτσυ μελέτη.[1] Indeed, without death there would hardly have been any philosophizing. It will therefore be quite in order for a special consideration of this subject to have its place here at the beginning of the last, most serious, and most important of our books.

The animal lives without any real knowledge of death; therefore the indi-

---

*Arthur Schopenhauer, "On Death and Its Relation to the Indestructibility of Our Inner Nature," from *The World as Will and Representation*, Vol. II, trans. E. F. J. Payne (Indian Hills, Colo.: Falcon's Wing Press, 1958). Reprinted by permission of the Barth Foundation.

[1]"Preparation for death." [Tr.]

vidual animal immediately enjoys the absolute imperishableness and immortality of the species, since it is conscious of itself only as endless. With man the terrifying certainty of death necessarily appeared along with the faculty of reason. But just as everywhere in nature a remedy, or at any rate a compensation, is given for every evil, so the same reflection that introduced the knowledge of death also assists us in obtaining *metaphysical* points of view. Such views console us concerning death, and the animal is neither in need of nor capable of them. All religions and philosophical systems are directed principally to this end, and are thus primarily the antidote to the certainty of death which reflecting reason produces from its own resources. The degree in which they attain this end is, however, very different, and *one* religion or philosophy will certainly enable man, far more than the others will, to look death calmly in the face. Brahmanism and Buddhism, which teach man to regard himself as Brahman, as the original being himself, to whom all arising and passing away are essentially foreign, will achieve much more in this respect than will those religions that represent man as being made out of nothing and as actually beginning at his birth the existence he has received from another. In keeping with this we find in India a confidence and a contempt for death of which we in Europe have no conception. It is indeed a ticklish business to force on man through early impression weak and untenable notions in this important respect, and thus to render him for ever incapable of adopting more correct and stable views. For example, to teach him that he came but recently from nothing, that consequently he has been nothing throughout an eternity, and yet for the future is to be imperishable and immortal, is just like teaching him that, although he is through and through the work of another, he shall nevertheless be responsible to all eternity for his commissions and omissions. Thus if with a mature mind and with the appearance of reflection the untenable nature of such doctrines forces itself on him, he has nothing better to put in their place; in fact, he is no longer capable of understanding anything better, and in this way is deprived of the consolation that nature had provided for him as compensation for the certainty of death. In consequence of such a development, we now (1844) see in England the Socialists among the demoralized and corrupted factory workers, and in Germany the young Hegelians among the demoralized and corrupted students, sink to the absolutely physical viewpoint. This leads to the result: *edite, bibite, post mortem nulla voluptas,* [2] and to this extent can be described as bestiality.

According, however, to all that has been taught about death, it cannot be denied that, at any rate in Europe, the opinion of men, often in fact even of the same individual, very frequently vacillates afresh between the conception of death as absolute annihilation and the assumption that we are, so to speak with skin and hair, immortal. Both are equally false, but we have not

[2]"Eat and drink, after death there is no more rejoicing." [Tr.]

so much to find a correct mean as rather to gain the higher standpoint from which such views disappear of themselves.

With these considerations, I wish to start first of all from the entirely empirical viewpoint. Here we have primarily before us the undeniable fact that, according to natural consciousness, man not only fears death for his own person more than anything else, but also weeps violently over the death of his friends and relations. It is evident, indeed, that he does this not egoistically over his own loss, but out of sympathy for the great misfortune that has befallen them. He therefore censures as hard-hearted and unfeeling those who in such a case do not weep and show no grief. Parallel with this is the fact that, in its highest degrees, the thirst for revenge seeks the death of the adversary as the greatest evil that can be inflicted on him. Opinions change according to time and place, but the voice of nature remains always and everywhere the same, and is therefore to be heeded before everything else. Now here it seems clearly to assert that death is a great evil. In the language of nature, *death* signifies annihilation; and that death is a serious matter could already be inferred from the fact that, as everyone knows, life is no joke. Indeed we must not deserve anything better than these two.

The fear of death is, in fact, independent of all knowledge, for the animal has it, although it does not know death. Everything that is born already brings this fear into the world. Such fear of death, however, is *a priori* only the reverse side of the will-to-live, which indeed we all are. Therefore in every animal the fear of its own destruction, like the care for its maintenance, is inborn. Thus it is this fear of death, and not the mere avoidance of pain, that shows itself in the anxious care and caution with which the animal seeks to protect itself, and still more its brood, from everyone who might become dangerous. Why does the animal flee, tremble, and try to conceal itself? Because it is simply the will-to-live, but as such it is forfeit to death and would like to gain time. By nature man is just the same. The greatest of evils, the worst thing that can threaten anywhere, is death; the greatest anxiety is the anxiety of death. Nothing excites us so irresistibly to the most lively interest as does danger to the lives of others; nothing is more dreadful than an execution. Now the boundless attachment to life which appears here cannot have sprung from knowledge and reflection. To these, on the contrary, it appears foolish, for the objective value of life is very uncertain, and it remains at least doubtful whether existence is to be preferred to non-existence; in fact, if experience and reflection have their say, non-existence must certainly win. If we knocked on the graves and asked the dead whether they would like to rise again, they would shake their heads. In Plato's *Apology* this is also the opinion of Socrates, and even the cheerful and amiable Voltaire cannot help saying: *On aime la vie; mais le néant ne laisse pas d'avoir du bon:* and again: *Je ne sais pas ce que c'est que la vie éternelle, mais celle-ci est une mauvaise plaisanterie.* [3] Moreover, in any case life must end soon, so that the few years which possibly we have still to exist vanish entirely before the endless time when we shall be no more. Accordingly, to reflection it appears even ludicrous for us to be so very anxious about this span of time, to tremble so much when our own life or another's is endangered, and to write tragedies whose terrible aspect has as its main theme merely the fear of death. Consequently, this powerful attachment to life is irrational and blind; it can be explained only from the fact that our whole being-in-itself is the will-to-live, to which life therefore must appear as the highest good, however embittered, short, and uncertain it may be; and that that will is originally and in itself without knowledge and blind. Knowledge, on the contrary, far from being the origin of that attachment to life, even opposes it, since it discloses life's worthlessness, and in this way combats the fear of death. When it is victorious, and man accordingly faces death courageously and calmly, this is honoured as great and noble. Therefore we then extol the triumph of knowledge over the blind will-to-live which is nevertheless the kernel of our own inner being. In the same way we despise him in whom knowledge is defeated in that conflict, who therefore clings unconditionally to life, struggles to the utmost against approaching death, and receives it with despair;[4] yet in him is expressed only the original inner being of our own self and of nature. Incidentally, it may here be asked how the boundless love of life and the endeavour to maintain it in every way as long as possible could be regarded as base and contemptible, and likewise considered by the followers of every religion as unworthy thereof, if life were the gift of the good gods to be acknowledged with thanks. How then could it appear great and noble to treat it with contempt? Meanwhile, these considerations confirm for us: (1) that the will-to-live is the innermost essence of man; (2) that in itself the will is without knowledge and blind; (3) that knowledge is an adventitious principle, originally foreign to the will; (4) that knowledge conflicts with the will, and our judgement applauds the triumph of knowledge over the will.

If what makes death seem so terrible to us were the thought of *non-existence*, we should necessarily think with equal horror of the time when as yet we did not exist. For it is irrefutably certain that non-existence after death cannot be different from non-existence before birth, and is therefore

---

[3]"We like life, but all the same nothingness also has its good points. . . . I do not know what eternal life is, but this present life is a bad joke." [Tr.]

[4]*In gladiatoriis pugnis timidos et supplices, et, ut vivere liceat, obsecrantes etiam odisse solemus; fortes et animosos, et se acriter ipsos morti offerentes servare cupimus.* Cicero, *Pro Milone*, c. 34.

["In gladiatorial conflicts we usually abhor and abominate the cowards who beg and implore us to let them live. On the other hand, we seek to preserve the lives of the brave, the courageous, and those who of their own free will impetuously face death." Tr.]

no more deplorable than that is. An entire infinity ran its course when we did *not yet* exist, but this in no way disturbs us. On the other hand, we find it hard, and even unendurable, that after the momentary intermezzo of an ephemeral existence, a second infinity should follow in which we shall exist *no longer*. Now could this thirst for existence possibly have arisen through our having tasted it and found it so very delightful? As was briefly set forth above, certainly not; the experience gained would far rather have been capable of causing an infinite longing for the lost paradise of non-existence. To the hope of immortality of the soul there is always added that of a "better world"; an indication that the present world is not worth much. Notwithstanding all this, the question of our state after death has certainly been discussed verbally and in books ten thousand times more often that that of our state before birth. Theoretically, however, the one is a problem just as near at hand and just as legitimate as the other; moreover, he who answered the one would likewise be fully enlightened about the other. We have fine declamations about how shocking it would be to think that the mind of man, which embraces the world and has so many excellent ideas, should sink with him into the grave; but we hear nothing about this mind having allowed a whole infinity of time to elapse before it arose with these its qualities, and how for just as long a time the world had to manage without it. Yet to knowledge uncorrupted by the will no question presents itself more naturally than this, namely: An infinite time has run its course before my birth; what was I throughout all that time? Metaphysically, the answer might perhaps be: "I was always I; that is, all who throughout that time said I, were just I." But let us turn away from this to our present entirely empirical point of view, and assume that I did not exist at all. But I can then console myself for the infinite time after my death when I shall not exist, with the infinite time when I did not as yet exist, as a quite customary and really very comfortable state. For the infinity *a parte post*[5] without me cannot be any more fearful than the infinity *a parte ante*[5] without me, since the two are not distinguished by anything except by the intervention of an ephemeral life-dream. All proofs of continued existence after death may also be applied just as well *in partem ante*, where they then demonstrate existence before life, in assuming which the Hindus and Buddhists therefore show themselves to be very consistent. Only Kant's ideality of time solves all these riddles; but we are not discussing this at the moment. But this much follows from what has been said, namely that to mourn for the time when we shall no longer exist is just as absurd as it would be to mourn for the time when we did not as yet exist; for it is all the same whether the time our existence does not fill is related to that which it does fill as future or as past.

But quite apart even from these considerations of time, it is in and by itself absurd to regard non-existence as an evil; for every evil, like every good, presupposes existence, indeed even consciousness. But this ceases with life,

[5]"After life"; "before life." [Tr.]

as well as in sleep and in a fainting fit; therefore the absence of consciousness is well known and familiar to us as a state containing no evil at all; in any case, its occurrence is a matter of a moment. Epicurus considered death from this point of view, and therefore said quite rightly: ὁ θάνατοζ μηδέν πρὸζ ἡμᾶζ (Death does not concern us), with the explanation that when we are, death is not, and when death is, we are not (Diogenes Laërtius, x, 27). To have lost what cannot be missed is obviously no evil; therefore we ought to be just as little disturbed by the fact that we shall not exist as by the fact that we did not exist. Accordingly, from the standpoint of knowledge, there appears to be absolutely no ground for fearing death; but consciousness consists in knowing, and thus for consciousness death is no evil. Moreover, it is not really this *knowing* part of our *ego* that fears death, but *fuga mortis* comes simply and solely from the blind *will*, with which every living thing is filled. But, as already mentioned, this *fuga mortis* is essential to it, just because it is the will-to-live, whose whole inner nature consists in a craving for life and existence. Knowledge is not originally inherent in it, but appears only in consequence of the will's objectification in animal individuals. Now if by means of knowledge the will beholds death as the end of the phenomenon with which it has identified itself, and to which it therefore sees itself limited, its whole nature struggles against this with all its might. We shall investigate later on whether it really has anything to fear from death, and shall then remember the real source of the fear of death which is indicated here with a proper distinction between the willing and knowing part of our true nature.

According to this, what makes death so terrible for us is not so much the end of life—for this cannot seem to anyone specially worthy of regret—as the destruction of the organism, really because this organism is the will itself manifested as body. But actually, we feel this destruction only in the evils of illness or of old age; on the other hand, for the *subject*, death itself consists merely in the moment when consciousness vanishes, since the activity of the brain ceases. The extension of the stoppage to all other parts of the organism which follows this is really already an event after death. Therefore, in a subjective respect, death concerns only consciousness. Now from going to sleep everyone can, to some extent, judge what the vanishing of consciousness may be; and whoever has had a real fainting fit knows it even better. The transition here is not so gradual, nor is it brought about by dreams; but first of all, while we are still fully conscious, the power of sight disappears, and then immediately supervenes the deepest unconsciousness. As far as the accompanying sensation goes, it is anything but unpleasant; and undoubtedly just as sleep is the brother of death, so is the fainting fit its twin-brother. Violent death also cannot be painful, for, as a rule, even severe wounds are not felt at all till some time afterwards, and are often noticed only from their external symptoms. If they are rapidly fatal, consciousness will vanish before this discovery; if they result in death later, it is the same as with other illnesses. All who have lost consciousness in water, through charcoal fumes, or through hanging, also state, as is well known, that it happened without pain. And finally, even death through natural causes proper, death through old age, euthanasia, is a gradual vanishing and passing out of existence in an imperceptible manner. In old age, passions and desires, together with the susceptibility to their objects, are gradually extinguished; the emotions no longer find any excitement, for the power to make representations or mental pictures becomes weaker and weaker, and its images feebler. The impressions no longer stick to us, but pass away without a trace; the days roll by faster and faster; events lose their significance; everything grows pale. The old man, stricken in years, totters about or rests in a corner, now only a shadow, a ghost, of his former self. What still remains there for death to destroy? One day a slumber is his last, and his dreams are ————. They are the dreams that Hamlet asks about in the famous monologue. I believe that we dream them just now.

I have still to observe that, although the maintenance of the life-process has a metaphysical basis, it does not take place without resistance, and hence without effort. It is this to which the organism yields every evening, for which reason it then suspends the brain-function, and diminishes certain secretions, respiration, pulse, and the development of heat. From this it may be concluded that the entire cessation of the life-process must be a wonderful relief for its driving force. Perhaps this is partly responsible for the expression of sweet contentment on the faces of most of the dead. In general, the moment of dying may be similar to that of waking from a heavy nightmare.

So far, the result for us is that death cannot really be an evil, however much it is feared, but that it often appears even as a good thing, as something desired, as a friend. All who have encountered insuperable obstacles to their existence or to their efforts, who suffer from incurable disease or from inconsolable grief, have the return into the womb of nature as the last resource that is often open to them as a matter of course. Like everything else, they emerged from this womb for a short time, enticed by the hope of more favourable conditions of existence than those that have fallen to their lot, and from this the same path always remains open to them. That return is the *cessio bonorum*[6] of the living. Yet even here it is entered into only after a physical or moral conflict, so hard does everyone struggle against returning to the place from which he came forth so readily and willingly to an existence that has so many sorrows and so few joys to offer. To Yama, the god of death, the Hindus give two faces, one very fearful and terrible, one very cheerful and benevolent. This is already explained in part from the observations we have just made.

From the empirical standpoint, at which we are still placed, the following consideration is one which presents itself automatically, and therefore merits

[6]"Surrender of property." [Tr.]

being defined accurately by elucidation, and thus kept within its limits. The sight of a corpse shows me that sensibility, irritability, blood circulation, reproduction, and so on in it have ceased. From this I conclude with certainty that that which previously actuated them, which was nevertheless something always unknown to me, now actuates them no longer, and so has departed from them. But if I now wished to add that this must have been just what I have known only as consciousness, and consequently as intelligence (soul), this would be a conclusion not merely unjustified, but obviously false. For consciousness has always shown itself to me not as the cause, but as a product and result of organic life, since it rose and sank in consequence thereof at the different periods of life, in health and sickness, in sleep, in a faint, in awaking, and so on. Thus it always appeared as the effect, never as a cause, of organic life, always showed itself as something arising and passing away and again arising, so long as the conditions for this still exist, but not apart from them. Indeed, I may also have seen that the complete derangement of consciousness, madness, far from dragging down with it and depressing the other forces, or even endangering life, greatly enhances these, especially irritability or muscular force, and lengthens rather than shortens life, if there are no other competing causes. Then I knew individuality as a quality or attribute of everything organic, and when this was a self-conscious organism, of consciousness also. But there exists no occasion for concluding now that individuality is inherent in that vanished principle which imparts life and is wholly unknown to me; the less so, as everywhere in nature I see each particular phenomenon to be the work of a universal force active in thousands of similar phenomena. But on the other hand there is just as little occasion for concluding that, because organized life has here ceased, the force that actuated it hitherto has also become nothing; just as little as there is to infer from the stopping of the spinning-wheel the death of the spinner. If, by finding its centre of gravity again, a pendulum finally comes to rest, and thus its individual apparent life has ceased, no one will suppose that gravitation is annihilated, but everyone sees that now as always it is active in innumerable phenomena. Of course, it might be objected to this comparison that even in the pendulum gravitation has not ceased to be active, but has merely given up manifesting its activity visibly. He who insists on this may think, instead, of an electrical body in which, after its discharge, electricity has really ceased to be active. I wished only to show by this that we directly attribute an eternity and ubiquity even to the lowest forces of nature; and the transitoriness of their fleeting phenomena does not for a moment confuse us with regard thereto. So much the less, therefore, should it occur to us to regard the cessation of life as the annihilation of the living principle, and thus death as the entire destruction of man. Because the strong arm that three thousand years ago bent the bow of Ulysses no longer exists, no reflective and well-regulated understanding will look upon the force that acted so energetically in it as entirely annihilated. Therefore, on further reflection, it will not be assumed that the force that bends the bow today, first began to exist with that arm. Much nearer to us is the idea that the force that formerly actuated a life now vanished is the same force that is active in the life now flourishing; indeed this thought is almost inevitable. However, we certainly know that, as was explained in the second book, only that is perishable which is involved in the causal chain; but merely the states and forms are so involved. Untouched, however, by the change of these, which is produced by causes, there remain matter on the one hand, and the natural forces on the other; for both are the presupposition of all those changes. But the principle that gives us life must first be conceived at any rate as a force of nature, until a profounder investigation may perhaps let us know what it is in itself. Thus, taken already as a force of nature, vital force remains entirely untouched by the change of forms and states, which the bond of cause and effect introduces and carries off again, and which alone are subject to arising and passing away, just as these processes lie before us in experience. To this extent, therefore, the imperishableness of our true inner nature could already be certainly demonstrated. But this, of course, will not satisfy the claims usually made on proofs of our continued existence after death, nor will it afford the consolation expected from such proofs. Yet it is always something, and whoever fears death as his absolute annihilation cannot afford to disdain the perfect certainty that the innermost principle of his life remains untouched by it. In fact, we might advance the paradox that that second thing which, like the forces of nature, remains untouched by the continuous change of states under the guidance of causality, i.e., matter, also assures us through its absolute permanence of an indestructibility; and by virtue of this, he who might be incapable of grasping any other could yet be confident of a certain imperishability. But it will be asked: "How is the permanence of mere dust, of crude matter, to be regarded as a continuance of our true inner nature?" Oh! do you know this dust then? Do you know what it is and what it can do? Learn to know it before you despise it. This matter, now lying there as dust and ashes, will soon form into crystals when dissolved in water; it will shine as metal; it will then emit electric sparks. By means of its galvanic tension it will manifest a force which, decomposing the strongest and firmest combinations, reduces earths to metals. It will, indeed of its own accord, form itself into plant and animal; and from its mysterious womb it will develop that life, about the loss of which you in your narrowness of mind are so nervous and anxious. Is it, then, so absolutely and entirely nothing to continue to exist as such matter? Indeed, I seriously assert that even this permanence of matter affords evidence of the indestructibility of our true inner being, although only as in an image and simile, or rather only as in a shadowy outline. . . .

The considerations which have brought us to this point, and with which the further discussions are connected, started from the remarkable fear of death which affects all living beings. But now we wish to alter the point of view, and to consider how, in contrast to individual beings, the *whole* of nature behaves with regard to death; yet here we still remain always on the ground and soil of the empirical.

We know, of course, of no higher gamble than that for life and death. We watch with the utmost attention, interest, and fear every decision concerning them; for in our view all in all is at stake. On the other hand, *nature*, which never lies, but is always frank and sincere, speaks quite differently on this theme, as Krishna does in the *Bhagavadgita*. Her statement is that the life or death of the individual is of absolutely no consequence. She expresses this by abandoning the life of every animal, and even of man, to the most insignificant accidents without coming to the rescue. Consider the insect on your path; a slight unconscious turning of your foot is decisive as to its life or death. Look at the wood-snail that has no means of flight, of defence, of practising deception, of concealment, a ready prey to all. Look at the fish carelessly playing in the still open net; at the frog prevented by its laziness from the flight that could save it; at the bird unaware of the falcon soaring above it; at the sheep eyed and examined from the thicket by the wolf. Endowed with little caution, all these go about guilelessly among the dangers which at every moment threaten their existence. Now, since nature abandons without reserve her organisms constructed with such inexpressible skill, not only to the predatory instinct of the stronger, but also to the blindest chance, the whim of every fool, and the mischievousness of every child, she expresses that the annihilation of these individuals is a matter of indifference to her, does her no harm, is of no significance at all, and that in these cases the effect is of no more consequence than is the cause. Nature states this very clearly, and she never lies; only she does not comment on her utterances, but rather expresses them in the laconic style of the oracle. Now if the universal mother carelessly sends forth her children without protection to a thousand threatening dangers, this can be only because she knows that, when they fall, they fall back into her womb, where they are safe and secure; therefore their fall is only a jest. With man she does not act otherwise than she does with the animals; hence her declaration extends also to him; the life or death of the individual is a matter of indifference to her. Consequently, they should be, in a certain sense, a matter of indifference to us; for in fact, we ourselves are nature. If only we saw deeply enough, we should certainly agree with nature, and regard life or death as indifferently as does she. Meanwhile, by means of reflection, we must attribute nature's careless and indifferent attitude concerning the life of individuals to the fact that the destruction of such a phenomenon does not in the least disturb its true and real inner being.

As we have just been considering, not only are life and death dependent on the most trifling accidents, but the existence of organic beings generally is also ephemeral; animal and plant arise today and tomorrow pass away; birth and death follow in quick succession, whereas to inorganic things, standing so very much lower, an incomparably longer duration is assured, but an infinitely long one only to absolutely formless matter, to which we attribute this even *a priori*. Now if we ponder over all this, I think the merely empirical, but objective and unprejudiced, comprehension of such an order of things must be followed as a matter of course by the thought that this order is only a superficial phenomenon, that such a constant arising and passing away cannot in any way touch the root of things, but can be only relative, indeed only apparent. The true inner being of everything, which, moreover, evades our glance everywhere and is thoroughly mysterious, is not affected by that arising and passing away, but rather continues to exist undisturbed thereby. Of course, we can neither perceive nor comprehend the way in which this happens, and must therefore think of it only generally as a kind of *tour de passe-passe* [7] that took place here. For whereas the most imperfect thing, the lowest, the inorganic, continues to exist unassailed, it is precisely the most perfect beings, namely living things with their infinitely complicated and inconceivably ingenious organizations, which were supposed always to arise afresh from the very bottom, and after a short span of time to become absolutely nothing, in order to make room once more for new ones like them coming into existence out of nothing. This is something so obviously absurd that it can never be the true order of things, but rather a mere veil concealing such an order, or more correctly a phenomenon conditioned by the constitution of our intellect. In fact, the entire existence and non-existence of these individual beings, in reference to which life and death are opposites, can be only relative. Hence the language of nature, in which it is given to us as something absolute, cannot be the true and ultimate expression of the quality and constitution of things and of the order of the world, but really only a *patois du pays*, [8] in other words, something merely relatively true, something self-styled, to be understood *cum grano salis*, or properly speaking, something conditioned by our intellect. I say that an immediate, intuitive conviction of the kind I have here tried to describe in words will force itself on everyone, of course only on everyone whose mind is not of the utterly common species. Such common minds are capable of knowing absolutely only the particular thing, simply and solely as such, and are strictly limited to knowledge of individuals, after the manner of the animal intellect. On the other hand, whoever, through an ability of an only somewhat higher power, even just begins to see in individual beings their universal, their Ideas, will also to a certain extent participate in that conviction, a conviction indeed that is immediate and therefore certain. Indeed, it is also only small,

----

[7]"Conjuring trick." [Tr.]
[8]"Provincial dialect." [Tr.]

narrow minds that quite seriously fear death as their annihilation; those who are specially favoured with decided capacity are entirely remote from such terrors. Plato rightly founded the whole of philosophy on knowledge of the doctrine of Ideas, in other words, on the perception of the universal in the particular. But the conviction here described and arising directly out of the apprehension of nature must have been extremely lively in those sublime authors of the *Upanishads* of the *Vedas*, who can scarcely be conceived as mere human beings. For this conviction speaks to us so forcibly from an immense number of their utterances that we must ascribe this immediate illumination of their mind to the fact that, standing nearer to the origin of our race as regards time, these sages apprehended the inner essence of things more clearly and profoundly than the already enfeebled race, οἷοι νῦν βροτοί εισίν, [9] is capable of doing. But, of course, their comprehension was also assisted by the natural world of India, which is endowed with life in quite a different degree from that in which our northern world is. Thorough reflection , however, as carried through by Kant's great mind, also leads to just the same result by a different path; for it teaches us that our intellect, in which that rapidly changing phenomenal world exhibits itself, does not comprehend the true, ultimate essence of things, but merely its appearance or phenomenon; and indeed, as I add, because originally such an intellect is destined only to present motives to our will, in other words, to be serviceable to it in the pursuit of its paltry aims.

But let us continue still farther our objective and unprejudiced consideration of nature. If I kill an animal, be it a dog, a bird, a frog, or even only an insect, it is really inconceivable that this being, or rather the primary and original force by virtue of which such a marvellous phenomenon displayed itself only a moment before in its full energy and love of life, could through my wicked or thoughtless act have become nothing. Again, on the other hand, the millions of animals of every kind which come into existence at every moment in endless variety, full of force and drive, can never have been absolutely nothing before the act of their generation, and can never have arrived from nothing to an absolute beginning. If in this way I see one of these creatures withdraw from my sight without my ever knowing where it goes to, and another appear without my ever knowing where it comes from; moreover, if both still have the same form, the same inner nature, the same character, but not the same matter, which they nevertheless continue to throw off and renew during their existence; then of course the assumption that what vanishes and what appears in its place are one and the same thing, which has experienced only a slight change, a renewal of the form of its existence, and consequently that death is for the species what sleep is for the individual—this assumption, I say, is so close at hand, that it is impossible

[9] "As mortals now are." [Tr.]

for it not to occur to us, unless our minds, perverted in early youth by the impression of false fundamental views, hurry it out of the way, even from afar, with superstitious fear. But the opposite assumption that an animal's birth is an arising out of nothing, and accordingly that its death is an absolute annihilation, and this with the further addition that man has also come into existence out of nothing, yet has an individual and endless future existence, and that indeed with consciousness, whereas the dog, the ape, and the elephant are annihilated by death—is really something against which the sound mind must revolt, and must declare to be absurd. If, as is often enough repeated, the comparison of a system's result with the utterances of common sense is supposed to be a touchstone of its truth, I wish that the adherents of that fundamental view, handed down by Descartes to the pre-Kantian eclectics, and indeed still prevalent even now among the great majority of cultured people in Europe, would once apply this touchstone here.

The genuine symbol of nature is universally and everywhere the circle, because it is the schema or form of recurrence; in fact, this is the most general form in nature. She carries it through in everything from the course of the constellations down to the death and birth of organic beings. In this way alone, in the restless stream of time and its content, a continued existence, i.e., a nature, becomes possible.

In autumn we observe the tiny world of insects, and see how one prepares its bed, in order to sleep the long, benumbing winter-sleep; another spins a cocoon, in order to hibernate as a chrysalis, and to awake in spring rejuvenated and perfected; finally, how most of them, intending to rest in the arms of death, carefully arrange a suitable place for depositing their eggs, in order one day to come forth from these renewed. This is nature's great doctrine of immortality, which tries to make it clear to us that there is no radical difference between sleep and death, but that the one endangers existence just as little as the other. The care with which the insect prepares a cell, or hole, or nest, deposits therein its egg, together with food for the larva that will emerge from it in the following spring, and then calmly dies, is just like the care with which a person in the evening lays out his clothes and his breakfast ready for the following morning, and then calmly goes to bed; and at bottom it could not take place at all, unless the insect that dies in autumn were in itself and according to its true essence just as identical with the insect hatched in spring as the person who lies down to sleep is with the one who gets up.

After these considerations, we now return to ourselves and our species; we then cast our glance forward far into the future, and try to picture to ourselves future generations with the millions of their individuals in the strange form of their customs and aspirations. But then we interpose with the question: Whence will all these come? Where are they now? Where is the abundant womb of that nothing which is pregnant with worlds, and which still conceals them, the coming generations? Would not the smiling and true answer to this be: Where else could they be but there where alone the real always was and will be, namely in the present and its content?—hence with you, the deluded questioner, who in this mistaking of his own true nature is like the leaf on the tree. Fading in the autumn and about to fall, this leaf grieves over its own extinction, and will not be consoled by looking forward to the fresh green which will clothe the tree in spring, but says as a lament: "I am not these! These are quite different leaves!" Oh, foolish leaf! Whither do you want to go? And whence are the others supposed to come? Where is the nothing, the abyss of which you fear? Know your own inner being, precisely that which is so filled with the thirst for existence; recognize it once more in the inner, mysterious, sprouting force of the tree. This force is always *one* and the same in all the generations of leaves, and it remains untouched by arising and passing away. And now

οἴη περ φύλλων γενεή, τοίη δὲ χαὶ ἀνδρῶν
(Qualis foliorum generatio, talis et hominum.)[10]

Whether the fly now buzzing round me goes to sleep in the evening and buzzes again the following morning, or whether it dies in the evening and in spring another fly buzzes which has emerged from its egg, this in itself is the same thing. But then the knowledge that presents these as two fundamentally different things is not unconditioned, but relative, a knowledge of the phenomenon, not of the thing-in-itself. In the morning the fly exists again; it also exists again in the spring. For the fly what distinguishes the winter from the night? In Burdach's *Physiologie*, Vol. I, Sec. 275, we read: "Up till ten o'clock in the morning no *Cercaria ephemera* (one of the infusoria) is yet to be seen (in the infusion), and at twelve the whole water swarms with them. In the evening they die, and the next morning new ones come into existence again. It was thus observed for six days in succession by Nitzsch."

Thus everything lingers only for a moment, and hurries on to death. The plant and the insect die at the end of the summer, the animal and man after a few years; death reaps unweariedly. But despite all this, in fact as if this were not the case at all, everything is always there and in its place, just as if everything were imperishable. The plant always flourishes and blooms, the insect hums, animal and man are there in evergreen youth, and every summer we again have before us the cherries that have already been a thousand times enjoyed. Nations also exist as immortal individuals, though sometimes they change their names. Even their actions, what they do and suffer, are always the same, though history always pretends to relate something different; for it is like the kaleidoscope, that shows us a new configuration at every

---

[10]"As the leaves on the tree, so are the generations of human beings." [*Iliad*, vi, 146. Tr.]

turn, whereas really we always have the same thing before our eyes. There-fore, what forces itself on us more irresistibly than the thought that that arising and passing away do not concern the real essence of things, but that this remains untouched by them, hence is imperishable, consequently that each and every thing that *wills* to exist actually does exist continuously and without end? Accordingly, at every given point of time all species of animals, from the gnat to the elephant, exist together complete. They have already renewed themselves many thousands of times, and withal have remained the same. They know nothing of others like them who have lived before them, or who will live after them; it is the species that always lives, and the individu-als cheerfully exist in the consciousness of the imperishability of the species and their identity with it. The will-to-live manifests itself in an endless present, because this is the form of the life of the species, which therefore does not grow old, but remains always young. Death is for the species what sleep is for the individual, or winking for the eye; when the Indian gods appear in human form, they are recognized by their not winking. Just as at nightfall the world vanishes, yet does not for a moment cease to exist, so man and animal apparently pass away through death, yet their true inner being continues to exist just as undisturbed. Let us now picture to ourselves that alternation of birth and death in infinitely rapid vibrations, and we have before us the persistent and enduring objectification of the will, the perma-nent Ideas of beings, standing firm like the rainbow on the waterfall. This is temporal immortality. In consequence of this, in spite of thousands of years of death and decay, there is still nothing lost, no atom of matter, still less anything of the inner being exhibiting itself as nature. Accordingly we can at any moment cheerfully exclaim: "In spite of time, death, and decay, we are still all together!"

Perhaps an exception would have to be made of the man who should once have said from the bottom of his heart with regard to this game: "I no longer like it." But this is not yet the place to speak of that.

Attention, however, must indeed be drawn to the fact that the pangs of birth and the bitterness of death are the two constant conditions under which the will-to-live maintains itself in its objectification, in other words, our being-in-itself, untouched by the course of time and by the disappearance of generations, exists in an everlasting present, and enjoys the fruit of the affirmation of the will-to-live. This is analogous to our being able to remain awake during the day only on the condition that we sleep every night; indeed, this is the commentary furnished by nature for an understanding of that difficult passage. For the suspension of the animal functions is sleep; that of the organic functions is death.

The substratum or filling out, the $\pi\lambda\acute{\eta}\rho\omega\mu\alpha$ or material of the *present*, is really the same through all time. The impossibility of directly recognizing this identity is just *time*, a form and limitation of our intellect. The fact that by virtue of it, for example, the future event does not as yet exist, rests on a delusion of which we become aware when the event has come to pass. The essential form of our intellect produces such a delusion, that this is explained and justified from the fact that the intellect has come forth from the hands of nature by no means for the purpose of comprehending motives, and hence to serve an individual and temporal phenomenon of will. . . .

There is no greater contrast than that between the ceaseless, irresistible flight of time carrying its whole content away with it, and the rigid immobility of what is actually existing, which is at all times one and the same; and if, from this point of view, we fix our really objective glance on the immediate events of life, the *Nunc stans* becomes clear and visible to us in the centre of the wheel of time. To the eye of a being who lived an incomparably longer life and took in at a single glance the human race in its whole duration, the constant alternation of birth and death would present itself merely as a continuous vibration. Accordingly, it would not occur to it at all to see in it a constantly new coming out of nothing and passing into nothing, but, just as to our glance the rapidly turning spark appears as a continuous circle, the rapidly vibrating spring as a permanent triangle, the vibrating cord as a spindle, so to its glance the species would appear as that which is and remains, birth and death as vibrations.

We shall have false notions about the indestructibility of our true nature through death, so long as we do not make up our minds to study it first of all in the animals, and claim for ourselves alone a class apart from them under the boastful name of immortality. But it is this presumption alone and the narrowness of view from which it proceeds, on account of which most people struggle so obstinately against recognizing the obvious truth that, essentially and in the main, we are the same as the animals; in fact that such people recoil at every hint of our relationship with these. Yet it is this denial of the truth which, more than anything else, bars to them the way to real knowledge of the indestructibility of our true nature. For if we seek anything on a wrong path, we have in so doing forsaken the right; and on the wrong path we shall never attain to anything in the end but belated disillusionment. Therefore, pursue truth straight away, not according to preconceived freaks and fancies, but guided by the hand of nature! First of all learn to recognize, when looking at every young animal, the never-ageing existence of the species, which, as a reflection of its own eternal youth, bestows on every new individual a temporal youth, and lets it step forth as new, as fresh, as if the world were of today. Ask yourself honestly whether the swallow of this year's spring is an entirely different one from the swallow of the first spring, and whether actually between the two the miracle of creation out of nothing has been renewed a million times, in order to work just as often into the hands of absolute annihilation. I know quite well that anyone would regard me as mad if I seriously assured him that the cat, playing just now in the yard, is still the

same one that did the same jumps and tricks there three hundred years ago;
but I also know that it is much more absurd to believe that the cat of today is
through and through and fundamentally an entirely different one from that
cat of three hundred years ago. We need only become sincerely and seriously engrossed in the contemplation of one of these higher vertebrates, in
order to become distinctly conscious that this unfathomable inner being,
taken as a whole as it exists, cannot possibly become nothing, and yet, on the
other hand, we know its transitoriness. This rests on the fact that in this
animal the eternity of its Idea (species) is distinctly marked in the finiteness
of the individual. For in a certain sense it is of course true that in the
individual we always have before us a different being, namely in the sense
resting on the principle of sufficient reason, under which are also included
time and space; these constitute the *principium individuationis*. But in
another it is not true, namely in the sense in which reality belongs only to
the permanent forms of things, to the Ideas, and which was so clearly evident to Plato that it became his fundamental thought, the centre of his
philosophy; the comprehension of it became his criterion for the ability to
philosophize generally. . . .

Finally, this explanation agrees also with that daily moral experience,
teaching us that the will alone is real, while its objects on the other hand, as
conditioned by knowledge, are only phenomena, mere froth and vapour, like
the wine provided by Mephistopheles in Auerbach's cellar; thus after every
pleasure of the senses we say; "And yet it seemed as I were drinking wine."

The terrors of death rest for the most part on the false illusion that then the
I or ego vanishes, and the world remains. But rather is the opposite true,
namely that the world vanishes; on the other hand, the innermost kernel of
the ego endures, the bearer and producer of that subject in whose representation alone the world had its existence. With the brain the intellect
perishes, and with the intellect the objective world, this intellect's mere
representation. The fact that in other brains a similar world lives and moves,
now as before, is a matter of indifference with reference to the intellect that
is perishing. If, therefore, reality proper did not lie in the *will*, and if the
moral existence were not that which extended beyond death, then, as the
intellect and with it its world are extinguished, the true essence of things
generally would be nothing more than an endless succession of short and
troubled dreams without connexion among themselves; for the permanence
of nature-without-knowledge consists merely in the time-representation of
nature that knows. Therefore a world-spirit, dreaming without aim or purpose dreams that are often heavy and troubled, would then be all in all.

When an individual experiences the dread of death, we really have the
strange, and even ludicrous, spectacle of the lord of the worlds, who fills
everything with his true nature, and through whom alone everything that is
has its existence, in despair and afraid of perishing, of sinking into the abyss

of eternal nothingness; whereas, in truth, everything is full of him, and there is no place where he would not be, no being in whom he would not live, for existence does not support him, but he existence. Yet it is he who despairs in the individual who suffers the dread of death, since he is exposed to the illusion, produced by the *principium individuationis*, that his existence is limited to the being that is now dying. This illusion is part of the heavy dream into which he, as will-to-live, has fallen. However, we might say to the dying individual: "You are ceasing to be something which you would have done better never to become."

As long as no denial of that will has taken place, that of us which is left over by death is the seed and kernel of quite another existence, in which a new individual finds himself again so fresh and original, that he broods over himself in astonishment. Hence the enthusiastic, visionary, and dreamy disposition of noble youths at the time when this fresh consciousness has just been fully developed. What sleep is for the individual, death is for the will as thing-in-itself. It could not bear to continue throughout endless time the same actions and sufferings without true gain, if memory and individuality were left to it. It throws them off; this is Lethe; and through this sleep of death it reappears as a new being, refreshed and equipped with another intellect; "A new day beckons to a newer shore!"[11]. . .

Death is the great reprimand that the will-to-live, and more particularly the egoism essential thereto, receive through the course of nature; and it can be conceived as a punishment for our existence.[12] Death is the painful untying of the knot that generation with sensual pleasure had tied; it is the violent destruction, bursting in from outside, of the fundamental error of our true nature, the great disillusionment. At bottom, we are something that ought not to be; therefore we cease to be. Egoism really consists in man's restricting all reality to his own person, in that he imagines he lives in this alone, and not in others. Death teaches him something better, since it abolishes this person, so that man's true nature, that is his will, will henceforth live only in other individuals. His intellect, however, which itself belonged only to the phenomenon, i.e., to the world as representation, and was merely the form of the external world, also continues to exist in the condition of being representation, in other words, in the *objective* being, *as such*, of things, hence also only in the existence of what was hitherto the external world. Therefore, from this time forward, his whole ego lives only in what he had hitherto regarded as non-ego; for the difference between external and internal ceases. Here we recall that the better person is the one who makes the least difference between himself and others, and does not regard them as absolutely non-ego; whereas to the bad person this difference is

[11]Goeth's *Faust*, Bayard Taylor's translation. [Tr.]
[12]Death says: You are the product of an act that ought not to have taken place; therefore, to wipe it out, you must die.

great, in fact absolute. I have discussed this at length in the essay *On the Basis of Morality*. The conclusion from the above remarks is that the degree in which death can be regarded as man's annihilation is in proportion to this difference. But if we start from the fact that the difference between outside me and inside me, as a spatial difference, is founded only in the phenomenon, not in the thing-in-itself, and so it is not an absolutely real difference, then in the losing of our own individuality we shall see only the loss of a phenomenon, and thus only an apparent loss. However much reality that difference has in empirical consciousness, yet from the metaphysical standpoint the sentences "I perish, but the world endures," and "The world perishes, but I endure," are not really different at bottom.

But beyond all this, death is the great opportunity no longer to be I; to him, of course, who embraces it. During life, man's will is without freedom; on the basis of his unalterable character, his conduct takes place with necessity in the chain of motives. Now everyone carries in his memory very many things which he has done, about which he is not satisfied with himself. If he were to go on living, he would go on acting in the same way by virtue of the unalterability of his character. Accordingly, he must cease to be what he is, in order to be able to arise out of the germ of his true nature as a new and different being. Death, therefore, loosens those bonds; the will again becomes free, for freedom lies in the *esse*, not in the *operari*. *Finditur nodus cordis, dissolvuntur omnes dubitationes, ejusque opera evanescunt,*[13] is a very famous saying of the *Veda* often repeated by all Vedantists. Dying is the moment of that liberation from the one-sidedness of an individuality which does not constitute the innermost kernel of our true being, but is rather to be thought of as a kind of aberration thereof. The true original freedom again enters at this moment which in the sense stated can be regarded as a *restitutio in integrum.*[14] The peace and composure on the countenance of most dead people seem to have their origin in this. As a rule, the death of every good person is peaceful and gentle; but to die willingly, to die gladly, to die cheerfully, is the prerogative of the resigned, of him who gives up and denies the will-to-live. For he alone wishes to die *actually* and not merely *apparently*, and consequently needs and desires no continuance of his person. He willingly gives up the existence that we know; what comes to him instead of it is in our eyes *nothing*, because our existence in reference to that one is *nothing*. The Buddhist faith calls that existence *Nirvana*, that is to say, extinction.

[13]"[Whoever beholds the highest and profoundest], has his heart's knot cut, all his doubts are resolved, and his works come to nought." [Tr.]
[14]"Restoration to the former state." [Tr.]

20

A. L. HERMAN

---

introduction

A. L. Herman, the translator of this section, has written concerning it as follows:

> The *Katha Upanishad* has been called the most philosophical of the *Upanishads*. The work is pre-Buddhist and belongs to the seventh or sixth century B.C. "Upanishad" means literally "to sit down near" and probably refers to the method of sitting and learning at the feet of a teacher. "Katha" is the name of a Vedic school. The *Katha Upanishad* is really a dialogue between a Brahmin boy, Naciketas, and the Lord of the Dead, Yama. Naciketas has been sent to Yama as a consequence of the anger of Naciketas' father, Vajaśravasa. The latter had given away, as religious gifts, all of his worldly possessions when suddenly his son, Naciketas, seeing everything being thus sacrificed, asks his father, "Father, to whom will you give me?" Receiving no reply, he again asks the same question and then, when his father still remains silent, he finally asks him a third time, "Father, to whom will you give me?" The father in anger cries out, "I will give you to Death." Because a Brahmin is obedient as well as truthful, the unfortunate Naciketas must now, in response to his father's directive, journey to the house of Yama, the Lord of the Dead. The translation that follows is cast as a dialogue in which some dramatic license has been taken, putting the *Upanishad* into the form of a short play. The lines spoken by the servant and the response to him are not part of the original text but otherwise

the translation is a fair and faithful rendering of this very early and very influential *Upanishad*.

Dr. Herman's conversion of this profound dialogue into a short play is brilliant, perfectly expressing the dramatic theme. It would be largely self-defeating to attempt formulating that theme in straightforward declarative statements, yet the following comments may be helpful to the reader in understanding it.

This ancient work is not only much older than all Western philosophy, it is also older then Buddhism, which predates Christianity. Its theme is identical to one of the central themes of Buddhism—namely, that the problem of life, which for Gotama Buddha was the problem of suffering, arises from desire, appetite, "grasping," or what is here expressed simply as being "bound" to the world. The simplest expression of this bond is the vain and ceaseless search for pleasure. If, however, one turns instead to religion, as it is usually understood—to rites and rituals or to the church—then he is still bound to the world, for he has merely replaced the love for worldly pleasure with a love for something hardly less worldly.

The Brahmin youth of this story is tempted, first, with every worldly good, if he will but forsake his wish to understand death. Failing that, he is tempted with worldly religion. Rejecting that, he is told, in terms that are, strictly speaking, meaningless, the nature of death and of life. But the instruction is meaningless only in terms of ordinary intelligence, sense, and experience. No one can ever be *told*, in such terms, what death is, or what life is. Yet understanding is possible by other means, of which some hint is given, the initial step being to relinquish attachment to the world. The deep truth underlying the mysteries of birth and death is suggested in the dramatic ending of the story, wherein life and death, as personified, are found to be one and the same thing!

A. L. Herman, who has translated and edited extensively from Indian thought, is Professor of Philosophy at the University of Wisconsin.

The Illusion of Death*

SCENE I

The house of Yama, King of the Dead. Naciketas is seated on the floor. The walls are hung in black, a servant enters and bows to Naciketas.

SERVANT: You are brave indeed to journey thus to this house. Yama, the Lord of the Dead, was not expecting you.

Katha Upanishad, trans. by A. L. Herman, in *Problems in Philosophy West and East*, ed. by R. T. Blackwood and A. L. Herman (Englewood Cliffs, N.J.: Prentice-Hall, Inc., 1975). Reprinted by permission of the publisher.

NACIKETAS: I have waited. I will wait longer.

SERVANT: Again I ask you, why have you come here? Why have you waited these three days for my master?

NACIKETAS: I come to fulfill my father's command.

SERVANT: Three days I have wanted to speak to you. Please tell me why you have come; and come so unexpectedly. My master will be angry that he was not here to receive a Brahmin youth. Expected or not, the laws of hospitality decree that the host should be here. I can do nothing for you until he returns.

NACIKETAS: I am patient. I have nowhere else to go, now that I have done the deed that sent me here.

SERVANT: But why? Tell me why you have come? My master will be so angry that he was not here to receive you that first day.

NACIKETAS: I look back and see men come hither and I see them no more. I look ahead and I see that all must finally come here. Mortal man withers and dies like the grasses of the field. But like that grass he will be born again. I wait patiently.

SERVANT: But why have you come? All unannounced, all unprepared are we here. Three days you wait. Oh my master will be vexed.

NACIKETAS: (*Rising and moving about rubbing his legs*). My father has renounced the world. Full of sorrow and fear he has given me to death. Full of anger he sent me forth.

SERVANT: And you came? But how? How could you find this dreaded place, young sir?

NACIKETAS: Among many who will some day die I go as the first. Among many who are dying now I go with them. (*He turns.*) What will Yama do to me who came in this way, dead by his own hand?

SERVANT: But why? A youth to this house, a Brahmin youth, young sprouting seedling, hardly ripe for dooming yet. Why have you come here?

NACIKETAS: My father in haste and anger sent me here. Upon my asking him, as he gave away his goods, he sent me here. Three times I asked to whom he would send me. And then but once he said, "To death." To death have I come, to Yama have I come.

SERVANT: But why, why, young sir?

NACIKETAS: A Brahmin is ever truthful. Holding fast to truth he never swerves from promises made. To keep my father's word, to obey my father's command, to make my father's truth, here I have come. (*Walks about rubbing his hands and arms.*) What will Yama do with me?

SERVANT: He will be angry that he was not here to greet a truth-protecting Brahmin youth. Oh, he will be vexed. (*Exits.*)

NACIKETAS: How cold the earth is here. How warm and sweet the sun that I miss. Death's house is not my home. And though he is not here I fear the moment when he shall return. What is it that Yama will do to me this day?

[*Enter Yama bearing a bowl of water. He is agitated and upset at not having been present when his guest arrived.*]

YAMA: Welcome my young Brahmin. (*Offering water to Naciketas.*)

> The Brahmin who enters a house as a guest
> Is like holy fire in the houses of men.
> Such a guest should be greeted with the gift of water.
> Welcome, my young Brahmin.
> (*Offers the bowl to Naciketas.*)

NACIKETAS: Sir, I am honored. (*He moistens his lips with the water.*)

YAMA: It is well said in the holy scriptures, that should a Brahmin dwell in the house of an inhospitable man who neglects his guest, then that foolish host shall lose his hopes and expectations, his possessions and his heavenly merit, his friendships and his loves. Such a one shall have his sons, his cattle, everything torn pitilessly from him. Even I, Yama, am subject to this law. Therefore welcome to my house.

NACIKETAS: My lord, it was not intended that . . . I am an unexpected guest, my lord.

YAMA:

> Nonetheless I am the absent host.
> Three nights you have spent in this my house, without hospitality's food or comfort.
> You are, Oh Brahmin, a guest most worthy of reverence.
> Having neglected you thus for three days, let me do you honor now.

NACIKETAS: If you so wish, my Lord, let it be thus.

YAMA: And let it be thus as you desire three times. To make amends, to honor you aright I grant you three boons, three wishes as you see fit.

NACIKETAS: My lord Yama, most dreadful of the holy Gods. I know not . . . three boons . . . my Lord . . . (*He is at a loss for words.*)

YAMA: Three boons to repair my tardiness, to honor you. Come, choose. Choose rightly three times.

NACIKETAS:

> Three days have I been in this your house, Oh Yama,
> Three days in darkness, cold and gloom,
> I who came here by his own choice, his own hand.
> I miss the sun my Lord,
> I miss the sweet warm earth, my father, and my life.

YAMA: Yes, choose, go on, choose now rightly.

NACIKETAS: Oh Death, as the first of my wishes, I choose to be returned to my father: let him be free from anger towards me; let his warm face and his gentle smile greet me as the sweet sun shall also greet me. This I would wish, Oh Death, to be thus returned to earth, to father and to life.

YAMA: You will find your father as before, but cheerful, warm, and loving. His passions departed, his anger flown, he will greet you full well as you return from this cold, lifeless realm, to earth, to father and to life. Granted. Now choose the second. Come, choose wisely.

NACIKETAS: (*Warming to his two remaining wishes as the possibilities unfold.*) My Lord Yama. There is a second wish that I would press.

YAMA: Say it. Say it.

NACIKETAS: It is said, my Lord, that in heaven there is no fear at all, no anxiety, no pain or sorrow. There in that world there is no old age to fear, no hunger, no thirst, no pain and torment of impending death. There in that realm one has gone beyond all these, but especially has one gone beyond old age and death.

YAMA: That is true. You declare the heavenly world well and truly.

NACIKETAS: Oh Yama, the way to that heavenly world, that world beyond sorrow and death, the way to that happiness is by understanding the great fire sacrifice.

YAMA: The fire sacrifice and the understanding of that great rite is truly the way to immortality. You speak the truth once again, my young Brahmin.

NACIKETAS: Then I would have you teach me the fire sacrifice, the knowing of which brings immortality and freedom. Teach me that fire wisdom, that is my second wish.

YAMA: To you I will declare the fire sacrifice, and you shall learn it and have the understanding of the fire which shall lead to immortality. Granted. Now choose the third. Come, choose wisely once again.

NACIKETAS: Oh Yama, Lord of the Dead, for my third boon I would choose the most difficult knowledge of all.

YAMA: Go on. Choose. I have promised you three boons. You have chosen well for two, first earth and then heaven. Say on, what is your third wish?

NACIKETAS: Oh Yama, this is my third wish. Among men there is doubt about what happens to a man when he dies.

YAMA: Ah, but careful, now, good Brahmin.

NACIKETAS: Some say a man exists when dead, others that he exists not. This I would know, Oh Death, when a man dies what then? What happens to a man when dead?

YAMA: My good Naciketas. Even the Gods themselves have not understood this matter. It is not easy to comprehend. The truth of it is subtle and difficult. So come choose another boon, choose another.

NACIKETAS: I would know that, my Lord.

YAMA: Oh Naciketas, do not press me here. Let me off that boon. Choose another, any other, please.

NACIKETAS: My Lord, I would know that. What happens to a man when his body dies. Does he yet live?

YAMA: *(Agitated, moving about.)* Naciketas, choose another, I urge you. Choose sons and grandsons who shall live a hundred years, choose herds of cattle, elephants, gold and horses. Choose any of these, choose all of these.

NACIKETAS: My Lord, I would know about man.

YAMA: Choose all the wide and open earth; choose that and live as long as your mind and heart desire. Choose that!

NACIKETAS: My Lord, I have chosen.

YAMA: Choose any other boon; choose wealth and long life. Be King, if you wish, of the entire earth! I will make you an enjoyer of all desires! Think of that, Oh Naciketas, any desire you wish I will grant. Any desire.

NACIKETAS: My Lord. . . .

YAMA: Whatever is hard to get in the mortal world, think on it, Naciketas, that will I get for you. Tell me what you would have. Lovely maidens, together with chariots and sweet musical sounds—such lovely ones are never to be obtained by mortals. But you, Naciketas, you can have them all. They will wait on your every desire. Choose them, I beg of you. But do not question me about dying.

NACIKETAS: These things and all that you have mentioned come to an end. Whatever power and vigor and manliness one possesses, all that passes away, all that ends some day. For you, Oh Yama, *you* are these chariots, *you* are these lovely maidens, *you* are their dancing, their music, their singing.

Man is not to be satisfied with wealth and riches and life. Shall we these possess when we meet finally with you? Shall we live and taste pleasure when we meet finally with you. No, Lord Yama. Only that boon, that choice that I have made, only that is what I have chosen, nothing else.

YAMA: You are difficult to be put off. For one so young you are truly difficult.

NACIKETAS: What use, Oh Lord of Death, is this slowly decaying body dwelling on this unhappy earth, when one knows that the ageless Gods are free from death and decay. How then can I take delight in a long life and the pleasures that come from beauty and love and pleasure.

YAMA: Yes, you have understood after all.

NACIKETAS: Then, Lord Yama, tell me what I would know. Tell me what there is in the great Hereafter for man, tell me I pray you the secret that lies even now hidden from me. This boon I would have, my Lord, and nothing else.

YAMA: *(Resigned.)* Naciketas, it is granted.

SCENE II

We are in the house of Vājaśravasa, Naciketas' father. This is not immediately evident as the scene opens, however, but as the conversation progresses it becomes gradually obvious. Further, Yama, who carries on the dialogue with Naciketas, slowly reveals himself as Vājaśravasa, until by the end of the scene Vājaśravasa and not Yama stands before Naciketas. At the same time the servant changes from Yama's servant to Vājaśravasa's.

YAMA: Naciketas, you have seen already the difference between that which is merely pleasant and that which is truly best.

NACIKETAS: Explain this to me. I know it but I seem not to understand it.

YAMA: Both pleasure and the good bind a man to deeds and to this world. Both call forth rebirth. But of the two, the good is the best. That man fails who simply chooses the pleasanter thing.

NACIKETAS: And I have chosen the best, the good, and the right?

YAMA: By renouncing the things and materials of this world, the cattle, the elephants, the lovely maidens, the chariots, the wealth and the riches, by renouncing all these for the sake of knowledge of man, you have chosen the best, indeed.

NACIKETAS: But is knowledge not also binding? Have you not said that both the pleasant and the good bind the soul and bring one back to this world, one dreary round following one dreary round. Tell me truly now?

YAMA: And tell you I shall. But slowly . . . very slowly. You must see that between knowledge and ignorance, between the good and the pleasant there is a wide chasm indeed. For those who abide in the midst of ignorance, self-wise, puffed up with thinking themselves learned, stumbling about and turning hither and thither are they, going about deluded in company with many others just as deluded, they go like blind men led by the blind.

[Servant enters, goes up to Yama and bows.]

YAMA: For those deluded in this way in this world, for those charmed by wealth and ignorance and pleasures, for those thinking that this is the only world, that this life is the only life, that there is no other—again and again that one comes under my control.

SERVANT: My Lord Yama, you are needed elsewhere. Too long have you stayed.

YAMA: (Waving the servant aside.) To one thus deluded, with wealth, the world, there is no way out of the cycle of torments and rebirths. And you, beloved Naciketas, you have come to me for instruction in this matter. You have seen through the world's delusions and you have come to me, your teacher, to be taught not only the good and the best, but that which stands even beyond that and before that and is not binding nor enthralling.

NACIKETAS: I know that what is best excels what is pleasant. But now is there another that stands beyond the best?

YAMA: There is indeed. Beyond the right and the good there is another. Beyond the law, beyond religion, beyond God there is another that does not bind. That does not hold one to this world, nor to my world, nor to heaven.

NACIKETAS: But then doing the right, obeying the holy law of dharma is that not enough to set one forever free?

YAMA: It is not. Both good and evil come from desire. Desiring good is forever binding, just as is desiring the evil. Knowledge is just as binding as ignorance. Desiring knowledge is just as binding as desiring to remain ignorant. The best is just as binding as the pleasant. Desiring the best, the right, is just as binding as desiring the pleasant. All bind, all come from desire, all hold one to heaven, to my world, or to earth. But for the truly wise man these are not enough.

NACIKETAS: But what way out is there then? How can I escape rebirth if not by seeking knowledge, if not by obeying the holy commandments, if not by attending to the priestly sacrifices and holy rites? What way out is there then, Oh my teacher?

[*The servant comes forward again and bows.*]
YAMA:

> Him who is hard to see,
> Him who is hidden, set in the secret place of the heart,
> Him who is dwelling in the depths of you,
> Him who is really God, your true teacher,
> Him who through yoga-study one comes to see,
> Him one finally comes to by leaving both joy and sorrow, good and evil, the best and the pleasant, and knowledge and ignorance behind. By abandoning all these.

NACIKETAS: But what is the way, then, Lord Yama, to this hidden and secret place?

YAMA: (*Seeming not to hear.*) Apart from the right and the unright, apart from what has been done and will be done, apart from what has been and what will be, apart from all these, in your heart, look . . . look now, right now . . . and declare what you see.

NACIKETAS: I am unable to answer my Lord. I am overwhelmed, and stopped.

YAMA: Listen and I will declare it to you.

SERVANT: My Lord Yama, you are needed at once, my Lord. Too long have you been here now.

YAMA: Yes, yes I know. A bit longer.

SERVANT: My Lord, now. You are needed now.

YAMA: A moment more.

[*He waves the servant aside. Servant retires to the right.*]

The goal as well as the origin that all our sacred scriptures glorify, that our holy men go in search of, and for the hearing of which all men practice the holy life, that goal I will tell you in one word.

NACIKETAS: What word, my Lord?

YAMA: That source, that goal, that sacred sound is OM.

NACIKETAS: I don't understand. What does it mean?
YAMA:

> That syllable is Brahman, the spiritual power, the holy power of the universe.
> Knowing OM whatever one desires is his.
> OM is the chief and only support of the universe.
> Knowing that support, one becomes great in the world of Brahman.

NACIKETAS: But where is that world, where does it lie?
YAMA:

> That OM dwells in you, Naciketas.
> It is not born, It does not die.
> It has not come from anywhere,
> It has not become anyone.
> Unborn, constant, eternal, the first and the last.
> It dies not when the bodies dies.
> That is what you searched for.

NACIKETAS: I do not yet see what this is to be. What is this Brahman, this OM? What does It do? What happens to It?
YAMA: My dear Naciketas, listen to me.
YAMA:

> If the slayer thinks that he slays,
> If the slain thinks himself slain,
> Both of these understand not.
> This One neither slays nor is It slain.
> Smaller than the smallest, greater than the greatest,
> Is this Brahman, this OM, this Atman that is set in the heart of every creature here.
> When once one is freed from sorrow and joy, from pain and pleasure, from all binding desire,
> Then and then only can one perceive this Atman, this OM, this true Self.

NACIKETAS:

> But tell me, what is the way to this, my true Self?
> How may I behold It, loosening all desire, giving up all joys and sorrows?
> Tell me what I must do.

YAMA: This true Self, this Atman is not to be obtained by instruction, nor by intellect, nor by learning. He is to be obtained only by those whom He chooses. Only to such a person, through His own favor is He to be seen, felt and understood.

[*The servant of Yama is now seen as the servant of Vājaśravasa, and at the same time Yama is seen as Vājaśravasa. The servant approaches.*]

SERVANT: My Lord, there are more things to do. Other guests are coming. There are other tasks to perform. You must be brief, my Lord.

YAMA-VĀJAŚRAVASA: Yes, yes, I am coming. But a moment more, now.

> Naciketas, my dearest, this Atman is not known by him who has be-
> come attached to bad conduct, nor to good conduct. But he who,
> through the practice of yoga, has a tranquil mind, who is inwardly
> peaceful, only that one can behold Him.
> Only when you perceive priests and princes as food for Death's eating,
> as all alike, indifferently, similar to one another at the banquet Yama
> has set for himself—
> Only then will you see the Truth, the OM, the Brahman.

NACIKETAS: I can only dimly see.

VĀJAŚRAVASA:

> Arise, Naciketas!
> Awake Naciketas! Seek further the answers to your question! Under-
> stand those answers!
> This path is like the sharpened edge of a glistening razor.
> It is hard to traverse, a path impossible to travel, the poets say.
> What is soundless, touchless, formless and imperishable,
> What is without taste, without odor, ever constant, ever abiding,
> What is without beginning, without end, higher than the highest,
> By seizing that, you shall be liberated from the mouth of death.

SERVANT: My Lord, Vājaśravasa, you must come. There are things to be distributed to the people. The wooden stool is still on the porch and awaits your choice of a new owner. The crowd of seekers and guests grows. You must come.

VĀJAŚRAVASA: Yes, I have finished here. (Rising). I am coming, too.

[End]